LANGUAGE, LITERATURE AND CRITICAL PRACTICE

Ways of Analysing Text

The INTERFACE Series

'A linguist deaf to the poetic function of language and a literary scholar indifferent to linguistic problems and unconversant with linguistic methods, are equally flagrant anachronisms.' – Roman Jakobson

This statement, made over twenty-five years ago, is no less relevant today, and 'flagrant anachronisms' still abound. The aim of the INTERFACE series is to examine topics at the 'interface' of language studies and literary criticism and in so doing to build bridges between these traditionally divided disciplines.

Contemporary philosophical, cultural, political and sociological influences have had a crucial impact on the way in which we approach and understand texts. *Language, Literature qand Critical Practice* examines the major consequences of these influences on textual analysis and the role of language within it, and provides an overview of developments in language-centred criticism in the twentieth century. Using a wide-ranging variety of texts David Brich reviews and evaluates an equally wide-ranging variety of approaches to textual commentary, introducing the reader to the fundamental distinction between 'actual' and 'virtual' worlds in critical practice, arguing for an unambiguous relation between critical practice and theories of language, and elucidating the critically important practices of *how* texts mean.

The Author
David Birch is a lecturer in English and Comparative Literature at Murdoch University, Western Australia. Previously he taught at the National University of Singapore, having completed his doctorate at the University of York, England.

The Series Editor
Ronald Carter is Senior Lecturer in English Studies and Director of the Centre for English Language Education at the University of Nottingham. He is Chair of the Poetics and Linguistics Association (PALA).

LANGUAGE, LITERATURE AND CRITICAL PRACTICE

Ways of Analysing Text

DAVID BIRCH

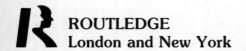

ROUTLEDGE
London and New York

First published 1989
by Routledge
11 New Fetter Lane, London EC4P 4EE
29 West 35th Street, New York, NY 10001

© David Birch 1989

Phototypeset in Linotron Souvenir Light 10/11
by Input Typesetting Ltd, London
Printed in Great Britain
by Cox & Wyman Ltd., Reading

Library of Congress Cataloging in Publication Data applied for

British Library Cataloguing in Publication Data
also available

ISBN 0–415–03121–4 (csd)
0–415–02941–4 (pbk)

For See Kam

激 扬 文 字

Contents

Series editor's introduction to the Interface series

There have been many books published this century which have been devoted to the interface of language and literary studies. This is the first *series* of books devoted to this area commissioned by a major international publisher; it is the first time a *group* of writers have addressed themselves to issues at the interface of language and literature; and it is the first time an international professional association has worked closely with a publisher to establish such a venture. It is the purpose of this general introduction to the series to outline some of the main guiding principles underlying the books in the series.

The first principle adopted is one of not foreclosing on the many possibilities for the integration of language and literature studies. There are many ways in which the study of language and literature can be combined and many different theoretical, practical and curricular objectives to be realized. Obviously, a close relationship with the aims and methods of descriptive linguistics will play a prominent part, so readers will encounter some detailed analysis of language in places. In keeping with a goal of much work in this field, writers will try to make their analysis sufficiently replicable for other analysts to see how they have arrived at the interpretive decisions they have reached and to allow others to reproduce their methods on the same or on other texts. But linguistic science does not have a monopoly in methodology and description any more than linguists can have sole possession of insights into language and its workings. Some contributors to this series adopt quite rigorous linguistic procedures; others proceed less rigorously but no less revealingly. All are, however, united by a belief that detailed scrutiny of the role of language in literary texts can be mutually enriching to language and literary studies.

Series of books are usually written to an overall formula or design. In the case of the Interface series this was considered to be not entirely appropriate. This is for the reasons given above, but also because, as the first series of its kind, it would be wrong to suggest that there are formulaic modes by which integration can be achieved. The fact that all the books address themselves to the integration of language and literature in any case imparts a natural and organic unity to the series. Thus, some of the books in this series will provide descriptive overviews; others will offer detailed case studies of a particular topic; others will involve single author studies; and some will be more pedagogically oriented.

This variety of design and procedure means that a wide variety of audiences is envisaged for the series as a whole, though, of course, individual books are necessarily quite specifically targeted. The general level of exposition presumes quite advanced students of language and literature. Approximately, this level covers students of English language and literature (though not exclusively English) at senior high-school/upper sixth form level to university students in their first or second year of study. Many of the books in the series are designed to be *used by students*. Some may serve as course books – these will normally contain exercises and suggestions for further work as well as glossaries and graded bibliographies which point the student towards further reading. Some books are also designed to be used by teachers for their own reading and updating, and to supplement courses; in some cases, specific questions of pedagogic theory, teaching procedure and methodology at the interface of language and literature are addressed.

From a pedagogic point of view it is the case in many parts of the world that students focus on literary texts, especially in the mother tongue, before undertaking any formal study of the language. With this fact in mind, contributors to the series have attempted to gloss all new technical terms and to assume on the part of their readers little or no previous knowledge of linguistics or formal language studies. They see no merit in not being detailed and explicit about what they describe in the linguistic properties of texts, but they recognise that formal language study can seem forbidding if it is not properly introduced.

A further characteristic of the series is that the authors engage in a direct relationship with their readers. The overall style of writing is informal and there is above all an attempt to lighten the usual style of academic discourse. In some cases this extends to the way in which notes and guidance for further work are presented. In all cases, the style adopted by authors is judged to be that most appropriate to the mediation of their chosen subject matter.

We now come to two major points of principle which underlie the conceptual scheme for the series. One is that the term 'literature' cannot be defined in isolation from an expression of ideology. In fact, no academic study, and certainly no description of the language of texts, can be neutral and objective, for the socio-cultural positioning of the analyst will mean that the description is unavoidably political. Contributors to the series recognize and, in so far as this accords with the aims of each book, attempt to explore the role of ideology at the interface of language and literature. Secondly, most writers also prefer the term 'literatures' to a singular notion of literature. Some replace 'literature' altogether with the term 'text'. It is for this reason that readers will not find exclusive discussion of the literary language of canonical literary texts; instead, the linguistic heterogeneity of literature and the permeation of many discourses with what is conventionally thought of as poetic or literary language will be a focus. This means that in places as much space can be devoted to examples of word play in jokes, newspaper editorials, advertisements, historical writing or a popular thriller as to a sonnet by Shakespeare or a passage from Jane Austen. It is also important to stress how the term 'literature' itself is historically variable and how different social and cultural assumptions can condition what is regarded as literature. In this respect the role of linguistic and literary theory is vital. It is an aim of the series to be constantly alert to new developments in the description and theory of texts.

Finally, as series editor, I have to underline the partnership and cooperation of the whole enterprise of the Interface series and acknowledge the advice and assistance received at many stages from the PALA Committee and from Wendy Morris at Routledge. In turn, we are all fortunate to have the benefit of three associate editors with considerable collective depth of experience in this field in different parts of the world: Professor Roger Fowler, Professor Mary Louise Pratt, Professor Michael Halliday. In spite of their own individual orientations, I am sure that all concerned with the series would want to endorse the statement by Roman Jakobson made over twenty-five years ago but which is no less relevant today.

A linguist deaf to the poetic function of language and a literary scholar indifferent to linguistic problems and unconversant with linguistic methods, are equally flagrant anachronisms.

The nature of David Birch's contribution to the Interface series is a potentially daunting one: that of providing an overview of developments in language-centred criticism in the twentieth century. His approach to the subject is an illuminating one which combines detailed attention to the particularities of textual analysis with an awareness of underlying theoretical considerations both in modern linguistics and literary theory. His fundamental distinction between *actual* and *virtual* worlds in critical practice provides key orientation for the reader across the range of diverse approaches to textual commentary which David Birch reviews and evaluates. The result is no bland and neutral survey but an argument that demonstrates a profound scepticism about the claims of much language-centred criticism and which argues for an unambiguous relation of critical practice to theories of language and of the nature of literature as well as to the central, informing impulse of the critic's own relationship to political ideologies. The range and depth of David Birch's coverage makes this book an ideal point of reference for the whole series.

Ronald Carter

Foreword

Language, Literature and Critical Practice was commissioned by Ronald Carter, the general editor of this series, to be a survey of the academic work that has been carried out at the ever-broadening interface of language and literary studies. Whilst I have attempted to write to that brief, I have also been conscious of the impossibility of the task.

Years ago, there may only have been *one* interface to handle, though I doubt it. Today, interfaces are legion – and that presents something of a dilemma. On the one hand, the very diversity of interests that inform contemporary critical practice is what makes text analysis such an exciting and dynamic occupation, on the other, no one individual can ever hope to be expert in all that diversity. With that in mind, then, *Language, Literature and Critical Practice* is *my* reading of how some of the major twentieth-century theoretical, philosophical, and critical/political positions have influenced textual analysis. Other positions, other assumptions, may preoccupy other people to greater or lesser extents.

David Birch

Acknowledgements

I would like to thank, in particular, John Frow for his detailed critique of the manuscript, and for the very stimulating discussions we had as a result of his readings. My thanks must also go to Michael O'Toole, Bob Hodge, Anthea Gupta, and Ron Carter for the very careful attention they paid to this book in typescript, and to Shirley and Don Murfitt for giving me a quiet cottage in the country in which to write it.

For permission to reprint material from works in copyright the author and publisher make grateful acknowledgement as follows:

'The Old Men admiring themselves in the Water' by W. B. Yeats is reprinted from *The Poems of W. B. Yeats* and the passage from 'Per Amica Silentia Lunae' by W. B. Yeats is reprinted from *Mythologies* by permission of A. P. Watt Ltd on behalf of Michael B. Yeats and Macmillan (London) Ltd; 'The Death of a Soldier' and the lines from 'The Motive for Metaphor' and 'Man Carrying Thing' by Wallace Stevens are reprinted by permission of Faber and Faber Ltd from *The Collected Poems of Wallace Stevens*; 'Note on Local Flora' by William Empson is reprinted from *Collected Poems* by permission of the estate of the author and Chatto and Windus Ltd; 'The Thought Fox' by Ted Hughes is reprinted by permission of Faber and Faber Ltd from *The Hawk in the Rain* by Ted Hughes; 'Lines on a Young Lady's Photograph Album' by Philip Larkin is reprinted from *The Less Deceived* by permission of the Marvell Press, England; 'There was a Saviour' by Dylan Thomas is reprinted from *The Poems* by permission of David Higham Associates on behalf of J. M. Dent & Sons Ltd; 'if everything happens that can't be done' by e. e. cummings is reprinted by permission of Grafton Books, a division of the Collins Publishing Group; 'Encapsulated' by Colin Johnson is reprinted by permission of Hyland House Publishing Pty. Ltd.

Text analyses

Preface

A book neither begins nor ends: at most it pretends to. (Derrida, 'Living on' in *Deconstruction and Criticism*, pp. 96–7)

I am acutely aware of the lack of fit that can exist very often between the progress of linguistic and literary theorists as intellectuals, and the curriculum and classroom practices they, and others influenced by them, are institutionally involved in. This book is an attempt to show to students, who are usually powerless in the institutional decisions and practices of teaching literary text analysis, the development of a critical practice/textual analysis that is becoming increasingly interdisciplinary, intertextual, historically and socially aware, and politically motivated – a critical practice that draws from a number of related and competing theoretical and methodological positions, and that questions those positions as part of its practice.

Language, Literature and Critical Practice foregrounds a number of these competing positions to demonstrate, in particular, that any form of textual analysis is grounded in theory and informed by ideology. More often than not books which cover the analysis of text do so as if the methodology of analysis exists in a theoryless vacuum, and techniques of analysis are presented without questioning the philosophical and ideological assumptions 'behind' the techniques (e.g. Cummings and Simmons 1983). In writing this book, I have tried to present a wide-ranging survey of textual analyses that is informed at all times by a social, historical, political, theoretical, and ideological awareness of 'where' the analysis 'is coming from'.

To that extent, then, this is not a traditional survey book written by someone who stands back from the work and comments 'objectively' on the 'progress' of a discipline. I have a distinct thesis that argues for an understanding of the history of textual analysis this century in terms of whether it is theoretically based in an *idealized* world or in an *actual* world. By actual, or real world I mean a world that is culturally, socially and institutionally determined; that is messy, noisy, and full of disturbances, surprises, and instabilities – I do not see reality as a psychological reality at all, but in relativist terms. My own position rejects idealization, and as a consequence I structure the book as a dialectic between a critical practice theoretically grounded in virtual-time analysis, and one that is theoretically grounded in real-time analysis. The consequence of this is that I draw together a number of theorists/analysts who privilege discourse analysis, and against their positions I survey the overall work of language analysis of literary texts.

Chapter 1 is an outline of a critical practice and an awareness that have developed in recent years as a reaction against the narrowness of the structuralist linguistic model of meaning and the moral orthodoxies of intrinsic criticism. It is this critical practice that I would offer as a reasonable and valuable means of analysing text. The subsequent chapters of the book are an account of the development of a number of theories and critical positions which inform, in one way or another, the practice outlined in Chapter 1, and that, in a variety of forms, are still practised in educational intitutions across the world.

Chapter 2 introduces the basic concepts of a theory of language founded on a philosophy of difference and contradiction. It is against this theory and its relation to a drive towards scientificity, that all major twentieth-century text analysis needs to be measured. Varieties of linguistic and literary theories based on a fundamental contrast between the idealized world of Saussurean *langue* and the actual world of Saussurean *parole* have been the dominant feature of twentieth-century text analysis. Understanding this background is crucial.

Chapters 3 and 4 examine some of the major traditions, assumptions and practices (and their consequences for text analysis) of a range of critical practices which, for the purposes of this book, I will consider as *intrinsic* criticism. The implicit distinction in using this label is that 'intrinsic' criticism is not extrinsic, i.e. it is not concerned with things 'outside' the text, but only with things 'inside' the text. Intrinsic criticism, as drama theorist Richard Hornby points out, 'examines the work in isolation and in considerable detail, with the only goal being, as T. S. Eliot put it 'to point out what the reader might otherwise have missed' (Hornby, 1977:16). This is necessarily a convenient fiction, suggesting a uniformity of thinking where often there is considerable dissention, but within the scope of this book I think it important to distinguish between a critical practice which is concerned, for the most part, with isolating the literary text as a 'verbal icon' i.e. a verbal work of art, and a critical practice which is concerned with the literary text in much the same way as it is with any other non-literary text (for example the analyses in Chapter 1).

Chapter 3 concentrates on the developing orthodoxies of Anglo-American New Criticism as part of an *intrinsic* critical practice, and Chapter 4 concentrates on the close reading techniques which were developed by more linguistically aware, though still intrinsic, critical practices.

Chapter 5 deals with the critical positions of analyses that are informed by specifically structuralist linguistic concerns.

The critical practices I present in the book, particularly the critical practice described in Chapter 1, are rarely taught in any coherent, disciplined way; they are often wrongly assumed to be already a part of a student's critical capabilities, even if only piecemeal from a number of positions.

The practice of text analysis I advocate in Chapter 1 is a critical practice which argues that textual analysis as an intellectual pursuit is not, nor should it ever be, assumed to be a quest for knowledge for its own sake. It is a practice which recognizes that intellectual activity has social and political responsibilities; similarly, the educational framework in which most of it takes place should not be considered, as it often is, as a separate, facilitating (but often handicapping) part of that activity. In short, it is a critical practice that recognizes that analysing literary text is first and foremost an institutional practice, requiring institutional skills – something that teachers in those institutions often seem blissfully unaware of. *Language, Literature and Critical Practice* is an account, in effect, of the development of a critically and politically aware analytic practice. And it is against this development that the survey of the interface of language and literature is positioned at any given moment in the book.

There are certain texts, theories, and practices that are valued by some people and institutions more highly than others, for a range of political, economic, social, and aesthetic reasons. Certain literary texts continue to be taught in universities, colleges, and schools as highly valued texts; over time some of these will be replaced, others will remain. Attitudes change, awarenesses change, theories change – but change is not absolute; the slate is never wiped completely clean, for there is always a trace that becomes an integral part of the practice of analysing text. This book is a collage of some of those traces.

These chapters are not indicative of moments in *past* time, of critical practices that no longer happen. They are about the 'here and now' of text analysis. A position developed by a critic in the 1920s doesn't just die out; in one way or another it informs contemporary practices. The variety of practices and theoretical assumptions discussed in *Language, Literature and Critical Practice* are not mutually exclusive practices that can be mapped in a historical line from then to now, but are rather practices that, in one way or another, are a continuing part of contemporary critical analyses.

My focus is on the literary text and on poetry in particular. Other texts such as film, television, the visual arts and so on, will no doubt be the concern of other books in this series. I concentrate on drawing together what I consider to be some of the more distinctive philosophical, political and sociological aspects of linguistic/literary theories and practices, and their consequences for text analysis, and I illustrate where possible by textual analyses drawn from a wide variety of sources. I refer in parentheses to as wide a range of related studies as I know for a given topic, and I include endnotes detailing sources for further study where insertion in the text would break the thread of my argument too much.

My main concern has been to focus on work which specifically analyses literary text in one way or another. I have not set out to write a survey of everything you ever wanted to know about linguistics, literature, philosophy, sociology, politics, and moral theology; neither is this a set of blueprints for reproducing text analysis. It is, I hope, a site for understanding some of the motivations which result in the analysis of text.

1 How texts mean: reading as critical/political practice

But it is not 'or', that is the point.
It is 'and'. Everything is. (Lessing, *Briefing for a Descent into Hell*, p. 141)

Language as showing

According to the philosopher Martin Heidegger, the world can for the most part be seen to mean in two ways: in terms either of 'things' or of 'ways of existing'. If you view the world as he did, in terms of ways of existing, then 'what it means to be in a world is more important than the classification of the world into a kind of entity' (Gelven, 1982:315). In terms of language this means that 'what it means to speak is prior to language; what it means to think comes before an understanding of the entity, mind' (Gelven, 1982:315). Language is therefore a means of understanding what it means *to be*. And this is highly resistant to formal/scientific (either sociologically or psychologically oriented) analysis. The world is not an object which scientists and critics – its subjects – can step out of and analyse, impassively and objectively, and then step back into when they go for lunch or go to the beach. Understanding the world is not simply a matter of end-stopped, closed-off classification of a dichotomy between object and subject. For Heidegger, language is not about representing something; 'it performs real actions in the world of beings' (Koelb, 1984:35). Analysis sets out to understand the whole of a text from its detail, and the detail of a text from its whole – the hermeneutic circle (see Szondi, 1978). This is an important point to understand, because it creates a method of reading and re-reading, that never closes its reading of a text (see, for example, Barthes, 1975; see also Eco, 1979; Riffaterre, 1978; Rosenblatt, 1978).

Understanding, for Heidegger, is a dynamic activity, an interaction or dialogue which is never fully completed, never finished, never closed off. Understanding, therefore, is not an activity which people can *perform*; it is not something that is *done*; it is a part of being, of existence, of language. In that sense it becomes anti-rationalist, almost mystical, and art and therefore literature – assumes a status 'where the truth of the world speaks itself' (Eagleton, 1983:64). Language *shows* rather than *tells* (Gelven, 1982:319).

'Telling' concentrates on the idea of language as *referential*; 'showing' concentrates on the idea of language as *manifestation*. Analysis therefore focuses not on the expression of language, but on what it means for language to speak. So, for example, in his book *Poetry, Language, Thought* (1971) Heidegger writes of the first stanza of Georg Trakl's 'A Winter Evening' that it is not the expression of snow or winter that is important in its meaning, but the 'mode of calling'.

> Window with falling snow is arrayed,
> Long tolls the vesper bell,
> The house is provided well,
> The table is for many laid.
>
> Wandering ones, more than a few,
> Come to the door on darksome courses.
> Golden blooms the tree of graces
> Drawing up the earth's cool dew.
>
> Wanderer quietly steps within;
> Pain has turned the threshold to stone.
> There lie, in limpid brightness shown,
> Upon the table bread and wine.

The first stanza shows itself as an invitation; its importance is not in what it tells (that is, the scene it describes) but how it *calls*. Similarly the second stanza continues 'the bidding things to come' (Heidegger, 1971:200), but in a different way from the first. The first invites things to come to the world of the poem, the second invites the world to come to the things, and the third binds together the world and the things.

What we are dealing with, therefore, is analysis that views text as a means by which writer and reader share an effect not described by a language, but *shown* by a language. This particular texts becomes a metaphor for understanding the struggle for meaning beyond referential language. Behind this 'reading' of the poem is a theory of language that is metaphysical (that is, concerned with being and knowing) rather than descriptive. It is a theory that presents 'a mode of writing without presence and absence – without history, cause, origin or telos – which would overturn all dialectic, theology, teleology, and ontology' (Derrida, 1970:93). In other words, it presents an idealized language constantly interrupted by 'two voices, each perpetually in search of, but unable to find or overcome, the other' (Silverman and Torode, 1980:135; see also, Bakhtin, 1981). Silverman and Torode write

> Heidegger plunges us into the midst of a play of languages, denying to us any secure sense of an outside reality to which we can cling, unless we remain outside that text, trapped within our own illusion of a reality outside the play of languages. (Silverman and Torode, 1980:135)

What is therefore crucial about this way of thinking is that it foregrounds not the individual subject, but an interaction, a struggle, a play, where understanding and meanings can never be fixed. The ego is therefore decentred, and reality becomes a play of languages, where neither voice can ever be determined as correct or incorrect. And it is here that we have a central, fundamental contrast to the traditional empiricist preoccupation with fixed, determinate, unchanging meanings of text (see, for example, Hirsch, 1967, 1976; Altieri, 1978; Fish, 1970; Bloom, 1986), for here is a preoccupation with indeterminacy and with changing, dynamic, meanings of text. The effect, for textual analysis, is to recognize language as *social* and *institutional*, not simply as an individualistic interiorization of meaning, and to recognize meanings as unstable – what Eagleton writes of as 'a continual flickering, spilling and defusing of meaning' (Eagleton, 1983:134).

The play of meanings

Jacques Derrida engaged with Heidegger's discussion of how texts *show*, and developed it into a discussion of how writing generates meaning through a constant process of *differing* and *deferring* – what he called *différance*. In effect this challenges the conception of texts as having fixed centres of meaning. It challenges, for example, the prioritizing of stable meanings and the sort of thinking, for example, that requires a locatable centre to a text; an idea, a philosophy or a religion – the sort of thinking that requires stability or that fears the unknown. What Derrida argues is that meaning is best understood in terms of the relationship (the play) between the known and the unknown, presence and absence, the stable and the unstable. This is not, as is often thought, anarchic: he doesn't suggest that the unstable should take over from the stable. If that happened then this would merely create a new centre, another form of meaning based on stability. His argument is that the constant deferring of presence means that the centre is never fixed. Hence a single, fixed meaning can never be determined; it is constantly postponed and deferred. (Derrida, 1967; 1973).

Texts are therefore decentred. Texts which have been set up as 'deeply mediated constructs not available to understanding except through a study of history or of the intertextual character of all writing' (Hartman, 1979:187) are deconstructed. 'Deconstruction' is a powerful expression used to describe a critical practice that rejects the traditional idea that assumes literary texts to be 'structures of determinate meaning accessible by objective critical procedures' (Raval, 1986:119). What this means in practice is that there is no such thing as a 'full', complete or determinate meaning, because finding the 'full' meaning would involve a never-ending search — just as tracing a word through a dictionary can result in a constant deferring of meaning by the dictionary suggesting another word, which you then have to trace, and then another and then another, and so on, leading to a continual postponement of the moment when you could say you had the full, complete meaning for the word.

In a discussion called 'Living on', Derrida engages with these ideas in some detail, developing them by reference to the meaning of *meaning* and to the meaning of *being*. In other words, does life have meaning? Does it have value? And if it does, then what is the essence of life, as Derrida calls the *'être-vivant'*, the 'living-ness' of life? (Derrida, 1979:79) Referring to *The Triumph of Life* by Shelley, Derrida problematizes these questions by problematizing the status of text, writer, and reading, suggesting that there is no single meaning of meaning which belongs to the poem written by Shelley, or which belongs to Shelley. There is no writerly or textual 'essence' of meaning which is fixed and determined for all time. The status of the text, for Derrida, can no longer be determined by its boundaries; where it starts or ends, for example, on a page, or where meanings start or end. His position is that no text is ever finished; meanings are never completed either by the text running out (at the end of the page or book, for example), or by the determinations of a writer intent on fixing a single meaning 'into' the text somewhere. Thus the text, for Derrida, is a complex network of unfinished meanings, 'a fabric of traces referring endlessly to something other than itself' (Derrida, 1979:84). The notion of text, is therefore, no longer an easy, comfortable one, in which openings and endings of meaning are recognizable by readers. Its openings and endings are, for Derrida, never actually found, and as a consequence reading becomes a much more dynamic, but uncertain, acitivity. In 'Border lines' which runs as a separate but related text at the foot of each page of 'Living on', Derrida writes: ' . . . no path comes back in its circle to a first step, none proceeds from the simple to the complex, none leads from a beginning to an end' (Derrida, 1979:96). Questions about text therefore demand other questions, resulting in what Paul de Man called a 'movement of effacing and forgetting' (de Man, 1979b:44) – a movement, therefore, of increasing uncertainty of being able to 'fix' meaning; 'an inability to know' (de Man, 1979b:51).

The importance of this notion of 'forgetting' is crucial, because it sets up a dialectic, between a state of knowing and a state of not-knowing, an indeterminacy about meanings and knowledge, which is crucial to the theory of deconstruction. In an article called 'Shelley disfigured', Paul de Man looks at *The Triumph of Life* not simply in terms of it as a text worth reading and analysing for its own sake, but as a text which enables him to develop arguments about the inability to determine meaning. *The Triumph of Life*, like many texts of the Romantics, has proved useful in the theorization of indeterminacy, because it seems to resist fixed meanings – *closure*. For example, lines II. 332–5.

Whether my life had been before that sleep
The heaven which I imagine, or a Hell

Like this harsh world in which I wake to weep
I know not.

allow de Man to argue that the polarities of waking/sleeping and remembering/forgetting are 'scrambled' with those of past/present, imagined/real and knowing/not knowing (de Man, 1979b:51). It is impossible to know, therefore, whether 'we are awake or asleep, dead or alive, forgetting or remembering. We cannot tell the difference between sameness and difference. . . .' (de Man,

1979:51). What is described, therefore, is a condition of indeterminacy, which accords perfectly with Derridean/deconstructivist ideas about meanings. Similarly, lines II.425–32:

> The presence of that Shape which on the stream
> Moved, as I moved along the wilderness.
>
> More dimly than a day-appearing dream,
> The ghost of a forgotten form of sleep,
> A light from heaven whose half-extinguished beam
>
> Through the sick day in which we wake to weep
> Glimmers, forever sought, forever lost.
> So did that shape its obscure tenour keep. . . .

allow de Man to argue that it is impossible to say 'how the polarities of light and dark are matched with those of waking and sleep' (de Man, 1979b:52). There is, he argues, a confusion of forgetting and remembering. The light is said to be like a dream, but it shines on a condition of awakening: ' . . . in this light, to be awake is to be as if one were asleep' (de Man, 1979b:52). This creates an experience, for de Man, similar to that of trying to read *The Triumph of Life* ' . . . as its meaning glimmers, hovers and wavers, but refuses to yield the clarity it keeps announcing' (de Man, 1979b:53). He calls this a 'play of veiling and unveiling – an image that stands well as a descriptor for the deconstructivist enterprise. The thematization of light in *The Triumph of Life* is therefore considered as a reading of the text, but also as a reading of the critical enterprise de Man is engaged in. Just as *The Triumph of Life* seems to set up clear, uncompromising themes and meanings, and then dissolve them into indeterminacies, so the deconstructivist enterprise sets up what appear to be firm readings of texts in order to demonstrate by deconstructing these readings, the play, rather than the inflexibility, of signification.

This necessarily demands a theory and practice of intertextuality; a recognition that 'one text reads another' (Derrida, 1979:107); a recognition that each text, each meaning, no matter how complete it might appear to be, is effectively always a fragment (de Man, 1979b:41). Derrida's reading of *The Triumph of Life* is therefore also a reading of many texts, some of which can be 'named', such as Maurice Blanchot's 'Celui qui ne m'accompagnait pas', and some which can't be named. These readings are interlarded with readings of other texts, including 'Living on' and 'Border lines', so that the beginning and end of the reading of *The Triumph of Life* are impossible to find 'within' the text 'Living on'. 'Each text', Derrida writes, 'is a machine with multiple reading heads for other texts' (Derrida, 1979:107).

What that also means for text analysis is that there is no final point at which you can declare that you have found *the* meaning or reached the final, definitive interpretation. And that, in the light of the other critical practices in operation, makes deconstruction a very exhilarating, but volatile, practice, as it turns its attention not just to literary texts, but also to literary criticisms (see Felperin, 1985; Norris, 1982; Leitch, 1983; Machin and Norris, 1987). Having said this, there are of course edges and borders to a text, and these are set not by the text or the writer, but by institutional practices that determine what constitutes meaning; what constitutes, for example, literature and what constitutes life. Deconstruction, for Derrida, does not simply entail the deconstruction of meanings associated with specific literary or philosophical texts, it involves deconstruction of philosophies and institutions, in particular the institution of myopic western intellectual practices.

This means, of course, that you have to ask yourself 'when and where do I stop the process of deconstruction, the process of interpretation?' And that allows critical decisions to be made that are not simply determined by a method, by a theory, or by a text. Those decisions have to be made by the analyst of the text and they therefore become political. They also throw into considerable doubt the privileged status of the writer (see Barthes, 1975, 1977; Foucault, 1975; Ricoeur, 1971: Riffaterre, 1973) and problematizes the status of both text (Barthes, 1975; 1981) and discourse (Foucault, 1971, 1972).

There is a danger of supposing that what is being said here is startlingly new – a product of the 70s and 80s. For the most part it isn't new. In his essay on William Wordsworth, 'Sense in *The Prelude*' (Empson, 1951b), William Empson makes the point that if an analyst were to follow a particular word through a text (as I suggested earlier for a dictionary) then there is a strong likelihood that its meanings will shift and alter, allowing no single meaning to dominate. He takes as an example the word 'sense' in *The Prelude* and looks at the 35 occurrences of it. The result is a range of meanings associated with the word 'sense' that suggests for Wordsworth an incoherence of a degree not normally associated with such a valorized writer.

This approach would have had serious repercussions for critical analysis had critics followed Empson's thinking. What they did, for the most part, was to reject it. In the preface to the 1951 (second) edition of *The Structure of Complex Words*, Empson cited some of the objections reviewers had levelled against his work: one of them wrote that he had a 'narrow or mechanical view of meaning' and as a result 'could never deal with images' (Empson, 1951a:xi), and that he was 'profiteering from the looseness of the word's meaning rather than profiting from its complexity,' (Empson, 1951a:xi) The decision by the majority of critics to steer clear of an approach that allowed for the 'play' of meanings kept criticism on its stable, determined quest for centred meanings for many years after. But Empson's point about meaning in the *Prelude* is an important one, signalling an attitude that recognized the impossibility of tying meanings down – an attitude that many deconstructionists have since theorized more thoroughly.

Paul de Man points out in his book *The Rhetoric of Romanticism* (de Man, 1984:83–92) that not only is there a literary canon, but there are canonical readings too – readings that are fixed and unchanged. In his chapter on Wordsworth he is interested in a canonical reading of Wordsworth that does not present the incoherence that Empson 'uncovered'. He picks up Empson's technique, and looks at a key word, 'face', in the corpus of *The Prelude*. He argues that it is used coherently throughout the corpus, but recognizes that others, like 'sense', can lead to 'near-total chaos', as Empson demonstrates. He concludes by writing

> It would be naive to believe that we could ever face Wordsworth, a poet of sheer language, outright. But it would be more naive still to think we can take shelter from what he knew by means of the very evasions which this knowledge renders impossible. (de Man, 1984:92)

What de Man is saying, therefore, developing Empson's undeveloped theory of indeterminacy, is that even in the apparently stable and coherent conditions of language in a text (as appears to be the case for 'face' compared to 'sense') critics can never be secure, can never find a fixed meaning.

Harold Bloom points out that 'our idealisms about texts are poor illusions' (Bloom, 1979:7) and that in practice there are no texts, just interpretations – a position that has led Geoffrey Hartman to argue that the critic, on reading a literary text, becomes the creator of the text (Hartman, 1975, 1980). This notion opens up a crucially important, and sensitive, area in literary studies, because the difference between literature and criticism, always central to the field, is now seemingly wiped away by the question 'what happens to "the concept of art"?' (see Hartman, 1975).

In effect, then, this sort of deconstructionist criticism is based on a theory of fictions 'all of which are shown not to be false but "undecidable" by virtue of the notion that referentiality is always totally internalized in the linguistic chain and meaning infinitely deferred' (Adams, 1983:198; cf. Jameson, 1972). We are, of course, in the world of the ideal, the closed world of a theory of language understood in terms of the arbitrariness of the sign. And we are in the world of the institutions of literary criticism and higher education, with their requirements, constraints and controls (see Kermode, 1979 and Culler, 1987). But the advantages for textual analysis are nevertheless considerable. A deconstructionist approach, following Nietzsche, allows a critic to interrogate 'the linguistic means by which a text or discourse comes to exercise its power' (Norris, 1980:282), but such an approach is, as Christopher Norris continues, 'only . . . as useful and enlightening as the mind which puts it to work' (Norris, 1980:291).

This notion of 'interrogation' is important in a deconstructionist approach to analysis, because central to the deconstructionist enterprise is a questioning of the underlying assumptions of a text.

What constitutes a text, of course, is a crucial issue. Jacques Derrida made the point that 'there is nothing outside the text', which on the one hand might seem to argue against recognizing context if, that is, text is considered simply as words, for example, 'in' a text. If the understanding of text is much larger than that, if it includes, for example signifying practices, and structures of representation (see Norris, 1984b:206) beyond the words on the page, then Derrida's statement becomes representative of a powerful political activity. In this case what is interrogated, therefore, is not simply the linguistic structure of a text, but the ideological, philosophical, economic, and historical practices of the text. So, for example, Edward Said, who would not consider himself a Derridean deconstructionist, has deconstructed the western construction of 'Orientalism', which he argues has presented a consistently distorted and stereotyped western image of oriental ideas, people, art, literature, and so on. In other words, he interrogates western texts about Orientalism to show how distorted they are. It is a process of deconstruction that demytho-logizes the text by using the resources of western scholarship against itself (see Said, 1978, 1979). The 'deconstructive force' (Norris, 1984b:210) of Said's work on western perceptions and writings about non-western societies is that it questions the assumptions at the base of the text in order to question the ideology 'behind' those texts.

Interdiscourse/Intertextualities

The developing critical practice of the last decade or so has incorporated a number of theoretical and methodological positions, including selected ideas from Derrida, Foucault, Bakhtin, Barthes, Freud, Kristeva, Lacan, Althusser, Habermas, Marx, Bourdieu, Irigaray, Pêcheux, Halliday and many others, and has resulted in a markedly different text analysis from that of intrinsic criticism. This developing critical practice has led to a far greater diversity of theoretical awareness, informed by a wide variety of discourses and political commitments (see Harland, 1987). It has also encouraged a deconstructing of the literary canon (cf. Fiedler and Baker, 1981; Hyland, 1986), with more and more critics turning their attention to other traditionally margi-nalized non-canonical texts and discourses.

The consequence is that many interests and disciplines that, for many working within intrinsic criticism, were usually considered separately are now combined (see, Leech, 1969, on the linguistics of English poetry and Leech, 1966, on advertising). Samuel Jay Keyser, for example, combines his interest in poetry (particularly in Wallace Stevens) with an interest in advertising in order to assess the extent to which modern advertising 'makes use of the many formal devices that literature and the visual arts do' (Keyser, 1983:305). Carol Edwards combines an interest in contemporary literary and ethnomethodological work on narrative with an interest in traditional folklore in a paper centred on joke analysis (Edwards, 1984; cf. Jakobson and Bogatyrev, 1971, for a struc-turalist/folklore interface, and Nash, 1985, for a close reading of comic discourse). Robert McCarl combines folklore theory, narrative analysis, performance analysis, and literary structuralism in a paper analysing the performance of participants in a fire-fighter's retirement dinner, situating the transcribed text of the whole proceedings with the institutional discourse of firefighting culture (McCarl, 1984). The dinner, the speeches, the running commentary of the MC, and the retirement process which set all of this in train are analysed as a text, which as a text is considered to be understandable only in terms of the larger discourse of firefighting culture. This is an important point and a crucial aspect of post-structuralist critical practice, following the work of Michel Foucault and Michel Pêcheux in particular (see, for example, Foucault, 1972, 1980; Pêcheux, 1975a, 1975b).

Indeed, one of the central aims of the work of Michel Foucault is to demonstrate that texts mean not because of their supposed 'objective' structures, but because they are the result of *discursive formations* 'which are intricated in the ideological system of a society' (Frow, 1983:94). Discourse is a social process; its subjects are 'interdiscourses' (Pêcheux, 1975a) determined ideologically and politically by a variety of discursive practices.

This signals a use of the term 'discourse' that is quite distinct from its use in 'everyday' practice. Discourse, in this sense, indicates formations that are much larger than individual language texts: the discourse of doctor–patient relationships, the discourse of apartheid, the discourse of feminism, the discourse of educational practices, and so on. This discourse can then be read as text. So, for example, John Fiske, in a fascinating article in the *Australian Journal of Cultural Studies*, reads the discourse of the Australian beach as a text. The 'author' of the beach 'text' is not a named individual, as is often the practice with other texts, but is a 'historically determined set of community practices' (Fiske, 1983: 120) that have produced a number of material objects and signs by which to read the text: kiosks, changing rooms, regulations, danger signs, concrete steps, and so on. The beach can therefore be read as a text by examining and analysing these signs and how together they *form* a discourse (discourse formations). What Fiske does for the beach can be done with any set of signs that form a distinctive discourse. So, for example, Bruce Gronbeck in an analysis of the Black Action Movement at the University of Michigan in 1970 (Gronbeck, 1973) demonstrates the daily activities of a group of people over a period of a few days bringing pressure to bear on a university (including a strike) to be a text. David Goldberg examining the language of apartheid (Goldberg, 1986/7), and Raymond Suttner exploring the role of the judiciary in South Africa (Suttner, 1984) treat their subjects as discourses to be analysed as texts; Robert Hodge uses a CND march as a text (Hodge, 1985). Discourse is therefore a social process; its subjects are 'interdiscourses' (Pecheux, 1975) determined ideologically and politically by a variety of discursive practices.

Analysis along these lines is therefore a political activity, in more obvious ways than theories of deconstruction, such analysis operates on a principle that all texts are political because all discursive formations are political (see Fairclough, 1988; Bourdieu, 1985). They are political because they are, following Nietzsche, involved in *power*, and power is immanent in discourse (Foucault, 1972:95). Understand that knowledge and you begin to understand what is involved in the play of power. Analysis of discourse, and of the discursive practices that generate text, is therefore an analysis of history, because history is basically a series of discursive practices, each with its particular ideologies and ways of controlling power (see Said, 1975, 1979, 1980, 1983).

There is therefore no room, in a critical practice that extends its notions of discourse so far, for the idea of an absolute, either in what is constituted as text or in terms of 'truth'; there is therefore no room for 'objectivity'. Knowledge is relative to a particular discursive practice that may change at a given time and in a given space. No knowledge is ever fixed for ever. Edward Said, following the work of Foucault, wrote:

> Monocentrism is practised when we mistake one idea as the only idea, instead of recognizing that an idea in history is always one among many. Monocentrism denies plurality, it totalizes structure, it sees profit where there is waste, it decrees the concentricity of Western culture instead of its eccentricity, it believes continuity to be given and will not try to understand, instead, how continuity as much as discontinuity, is made. (Said, 1979:188)

The negotiation of meanings

Georg Lukács, writing in 1936 and broadly following the theories of Karl Marx, argued for a recognition that the forms of literature (for example, the novel) do not change internally; that is, they do not change as a result of some autonomous force solely *within* the genre, but as a result of political, social and economic pressures upon the genre (though the genre itself may not necessarily keep pace with the changes in society)[1] (see Eagleton, 1976a, 1976b). Understanding meaning, therefore, is a question of recognizing social reality. But what constitutes 'social reality'? Broadly, a Marxist position grounds social reality in a history of struggles centred upon class and systems of production, reflecting at any given moment a dialectical relationship between history and society. The capitalist society of 'intrinsic' and extrinsic criticism in the west has been founded on a base of exploitation, and as a consequence Marxist analysis of that society is effectively centred on conflict of one form or another.

Pierre Macherey, following Louis Althusser, centred his theory of reading the relationship of the literary text and reality on a view that asserts that 'Literature "produces" ideology by writing it out' (Forgacs, 1982:148). In other words, this theory assumes that ideologies need a shape, a form, in which to exist. Conflict is therefore a part of the literary text, because 'literature challenges ideology by using it' (Macherey, 1978:133). This is a crucial point because it focuses not just on the status of literature, but also on the status of criticism. An intrinsic understanding of interpretation implies that a text has a coherent meaning that simply needs to be discovered by the critic. Macherey and Althusser would disagree and argue that meaning isn't simply located *within* the text, but is explained in terms of its larger site of production:

> . . . a true analysis does not remain within its object, paraphrasing what has already been said; analysis confronts the silences, the denials and the resistance in the object – not that compliant implied discourse which offers itself to discovery, but the condition which makes the work possible, which precedes the work so absolutely that it cannot be found in the work. (Macherey, 1978:150)

Central to this approach, then, is the analysis of ideology – and crucial to any understanding of ideology is the role of language. Macherey did not develop this idea to any great extent, but the work of Mikhail Bakhtin/Valentin Voloshinov did. (Bakhtin used several of his friends' names in order to publish some of his work, which might not have been published or banned if published under his own.)

The work of Bakhtin/Voloshinov, mostly written in the 1920s (Bakhtin/Voloshinov, 1930; 1968, 1973, 1981), has gained prominence in the 1980s, mainly through the work of Julia Kristeva (Kristeva, 1980) and Roger Fowler (Fowler, 1981), for a developing critical practice concerned with ideology. The theory of language established in this work rejects the dichotomies of structuralism and argues that the text is a site for the 'negotiation of meanings': meanings that result from a range of other texts and contexts – other 'voices'. The text is the product of *social* interaction and intertextualities; the basic unit of language is interactive (*dialogic*), 'a two-sided act' (Bakhtin, 1973:86).[2] The 'sign' is multi-accented (*heteroglossic*), resulting in discourse as an 'arena of struggle' (Threadgold 1986:23). Ideology for Bakhtin/ Voloshinov is 'the material embodiment of social interaction' (Forgacs, 1982:161), with the emphasis upon discourse, dialogue (see Bakhtin, 1981), and literature as practices rather than expressions of social reality. The subject is therefore a social subject constituted by material forces – ideology – rather than by some form of rational consciousness.

Feminist criticism

Analysis of literature as the product of social relations has found its strongest, and one of its most politically necessary, expressions, in feminist analysis of text. When Kate Millett read the work of D. H. Lawrence as 'a progression from misogynistic homo-eroticism in *Aaron's Rod* to the narcissistic cult of male supremacy in *Lady Chatterley's Lover*' in her book *Sexual Politics* (Millett, 1969), she was developing in criticism a polemicism which had found a voice in Simone de Beauvoir (de Beauvoir, 1949) and which would continue to develop in force in the 1970s and 1980s. These voices have a clear message: women are oppressed by the patriarchal order (see, for example, Eisenstein, 1979; Barrett, 1980; and the poetry of Atwood, 1972). Text analysis therefore needs to recognize that every reading is a *gendered* reading because all text production is gendered.[3] Speaking/writing is not neutral/neuter.

Oppression comes not simply with the obvious patriarchal structures; it can also come with the psychological and social formation of gendered subjects, who can be disabled as objects by controlling, dominant, but often unconscious, gendered interests (see Kelly-Gadol, 1976).[4] Analysis, therefore, is concerned with the construction and deconstruction of the political, social, psychological, and historical formations and processes of gendered text (see, for example, Moi, 1985; Marks and de Courtivron, 1981; Abel, 1982).

Analysis is therefore about conflicting ideologies. Elaine Showalter argues that 'The task of feminist critics is to find a new language, a new way of reading that can integrate our intelligence and our experience, our reason and our suffering, our skepticism and our vision' (Showalter, 1985a:141). Criticism and reading (see Fetterley, 1978, Flynn, 1983) is therefore 're-visionist, it questions the adequacy of existing conceptual structures' (Godard, 1985:168).

> The new sciences of the text based on linguistics, computers, generic structuralism, deconstruction, neoformalism and deformalism, affective stylistics, and psychoaesthetics have offered literary critics the opportunity to demonstrate that the work they do is as manly and aggressive as nuclear physics – not intuitive, expressive and feminine, but strenuous, rigorous, impersonal and virile. (Showalter, 1985a:140)

Her response:

> The appropriate task for feminist criticism, I believe, is to concentrate on women's access to language, on the available lexical range for which words can be selected, on the ideological and cultural determinants of expression. (Showalter, 1985c:255)

Language is of course one of the major means of oppression (see Lakoff, 1975; Cameron, 1985),[5] but a difficulty arises in the creation of 'new worlds from words' – Barbara Godard asks 'How can one be an object, be constructed by a ruling discourse and still constitute an opposition to it, be outside enough to mark an alternative? If outside, how can one be heard at all? (Godard, 1985:167). The answer, for her as for Luce Irigaray (Irigaray, 1977; 1985), lies in writers who 'redraw the circle for us, shift the relationships of centre and periphery, of authoritative word and marginal silence' (Godard, 1985:167).[6]

The challenge to the centre is not new, but in feminist analysis and criticism it is ideologically motivated, intent on seeing the concept of difference (by which that centre has been defined for so long as an opposition between presence and absence) changed. This, then, is more than just analysis aimed at demythologizing negative images of women; it is the development of a feminist ideology, a feminist poetics (see Showalter, 1985b).

As part of the move towards that poetics, some (though by no means all, cf. Irigaray, 1977) feminist critics have turned their attention to the psychoanalytic work of Jacques Lacan, who argues for understanding perception by means of recognizing the split subjectivity, divided between 'being' and the 'social speaking self' (the split between *moi/je*). The ego is constructed by perception of objects, it is not 'in' the perception already. This theory is important because it argues that meaning is not 'in' anything, it is a construction, a drama (Lacan, 1977; see also Gallop, 1982; Mitchell, 1975; Kristeva, 1974, 1980). It also enables the act of analysis to be more prominent. Freud assumed he was a neutral, innocent observer; his world was populated 'by activities without human agents' (Schwartz, 1978:7), but it is exactly this human agency that feminist criticism wishes to foreground. Furthermore, meaning is not considered to be immanent in a text, which therefore motivates a feminist criticism to construct meaning, not simply to 'discover' it. Lacanian psychoanalytics does not psychoanalyse a text (as Freudian psychoanalysis does) it 'rescrutinizes' the way meanings are made (Ragland-Sullivan, 1984:382).

Bearing this in mind, analysis of text is not just a matter of discussing certain effects of language in a text, it can be – needs to be – a powerful method for understanding the ways in which all sorts of realities are constructed through language (cf. Burton, 1982:201; see also Berger and Luckman, 1967; St Clair, 1982; Alexander, 1982; Fowler 1981, 1986; Kress, 1985a, 1988a. Hodge and Kress, 1982; Aers and Kress, 1982; Aers *et al.*, 1981). As Barbara Godard, citing Roland Barthes, writes: ' . . . every theory of language implies a whole philosophy of history: every form of practice implies and presupposes a form of theory whose denial is a mask' (Godard, 1985:165).

Language, text, coherence

Analysis requires a curiosity about the way language works in discourse, and it is this curiosity that requires an analyst not simply to describe by using a series of grammatical and linguistic labels, but to probe the language. This probing requires a quite dramatic shift of attention away from the idea that meanings are contained within the words and structures towards explaining and understanding meanings constructed by all producers of language – writers/readers, speakers/hearers. What that means in effect is recognizing from the beginning that when we are faced with analysis, for whatever reason, we need, in the first instance, to engage with (and, I would suggest, reject) two assumptions:

1 that there is a meaning *in* a text 'put in' by a writer which has to be 'fished out' by the reader/hearer/critic/analyst in order for the interpretive process to take place;

2 that a text can be treated as self-contained, a contextless artefact, a text 'in its own right'.

Central to this rejection is the crucial notion that analysing text is an activity which is concerned with understanding *how* a text means, not with *what* a text means (cf. Belsey, 1980, Easthope, 1983; Norris, 1982, 1984).

Analysing what a text means implies a position that involves finding and extracting meaning(s) from a text; it is a 'search and remove' activity. This undertaking is based on a theory that states that meanings have been 'put into' the text by the writer or speaker, and that it is the job of the reader/hearer/analyst/critic to discover them. It is effectively a static operation, and has produced over many years a wide variety of *formal* objective approaches, in which the personality, beliefs, background, the biases of the reader/critic are considered not only irrelevant, but a positive hindrance to textual interpretation.

Analysing how a text means involves a much more dynamic activity, whose underlying theory suggests that meanings aren't simply 'put into' a text by a writer/speaker, but are constructed by the reader/hearer. That doesn't mean that the writer/speaker has nothing to do with the text – what it means is that the only way we have of constructing a reading for a text is through our *own* socially determined language as reader/hearer. In effect, that means that each time a reader reads a text, a *new* text is created. Whose text is it? The writer/speaker's or yours? That of the editor of the book or yours? That of the performer in a poetry reading/ play or yours? Whose voice are you when you are reading? Yours? Or the writer's? When you are attempting to make a text coherent – to understand how it means – what criteria do you use for discarding what you don't think necessary or relevant? Criteria developed by the writer or developed by you?

You cannot make a statement about a particular idea *in* a text. What you can do is to make a statement about a particular idea that you have constructed *for* the text. You have to use your own language in order to get to the writer's, and in so doing you can never actually get to the writer's because your own language and the institutions which have created it get in the way. You cannot escape your own language, and you cannot stop using your own language in order to construct a reading of what you might consider to be someone else's text. What you construct is your own linguistic engagement with the text – your own language, which is itself constructed and determined by social, cultural, ideological, and institutional forces. The American critic Harold Bloom puts it this way: 'I only *know* a text, any text, because I know a reading of it, someone else's reading, my own reading, a composite reading' (Bloom, 1979:8).

This is a very important argument and one that stands against the idea that literature exists for its own sake – beyond a reader's experience of it. F. W. Bateson presents the other side of the argument in *Essays in Critical Dissent*:

> As the *Mona Lisa* exists both within and outside the various reactions to it by visitors to the Louvre, so there is an objective *Hamlet*, behind our individual experiences of it, which enables us to say of a particular performance that it is 'wrong-headed' or 'one-sided'. (Bateson, 1972:9–10)

But where is this objective text of the *Mona Lisa* or *Hamlet*? Is it the one constructed by the painter/writer? When the Louvre is closed for the night, the galleries in darkness and no one about, is the painting on the wall still the *Mona Lisa*, or does it require recognition as the *Mona Lisa* before it 'becomes' the *Mona Lisa*? Similarly for *Hamlet* – for any text. Do they exist beyond people's experiences of them? If they do, as Bateson and others would argue, where do they exist, and in what form do they exist?

In Marianne Dekoven's book *A Different Language, Gertrude Stein's Experimental Writing* (Dekoven, 1983:13–16) there is an interesting discussion of a sentence in Stein's 'Portrait of Mabel Dodge at the Villa Curonia' which I will use to develop this point.

As language users we tend to assume that texts are designed to mean, and as a consequence we construct coherences for a text which may well have little or nothing to do with writerly design or intention. In an extremely interesting experiment in his book *Telling How Texts Talk* (McHoul, 1982) Alec McHoul designs an exercise that offers to readers what appears to be a 14-line poem by Pierre Reverdy. Each line is offered cumulatively and readers are asked to comment as the 'poem' develops. The results are an interesting collection of commentaries, all of which seek to make the text work coherently. In practice, the poem is a collection of the randomly chosen first lines of fourteen separate poems.[7] Had the readers known that, their search for making the text coherent might well have taken quite different routes to the ones they took. And this is Dekoven's point in her discussion of Stein's sentence, which runs:

A bottle that has all the time to stand open is not so clearly shown when there is green color there.

Coherence, for the most part, is a central tenet of most cultures, and its overturning is often a mark of experimentation and the avant-garde. Dekoven offers a number of interpretations for what might 'usually' be considered an ambiguous sentence, but then asks, on behalf of someone interpreting Stein's poem, 'but what does it *really* mean?' In other words, 'what does Stein mean in the writing of this sentence?' From the outset, anyone involved in critical practice and analysis of texts needs to decide not just whether this is an important question, but whether it is a relevant one. If you accept it as relevant and important, as many critics do, then when faced with what appears to be a difficult and ambiguous text, like the Stein sentence, a range of interpretations can be offered in order to attempt to make accessible the seemingly inaccessible. And this is what Dekoven does. She offers a range of possible meanings for the sentence by suggesting different meanings for the main constituents of the sentence: 'A bottle'; the modifying phrase 'that has all the time to stand'; the 'green color' and so on. To do this she has only her own resources as reader to fall back on. Regardless of how much she might know about Gertrude Stein, she can never 'access' Stein's language resources and intertextuality. The list of possible meanings that she comes up with, or that you or I would come up with, are reader-specific. They are not necessarily the ones that Stein would come up with. So if you choose to make a selection from this list in order to find the one single meaning for the sentence that you think is the right one, you will still not be able to argue that this is the one the writer intended. Yet much critical practice has been and continues to be, a process of selection on behalf of a writer.

The argument is a familiar one: unless you actually uncover the meaning intended by the writer, you will never really be interpreting the text properly. Dekoven appears not to hold this view. She says of the various attempts to impose a meaning on the sentence: 'We can dispense with all of these translations and interpretations, and instead simply register, without any attempt to reconcile, order, extend, apply, or make sense of them, the various meanings the sentence offers' (Dekoven, 1983:13). But this seems not to take into account the way we, as readers, attempt to make sense of how texts mean. We do attempt to reconcile, order, extend and apply and make sense of meanings (as McHoul's experiments show), and this is exactly what Dekoven herself does when she declares, 'But by multiplying ambiguity well beyond what we are used to tolerating even in 'difficult' poetry, Stein's sentence absolutely prevents us from making sense' (Dekoven, 1983:16). In other words, Dekoven has catalogued a number of her readings for this text and decided that *her* ambiguities, *her* list of possible meanings have been created by Stein in order to allow Dekoven to declare Stein's own meaning for the text – that it is designed not to make sense. But we have no way of knowing whether this complies with what Gertrude Stein intended for the sentence, and if it does comply, it is irrelevant, given that Stein herself could well have many different readings of the text, depending on when, and how, she read it. All that Dekoven, or any of us, can actually talk about is *our* reading of a text. How a text means for us at a particular reading is all we can really attempt to articulate.

What Dekoven has done is accept the Derridean principle of pluridimensionality of meanings as part of the *reading* process, but she has been unable to accept this as part of the *writing* process. In her interpretation of Stein's sentence, she creates a centre for the text out of her readerly decentrings of the text – her plurality of meanings. Her critical practice appears to be reader-oriented but in practice is writer-centred. My position is that we can never make our critical practice writer-centred because we can never recover the writer's language. We can only work with a construction – a reading formation based on differing institutional constructions and ideologies. We can therefore only ever talk about *readings*, not *writings*.

The consequences of this position are that your language, your background, biases, ideas, beliefs, politics, education, etc. *determine* your understanding. But they are not invented by you. They are socially determined by the institutions and discursive practices that constitute the social networks you are involved in. Consequently, whatever you construct as a reading of a text is what you as reader/critic have created for that text, and it is the result of critical decisions that have been developed as an integral part of your background. They do not stand innocently and separately from who you are. As analyst you are not an archaeologist digging out other people's words and ideas; you are a critic actively engaged in understanding your reaction to a text which has been initially created by someone else. Much as you might want to talk about that 'someone else' you can only ever talk about your reading, your intertextuality. And no matter how appropriate you think your reading to be, there is no way that you can make that reading the 'correct one' by implying or declaring it to be the same as the writer's. As analyst and critic you are not a nameless and faceless explicator of someone else's meaning. You are involved in explaining how texts mean for *you* and no one else. And to do that requires that you are *known*.

This is a crucial idea and needs to be developed further because *how* a text means, and who you are, isn't theory-less. The way you construct meanings for texts depends on the way you construct theories about the world – about realities.

Classifications, realities and textual analysis

There isn't a single theory of the way the world works, and, just as crucially and relatedly, there isn't a single theory of the way language means. Following on from Derrida, there is no such thing as *the* single meaning, *the* correct meaning, *the* right meaning. There are many meanings associated with many theories of reality. And theories of reality are, like theories of language, a means of classification, a way of ordering the world. Different cultures, societies, and individuals classify and under-stand the world in different ways and this recognition needs to be a crucial part of the thinking involved in a *dynamic* textual interpretation. As readers/critics – as people living amongst other people – we make choices about the way we view the world, the way we classify, the way we order our lives, our political positions. These decisions are critical because we have made them – even if constrained and repressed by more powerful agencies than ourselves – from a position of choice. The 'rightness' of a decision, of an act of classifying something, of an idea about the world, is relative not to some inherent correct order for the world ordained somehow in nature, but to a theory, a position, a set of ideas, institutionally created and constructed. Put simply, there is nothing inherently correct or right about anything; there are levels of appropriateness relative to particular ideas, theories and systems of classifying. I'll develop this a little further by looking at an example of a text from Michael Halliday (1976) which at first appearance might seem to have a single 'straightforward' meaning:

1.1   THE TEACHER TAUGHT THE STUDENT ENGLISH

One of the traditional ways that linguists have of understanding how a text means is by classifying its grammatical structures according to a form of labelling that has its semantic roots in classical Greek philosophy. So the functions of the principal structures of this text might be classified as

1.2

THE TEACHER TAUGHT		THE STUDENT	ENGLISH
[subject]	[verb]	[indirect object]	[object]

The subject of the sentence – grammatically – is the teacher, though you might consider that the subject of the activity, supposing this text is describing a 'real event', is either the student (who is subjected to the teaching) or English (which is the subject being taught). Labelling the language in this way puts the teacher into a position of power – the teacher is the subject of the activity, that is, the process of teaching. The student is an object, like English, in the control of the teacher, and is not a part of the activity, but rather a passive receiver – in an indirect way – of an object, English. The grammatical classification of the elements of this text therefore suggests that these are not neutral, objective labels, 'simply' classifying an activity, but that they are a powerful means by which to create a world – that of an unequal power relationship in which a teacher controls the means of gaining knowledge, the knowledge itself, and the recipient of the knowledge. Neither the student nor English are an active part of the process of teaching, but are passive participants in someone else's activity. In other words, the means of classification are not formal – innocent – tools, but are a powerful way of expressing a particular reality – one that, in terms of education, and in many ways of the world at large, privileges unequal power relations and accords high status to certain members of society. *How* this 'simple' text means depends on you recognizing that its 'formal' grammatical classification of *subject, verb, object* is integrally connected to a philosophy of the world, and that the use of this classification system is a *critical* decision that implies that the critic accords with this world view. In other words, if you as critic/

analyst use this system, you are engaging in more than an innocent, objective, analytic process; you are expressing a particular
ideology from which, in the use of these labels, you cannot
escape. *How* this text means is therefore not 'simply' a question
of what the words mean, but how their functions and connections
are perceived and classified by the reader/critic. This is a crucial
point to understand if you are to engage at all with this type of
critical practice and interpretation.

The traditional grammatical classification is not the only classification choice open to you, though. There is nothing 'in' this text
which requires you to see it in that way. Classified as follows, the
text becomes a different text with new meanings, new world views.

THE TEACHER	TAUGHT	THE	STUDENT	ENGLISH	
[actor]	[material process]		[beneficiary]	[goal]	1.3

This, Halliday suggests, can be paraphrased as 'The teacher
imparted English to the student.'

Classifying 'taught' as a material process indicates that something more than the idle labelling of a word is happening here.
A material process implies that there is some sort of physical –
material – action involved, so that teaching might be considered
as a transaction, a handing over of a commodity to a recipient.
If you see that recipient as a beneficiary then you are signalling
that the act of receiving has benefits, though you are not normally
saying what those benefits are. At least there is no foregrounding
of an indirectness in the act of receiving, as there is in the first
example. With this type of labelling comes a sense that the classifying of processes and participants involves a view of the world
that is concerned with the apportioning of responsibilities. Here,
the responsibility is on the teacher to give the best possible
English, which is the goal of the activity. The prominent feature
here is therefore 'English' rather than 'the student'. And in that
sense this is a quite different text from the one that has subjects
and objects *even though the words may look the same.*

Take another look at the sentence:

THE TEACHER	TAUGHT	THE STUDENT	ENGLISH	
[actor]	[material process]	[goal]	[range]	1.4

This might be paraphrased as 'The teacher instructed the student
in English.'

The process is still considered to be material, but the teacher is now doing something to the student rather than to the language. The student, rather than the language being taught, is the goal, so the process involved here has more to do with the person than with the commodity. English is seen as the range, or scope, of the activity of teaching, thus specifying more precisely the concerns of the process of teaching. The action is now directed at the student, though the role is still passive inasmuch as the student isn't doing anything. The teacher is still the person controlling the activity and the student is still manipulated by the teacher and controlled by the range of the activity. Is this the 'same' text as in 1.2 and 1.3?

Another classification of the sentence might run as follows

	THE TEACHER	TAUGHT	THE STUDENT	ENGLISH
1.5	[initiator]	[material process]	[actor]	[range]

Paraphrased, this might read 'The teacher caused the student to learn English.'

The student, as actor, is now the person *doing* something so that the purpose of the teacher is to initiate a process whereby the student learns. The process is still a material process as action is involved and 'English' is still describing the range of this action, but unlike 1.2, 1.3 and 1.4 the student is perceived, through the classification system itself, as someone who is *actively* involved in the process of teaching, rather than as a passive receiver of a commodity.

So far we have moved from a classification system that puts all the power into the hands of a teacher to one that suggests teaching to be much more of an *interactive* process. There are, of course, pedagogical, social, and political consequences in a critical practice that seeks to understand how language means in this way. The labels you choose reflect the ideology you espouse. They are not, as indeed no word is, innocent of ideological consequences. The last example should indicate this quite clearly.

	THE TEACHER	TAUGHT	THE STUDENT	ENGLISH
1.6	[initiator]	[mental process]	[cognisant]	[range]

Paraphrased, this might read 'The teacher enabled the student to come to know English.'

The process is now considered to be a *mental* process, not a material action one. This signals that the student now participates more fully in the process because it is the student's cognitive faculties that are involved, rather than the physical actions of the teacher. The student is foregrounded, but is still involved interactively with a teacher who initiates the process of learning. Learning is now seen not as the passive receiving of a commodity, but as a cognitive activity involving interaction between student and teacher. This places the student in a quite different political position than in 1.2, 1.3, 1.4 and 1.5.

There are other classifications, other readings, other ways of articulating how this text means, but the point has been made, I think. There is no single text with a single meaning. Meaning is relative to ideology, and the way we classify a text as 'working' in a particular way says a great deal about the ideologies we are practising – consciously or otherwise. Analysis of how a text means is therefore analysis about how the world means, how ideas and institutions mean. What we are involved in here is therefore a critical practice that is both *political* and *historical*. The decisions you make about how you classify language are political ones that accord with the way you see, and wish others to see, the world. This political act is not something that should be swept under the carpet, it should be recognized for what it is – a crucial, necessary, and inescapable part of the interpretative process (see Jameson, 1976:36).

Politically committed analysis

What we are involved in as analysts of texts along these lines is therefore a socially and politically oriented *explanation* of language and not simply a neutral description of it. (See Kuhn, 1962, which develops a very powerful argument for rejecting the idea that language can be neutral.) As analysts we are involved in the articulation of *our* meanings of texts, *not* reconstructing by detailed surgery, other people's meanings. This form of analysis is therefore a *critical linguistics* (see Fowler *et al.*, 1979; Fowler, 1986; and cf. Steiner, 1985; Frow, 1984). It does not mean that writers are belittled or 'dead', or have become pointless and useless, or that their ideas and emotions are of no interest and that the writing process of no importance at all. Far from it – what it means is that as readers we can never speak on their behalf. We often (though not always) engage with texts because of the writer, but we can only explain and articulate our own understanding of how the text means, not theirs. And this attempt at explanation is, consciously or unconsciously, ideologically determined.

The relationship of ideology and meaning is something that has influenced a great deal of work in language and literature studies over the last twenty years or so, and many of the theoretical influences have come from disciplines like philosophy, sociology, and political science (see Coward and Ellis, 1977; Burton and Carlen, 1979; Silverman and Torode, 1980; Fowler and Marshall, 1985; Frow, 1986; Kress, 1985a, 1985b, 1988c). It is important to realize how the face of textual analysis has changed, and continues to change, because of a commitment to ideas and beliefs which at one time would have been considered totally inappropriate for 'literary' analysts. This has resulted not only in a broadening of the theoretical and philosophical interests in language and literature studies, but also in a considerable widening of the range of texts people are looking at. This has come about, for the most part, because many analysts are no longer interested in simply studying a text 'for its own sake'. The choice of text is no longer constrained by a traditional literary canon, but is very often made less because of the intrinsic – 'internal' – value of a text, than because an analyst has an interest *beyond* the text. A good example is the work of Deirdre Burton on a passage from Sylvia Plath's *The Bell Jar* (Burton, 1982).

Central to Burton's argument is that an analyst has to be politically committed, and that this commitment cannot be conveniently put on one side while the analysis is taking place. In fact, Burton, like many contemporary analysts of discourse, would argue that the choice of the particular text you are working on should not be arbitrary, but should be made because you actually have something to say that goes beyond the confines of the text. She says ' . . . I take it as axiomatic that *all* observation, let alone description, *must* take place within an already constructed theoretical framework of socially, ideologically and linguistically constructed reality' (Burton, 1982:196). There is no such thing, she argues, as a-political analysis. We cannot be politically neutral in anything we do as analysts, and, as a consequence, she believes (as I and many others do) that all academic work should be committed to influencing the better development and improving the rights of human beings. The established belief of 'knowledge for its own sake' is a self-indulgence that has no place in the work we do. All knowledge is ideologically determined and we are politically irresponsible if we do not recognize this. Her own position is stated clearly. She believes we live in a society that is classist, racist, and sexist, and responsible analysts should be working towards the elimination of these three major injustices. Linguists and literary critics are concerned with cultural processes and products, and as these processes and products are not innocent and immune from ideologies, so analysts should not pretend that they can assume a role of innocent, objective/scientific observer.

Burton works specifically on the processes and participants of her chosen passage from *The Bell Jar* because she is concerned with the power relations of the participants – i.e., the actors and the acted-upon – and their actions. Her argument is that linguistic structures – the way we construct realities through language – can be restructured in ways that are less damaging to people. Her interest is not simply in observing the processes (which appear in italics) and participants in the passage quoted, but in using an analysis as a base to argue for a greater political awareness of the way that language *as linguistically constructed reality* can be changed to remove classist, sexist, and racist injustices in the world.[8]

One segment of the Plath text reads:

The wall-eyed nurse *came* back. She *unclasped* my watch and *dropped* it in her pocket. Then she *started tweaking* the hairpins from my hair.

Doctor Gordon *was unlocking* the closet. He *dragged out* a table on wheels with a machine on it and *rolled* it behind the head of the bed. The nurse *started swabbing* my temples with a smelly grease.

As she *leaned over* to *reach* the side of my head nearest the wall, her fat breast *muffled* my face like a cloud or a pillow. A vague, medicinal stench *emanated* from her flesh.

'Don't worry,' the nurse *grinned* down at me. 'Their first time everybody's *scared* to death.'

I *tried to smile*, but my skin *had gone stiff*, like parchment.

Doctor Gordon *was fitting* two metal plates on either side of my head. He *buckled* them into place with a strap that *dented* my forehead, and *gave* me a wire *to bite*.

I *shut* my eyes.

There *was* a brief silence, like an indrawn breath.

Then something *bent down* and *took hold* of me, and *shook* me like the end of the world. Whee-ee-ee-ee-ee, it *shrilled*, through an air *crackling* with blue light, and with each flash a great jolt *drubbed* me till I *thought* my bones *would break* and the sap *fly out* of me like a split plant.

I *wondered* what terrible thing it *was* that I *had done*.

Burton gave the passage to a number of readers who responded that the patient appeared to be helpless, that she was distanced from her surroundings, and that the medical staff seemed more interested in getting the job done than in caring for her as patient. The question then is to ask why the readers responded in this way. What is it about the language that enabled them to construct the texts they did? Burton looks at three things: who (or what) is ' "doing" each process'; what sorts of process they are; and who the participants affected by the process are. The results are simple but effective because they immediately give a stronger image of who is doing what and when in the patient's world.

There are eight processes associated with the nurse, seven with the doctor, four with the electricity, and seven with the patient. Clearly we need to know what sorts of processes are involved here. Twenty of the thirty processes in the passage are *material action intention* processes, that is, they are processes in which someone intentionally *does* something to someone else. All of the processes associated with the nurse, the doctor, and the electricity are material action intention processes. The only material action intention process associated with the patient is when she shuts her eyes, thus shutting out the active world of the nurse, doctor and electricity. But who is affected by all of this? All of the processes associated with the nurse and the electricity affect the patient, but the doctor only affects the patient with one of the processes associated with him. For the rest he affects equipment. This is a clear example of how to articulate a response that the doctor is uncaring – his concerns are with equipment rather than with the person. And what of the patient? Effectively, she affects nothing at all.

This is a simple analysis requiring skills in linguistic *analysis* in one main area, but it is also an *explanation* of how a text means according to a particular response. Linguistic analysis along these lines gives a vocabulary to help explain a reading. This does not mean that Burton is any more likely to have a deeper insight into the text than anyone else, but it does mean that she can explain how a particular response was constructed *linguistically*. Compare, for example, what Jeremy Hawthorn has to say about his reading of *The Bell Jar* in his book *Multiple Personality and the Disintegration of Literary Character*.

> One important element in *The Bell Jar* is Plath's perception of the dehumanizing effect of commercial medicine; Joan tells Esther that she could see the dollar signs in her psychiatrist's eyes, and shortly after this a nurse tells Esther that when she has earned enough money to buy a car, she will clear out and take only private cases. The nurse's behaviour is classically contradictory; her friendly conversation implies that she sees the patients as human beings, but what she actually says implies that she sees them only as a means to an end, defines them only in cash terms. (Hawthorn, 1983:133)

The difference between Burton's approach and Hawthorn's approach is that Hawthorn, though saying similar things to Burton, uses quotation and paraphrase from the text to support his reading. We are therefore expected, as readers of Hawthorn, to construct the same conclusions as if we had a shared viewpoint, a shared vocabulary, a shared understanding of what Hawthorn views as intrinsically important in his quotations. On the other hand, Burton's approach, though it still requires a shared vocabulary, states quite clearly what the criteria for shared expectations are.

The next move, for Burton, is to use the information gained to rewrite the text according to different points of view (and Burton includes some in her article), making clear just how a linguisticaly constructed world can disadvantage people.[9] This is not an option Hawthorn takes up. Nor does his approach lend itself to such rewriting, given his authoritarian nature of pedagogy as compared to the openness of Deirdre Burton's.

Textually constructed realities

The notion of a linguistically constructed world is an important one. Beng Huat Chua in his paper 'Describing a national crisis: an exploration in textual analysis' (1979), uses a similar concept: 'textually constructed reality'. His concern in this paper is with the status of the written report, specifically a preliminary report of the Canadian Royal Commission on Bilingualism and Biculturalism (1965). This proved to be an important document because it concluded that Canada was going through the greatest crisis of its history. The report stated: 'If it should persist and gather momentum it could destroy Canada. On the other hand, if it is overcome, it will have contributed to the rebirth of a richer and more dynamic Canada' (Chua, 1979:49). Clearly this was a document that was likely to change people's lives; Chua's argument is that it did effect change and that this change was based on the constitution of a crisis that was in fact a *textually constructed reality*. In other words, the report constituted the crisis.

The report was based on what a group of commissioners had heard and read during a tour of the country. What they heard and read were opinions about the 'lack of equal partnership between the two "founding races" of Canada', that is, English and French (sic) (Chua, 1979:49). The commissioners' role was to produce a report 'reflecting' objectively and without bias what they had heard and read. And it is their *role* which is of crucial importance here, because as with many commissions, their brief was to produce a report – a written document. How their text means is therefore going to be determined by how they view report writing, and what they consider to be the components of a report. Some interesting work has been done, and continues to be done, on the way texts like records of evidence, police statements, parole reports, and so forth, have been determined by the extent to which the writer is concerned not with recording 'reality', but with producing a report (see Cicourel, 1968, Harris, 1984). The 'reality' of the opinions, the newspaper reports, the discussions the commissioners had with people were necessarily edited in certain ways, ordered in certain ways, and generally shaped and designed by the need to present a report. The consequence, according to Chua's analysis, was that opinions from 'both sides' of the perceived divide, which were reported verbatim and presented as objective evidence, were inevitably manipulated by the writers of the report to accommodate the 'reality' of the problem. In other words, the very presence of the Commission presupposed that there was a problem. The need to produce a written report 'confirmed' it. But more than this, the report constituted a crisis where before there had only been a perceived problem. 'We believe that there is a crisis, in the sense that Canada has come to a time when decisions must be taken and developments must occur leading either to its break-up or to a new set of conditions for its future existence' (Chua, 1979:58).

This understanding of a crisis depended upon documentary interpretation ' . . . of the meaning of the present in terms of its possible futures' (Chua, 1979:58). Chua draws upon the work of Harold Garfinkel here (see Garfinkel, 1967) and is able to demonstrate how the constitution of a crisis is a textually determined reality, that is, one created in and by language.[10]

Relevance

All discourse is ideologically and textually determined. It is also institutionally determined. Part of the work undertaken by contemporary analysts aims to break down the myth that the discourse of literary studies has to be dominated by an institutional literary canon. I raise this issue here because one of the criticisms levelled against people who move 'out of' the canon is that the texts they work with are trivial and often meaningless. But such judgements are tied very firmly to a theoretical position that needs to be questioned. What is at issue here is not the intrinsic worth of bus-ticket analysis against analysis of Wallace Stevens's poems, but the institutional positions that deny the validity – the *relevance* – of other texts. This is a crucial theoretical point. Relevance is determined for the most part in two ways: the first way looks at a number of rules of relevance that apply *internally* in a text, that is, the function and context of the text are not considered; I'll call this 'text-in-itself relevance'. The second way is the exact opposite: the text is considered as part of a much larger field of discourse and its relevance depends on social/historical institutions; I'll call this 'institutional relevance'. The first is a closed world – what Walter Ong calls 'the closed field' (Ong, 1976:150) – where a text is what it is because of its 'interior economy', with no reference to the world outside of the text; the second is an open one. To be precise, the second is the actual world and the first is an idealized (virtual) world that doesn't exist. The distinction between the actual and the virtual is of central importance in the philosophical and theoretical bases of most western ways of thinking, and which world you choose to make your priority as a theorist/analyst will quite radically affect the way you approach how texts mean.

Tanya Reinhart (1980) discusses an interesting text that perfectly illustrates this point. She is concerned with developing ways of recognizing coherent texts, that is, texts which from a certain position would be considered well-formed texts. The nature of that position is what interests me here, because it is a position that judges the coherence or incoherence of a text from the standpoint of an idealized world, *not* an actual, messy, noisy world filled with inconsistencies and unpredictable people.

Reinhart uses a number of maxims established by H. P. Grice (1975) in his discussion of the principle of cooperation, which he argues is at the base of conversation. These maxims represent *idealized* conversational behaviour, that is, the sort of conversation people would engage in if they wished to achieve the maximum effect in the most economical of ways in an ideal world.

These maxims are based on the four Kantian categories of quantity, quality, relation, and manner. *Quantity* basically states that you need to be as informative as possible in the most economical way, *quality* that you are basically honest in what you are saying, *relation* that you are relevant, and *manner* that you are unambiguous. Upsetting any of these maxims results in interaction that is not well-formed. Of course, in practice we violate these maxims all the time and are still involved in meaningful interaction. So what's the point of the maxims? They in fact illustrate a very important aspect of the way many of the theories involved in understanding the world work. Central to many of these theories is the distinction between a *virtual* world and a *real* world, that is, between an idealized world (where no one actually lives and talks) and an actual world (where we all live and talk). The actual world, the one filled with people and mess and noise and bodies and so on, is measured in terms of the virtual one. It is a way of trying to bring order to the chaos, as it were, of the messy real world. Grice's maxims exist in a virtual world and are used to try to explain in an ordered, neat way how the actual world works. We will come across this idea frequently in a number of ways throughout this book. There are problems with this approach, and I will cover them in some detail in later chapters. I raise the issue here because for the most part the establishment of a literary canon, that is, a set of texts deemed suitable for reading and studying by students and academics, is effectively a setting up of a virtual, idealized world of literature, excluding many of the texts produced in the real world, which break the rules – what we might call the maxims of literariness. This has developed in some areas to the extent that the notion of the ideal reader has been produced; a reader characterized by a literary competence associated not with the real world of reading and writing, but with a virtual world of literary rules (see Culler, 1975). But when we start to measure real worlds by virtual worlds we are on very dangerous ground. Virtual worlds require closed-off statements and completed paradigms. They require comprehensive accounts that cover every convenient aspect of a topic. They need to operate with self-contained discourses. The language, then, of how texts mean, becomes not the language of real people in real cultures, but an idealized language that doesn't actually exist.

The maxim that Reinhart concentrates on is that of relevance (for further applications of all Grice's maxims to literary texts see Weber, 1982, and Pratt, 1976), using interviewer/patient discourse. The following text is a fragment of an interview between a patient in a mental hospital and an interviewer not attached to the hospital.

Interviewer: You find it difficult talking to me.

Patient: Yes, to a man. (*When asked why she replied*:) Well I always get worried about it . . . (*After a pause she continued.*) I am thinking of Paisley. It's a nice town, it is quite warm. There are houses being built. They pull down the houses there, and are building fifteen- and twenty-storey flats. I think in Scotland and Glasgow there are twenty-storey flats because people are so crowded in houses and they can't breathe . . . and . . . in Paisley during the winter time in the flats, the heating, something went wrong . . . and the people didn't like it during the winter because Scotland is very crowded. . . . Queen Elizabeth II is depressed because . . . in Scotland, the Presbyterians, the non-Catholics, are trying to agree with Pope John because of mixed marriages. There is a lot of mixed marriages in Great Britain . . . the children can get on very well but some way they get out of it . . . of course a lot of them get out of it . . . of course a lot of them get out of it because there are many . . . mixed marriages . . . when the child is born some people say they are quite clever but many . . . five years old . . . in Britain they have from five years old so they are fifteen . . . fifteen. . . . You know children from five to fifteen there is a lot of them have to pass their test when they are eleven

years old.
Interviewer: You think of this interview as a test.
Patient: Yes, a test of faith and loyalty and understanding. I
see the recorder.

As there is no explicit reason why the speaker refers to England
and Scotland in the way that she does, Reinhart argues that it
fails the maxim of relevance because a listener/reader/analyst has
to go 'outside' of the text in order to *impose* relevance upon it.
A judgement is therefore made on the 'patient' (already classified
as schizophrenic[11] and her life is affected. The text is considered
cohesive – that is, it hangs together reasonably well grammatically
– but not coherent, because it fails the maxim of relevance.

A person is processed, therefore, according to how a text is
considered to mean, using rules established for ideal worlds, not
rules describing actual worlds. The effect of all this is that people's
lives are changed because of the convenience of a theoretical
modelling of the world which has little to do with reality.

'Text-in-itself-relevance' is rather more convenient for the
analysts than it is for the people whose lives are affected. I'll refer
to another text and its analysis, this time from Gunther Kress
(1979), to demonstrate my point here.

Central to Kress's argument in this paper is that most education
systems take the written language as a standard for measuring
the 'quality' of someone's spoken language, thus viewing, in his
useful phrase, 'speech . . . as a deformation of the norms of the
writing model' (Kress, 1979:56). Most of us will be familiar with
the sorts of judgements made about 'correct' spoken English that
suppose that the grammar of any variety of spoken English is the
same as the grammar of standard written English. It is not, of
course, and considerable work has been done in the last twenty
years or so that demonstrates the quite different grammars in
operation (see in particular Halliday, 1985a, 1985b; Stubbs,
1980). For the most part the judgements that are made don't
actually affect the course of most people's lives. But there are
situations in which value judgements are made by people in
control of others based on the fallacy that spoken language should
somehow approximate written language, and people's lives can
be affected as a result. Gunther Kress takes the example of a
transcript made by a speech therapist of a spoken text produced
by an 8-year-old boy. He was given a picture book and asked
to recount the story he saw there.

That's a bus and driving down the road and the drive round
road and try and mend them is stop try stop running away try
catch him and can't. He see engine him follow him. Make
funny funny funny er pictures and he run away and go in
tunnel and his bus go away.

Kress's initial point – and it's one we've already come across
in this chapter – is that this text is not a neutral, objective reflection
of reality. The production of this text requires a therapist to hold,
consciously or not, a theory of language that enables the therapist
to *shape* the text according to a set of principles underlying how
the therapist believes language works. The consequences of this
transcript are that they represent the boy as someone without
any coherent command of syntax: sentence structure is 'poor',
tense and time are confused, gender and number are mixed up.
The sorts of decisions that would be made by a therapist about
the child's command of English are likely to be made using these
observations as a base for developing a programme of 'corrective'
action. This, after all, is what speech therapists, presume their job
to be. The point that Kress makes is that decisions about a child's
spoken language are likely to be made using notions of what
constitutes 'good' grammar and coherent English in *written*
English. So, for example, conceptually the sentence is considered
to be the basic unit of thought, because this is how it is described
in written English. Consequently, judgements can easily be made
about the child's conceptual abilities, based on a perception that
he or she cannot make sentences. In practice, the sentence is
one of the least useful ways of describing how spoken language
is structured, but if you use it as a judgemental base the next
step is to argue that the child is unable to make logical connections
between sentences. Similarly, because a sentence is defined by
grammarians in terms of subject/actor, verb, and object/acted-
upon, decisions could be made about the child's undeveloped
notions of causality because of the absence of grammatically
expressed sentence constituents. Continuing in this way a therapist is likely to make judgements about the child's poor understanding of the notion of time because of problems with time and
tense in the text. In other words, judgements about how the text
means are made as if it were written language, and these linguistic
judgements are used as a base to make value judgements about
the child's conceptual abilities. The child can therefore be categorized as having mental problems which, in practice, are effec-

tively textually determined by the way a therapist decides to transcribe the data.

But Kress suggests that a transcript of the text based on information units of speech rather than on a sentence-based writing model might look something like this (underlining indicates major pitch movement and // marks major information units):

> //I saw a <u>bus</u>// a . . . driving down the <u>road</u>// and it <u>drives</u> there (that// round the (na) <u>road</u>// an try and <u>mend</u> them// is a stop p//<u>try</u>// that were running <u>away</u>// and try to (a) <u>catch</u> him// and <u>can't</u>// He see an <u>engine</u>// it <u>follow</u> him// make funny funny a funny a pictures// and he <u>ran</u> away// and he go in <u>tunnel</u>// and his bus go <u>away</u>//

What this transcript immediately does is to treat the grammar of spoken English in a radically different way from the grammar of written English. Kress also includes information from the tape that was 'cleaned up' in the therapist's version. Importantly, the passage is marked by clearly defined information units, consisting for the most part of a single clause. This is expected behaviour for spoken English. The child clearly has a good grasp of the basic units of speech and an ability to order these units in complex ways. As is common in speech, much is 'understood', for example ellipsed subjects, but more importantly, I think, this transcript demonstrates clearly that the child has a good understanding of direction and movement in storytelling, because the placing of intonation focus falls on the major components of the story: bus, road, drive, etc. Kress also makes the crucial point that the therapist's transcript takes no account of the child's dialect. It is in fact a variety of English from East Anglia in the UK (Norwich English). In this dialect verbs tend not to be marked for the third person or for past and present tense (see Trudgill, 1974). But Kress's point, and it is an important one, is that if you don't happen to be a speaker of Norwich English, and therefore don't know these features, the decisions you make about the speaker's language, and possibly their intellectual capacities, are influenced by a quite different model and theory of language. Consequently, you can construct, textually, a quite different picture of a child's linguistic and intellectual abilities or problems. The version from the therapist shows a child barely able to express himself through language; the other, by Kress, shows a competent 8-year-old speaker of Norwich English. Kress suggests, therefore, that an interpretation of the child's discourse, based on his transcript, would be something like this:

> I saw a bus, driving down the road; and it drives there, round the road, and try and mend them. It has stopped, try . . . (inaudible) running away, and try to catch him and can't. He see an engine, it follow him, make funny, funny, funny pictures. And he ran away and he go in tunnel, and his bus go away.

This is a text less likely to result in value judgements determining the child to be less capable than he really is. How this text means is quite different from how the therapist's text means. Quite different realities are presented with quite different ideological bases for modelling language and the world.

Manipulating – editing – textually determined realities in this way is not necessarily a conscious activity, but when it is it can prove to be a very effective – sometimes damaging, sometimes useful – political, cultural, and social strategy (see also Kress, 1982; Martin, 1985). For example, the exploitation of some of the differences between spoken and written language are used to particularly good effect in the following extract from *The Guardian*, a British newspaper more liberal than conservative in its editorial policy.[12] The report contains a series of excerpts from President Reagan's response when asked, in October 1981, if he thought an exchange of nuclear weapons between the United States and the Soviet Union could be limited or if escalation was inevitable:

> 'I don't honestly know. I think, again, until someplace – all over the world this is being, research going on, to try and find the defensive weapon. There never has been a weapon that someone hasn't come up with a defense. But it could – and the only defense is, well, you shoot yours and we'll shoot ours. . . . But these are weapons, these, now what I call strategic, these theater weapons, that are in the theater of war, potential war, but would be used strategically, that we want the weapons, and that's what we're going to start talking about on November 20.'
>
> *Asked if he thought there could be a battlefield exchange of nuclear weapons without an exchange of strategic nuclear weapons, Mr Reagan said:*
>
> 'Well, I would – if they realized that we – again, if – we led them back to that stalemate only because that our retaliatory

power, our seconds, or our strike at them after their first strike, would be so destructive that they couldn't afford it, that would hold them off.' (*The Guardian*, 1 November 1981)

People don't generally speak as they write, but the representation of speech in writing like this can be a very powerful tool for throwing doubt on a person's credibility. Edited by a sympathetic journalist Reagan could have been presented in a quite different light (see Halliday, 1985a; Tannen, 1982).

The view of language as determining, not simply reflecting, reality, is an important one, and central to much contemporary thinking abut the way language and society work (see Kress and Hodge, 1979; Fowler *et al.*, 1979). The theory that language is simply a means of representation – language as saying, if you like – is really a very inadequate one. Language does more than say; it does more than pass on information or reflect an already existing reality 'out there' somewhere in the world. Language is about action and interaction; it is about performance, about showing, about doing. Language is not a neutral instrument: it is biased in a thousand different ways, and those ways are of course determined by any number of differing ideologies, knowledge and power systems, and institutions. And it is the role, it seems to me, of a responsible critical linguistics to develop the means of understanding and explaining the mechanics of those thousand different ways.

Having said this, though, we should be cautious, we should not allow an enthusiasm for the 'power' of a discipline to lead us to assume that texts cannot be interpreted unless we have these specialized knowledges about how texts mean. We don't need linguistics to help us interpret a text – people have been doing that for years without linguistics. What linguistics can do is to give a vocabulary for understanding and explaining how the text means, and not everyone needs to be able to articulate this. Dwight Bolinger in *Language The Loaded Weapon* (1980), uses the analogy of a speaker who may live a lifetime without realizing that verbs agree in number with their subjects, but who would soon object if you tried to pass off ten eggs as if it were a dozen. One transaction matters to that person, whereas another doesn't. One piece of knowledge is powerful, whereas the other isn't. This does not mean that the linguist can have deeper insights into the text than anyone else, but rather that the linguist might be better able to articulate those insights, and in practice might well have different institutional reasons for wanting to articulate them.

To summarize the main points so far:

1 Language is a means of understanding what it means to 'be', rather than a means of expressing a 'given' reality.

2 What it means to 'be' is best seen in terms of socially constructed realities rather than in terms of the world as psychologically 'real'.

3 Analysis of text is therefore a dynamic activity, concerned with language as a dynamic *process*, not as a static *product*.

4 Analysis therefore concentrates not just on what language says, but on what language does.

5 What language does is not done through a single voice, but through a process of *interaction*; it is dialogic (to use Bakhtin's term), so the interactive voices, not the single, individual voice, become the focus of analysis. The ego is therefore decentred, and consequently social, institutional and textual constructions of reality are foregrounded.

6 Socially constructed realities are understandable only in terms of ideological variation. Such variation inevitably means that the construction of meanings for texts is a process of indeterminacy. There are no fixed, determinate meanings encoded within the texts; texts are best understood in terms of indeterminate meanings constructed by readers.

7 There is therefore no such thing as 'the' single, correct, meaning of a text.

8 This means that the status of the writer is deprivileged, and the role of the reader, governed by institutional and social discourses, is given a much more prominent role in the construction of meaning.

9 A critical practice informed by these factors therefore concentrates on the analysis of literary texts in terms of reading, not writing.

10 This type of criticism is therefore a political act, aiming to understand not simply what a text means but how a text means.

The main goal of this sort of analysis is much larger than that of simply being able to describe linguistic or stylistic structures in texts; such analysis plays a major part in understanding the nature of language, and hence in understanding people and the discursive practices they are engaged in.

The Cartesian view that we are individuals free from context is still a dominant one in many circles; it is a convenient means of maintaining classist and elitist views, of suggesting that a minority of people are more sensitive, more able to 'understand' the world than the larger mass of people. It is a view that is at the very roots of intrinsic literary criticism, and is something that is vital to any understanding of how certain views of how texts mean have developed, and continue to be developed, in linguistic and literary studies.

2 Language, literature and scientific fictions

> The final belief is to believe in a fiction, which you know to be a fiction, there being nothing else. The exquisite truth is to know that it is a fiction and you believe it willingly. (Stevens, *Opus Posthumous*, p. 163)

Scientificity

It's nearly sixty years since William Empson talked about the multiple meaning (polysemy) of grammatical structure and labelled it 'ambiguity' (Empson, 1930). There has been, and continues to be, a great deal of formal analysis associated with the description of such ambiguities, which has tended to throw into the shadows, in some linguistic and literary circles, one of the 'machinations of ambiguity' that Empson held dearest: the ambiguity constructed by readers when they are unable to fore-ground one particular meaning in a text as being of more value or significance than another. When applied to text analysis, the result is an analysis that doesn't just take notice of multiple meanings, it actively looks for, and expects to find, more than one meaning, more than one reading. In these circumstances, analysing text becomes quite a different activity from analysing text for *the*, single, determined meaning (see Bennett, 1987; Eagleton *et al.*, 1984; Felperin, 1985 for discussions of this).

This is because the theory of language that is behind it argues for considerably more 'play' and freedom in the way that language means. That 'play' doesn't just happen; rather, it is recognized because the theory of language recognizes what causes it. Institutions and people cause it. But in many linguistic/literary theories and practices people and institutional practices, and their potential for disturbing neatly worked out meanings, have been kept as far away as possible from the techniques and theories involved in the analysis of text. The almost single-minded pursuit of scientific status for studies in the humanities is the overriding feature of intellectual life in the twentieth century. This pursuit has shaped the direction of analysis and theory to such an extent that ideas about language, thrown up at the turn of the century and appropriated for the scientific cause, are now unquestioned by many and believed as fact by even more.

Formalism/Structuralism

The most dominant view of language, established at the turn of the century and developed and redirected over the years, is one that sees language as an objective system of signs related arbitrarily to what they signify. This idea has shaped almost all western twentieth-century thought. The effect on language and literature studies has been dramatic; it has been wrought, for the most part, by the twin forces of *formalism* and *structuralism*.

European and American structuralist linguistics was developed as a discipline this century by a number of people who were concerned with establishing a *science* of language. In the context of the university system this was a political act aimed at countering the positivist/historicist scholars who maintained that for the study of language to be considered a science, it should be concerned with answering the question of why languages are as they are — such a science, they argued, would only need to find historical answers to that question. Histories of linguistics tend to use Ferdinand de Saussure as a convenient moment to dramatize/ mobilize the reaction against this historicism. In practice, Saussure's influence at the time was probably minimal; a much louder voice had preceded his in the figure of Wilhelm von Humboldt, who argued very influentially for the *synchronic* study of languages to dominate theory and practice, that is, he argued for the need to look at the 'here and now' of a language rather than to view it historically.

It was really a question of causes and effects. Historicism aimed at explaining, scientifically, the causes of language. Synchronicity aimed at understanding, scientifically, the effects (structures) of language without being concerned about where it came from. Saussure built upon this position in his work, and a collection of notes written by his students was published in 1915 as *Cours de Linguistique Générale* (Saussure, 1959). This book has gained almost biblical status throughout this century, mostly, I would suggest, as much for its appropriation by a cause for political purposes, as for its 'scholarly' attraction. It was certainly never a statement of truth about the way a system of signification works (language being only a part of that system). But its influence has been shattering.

A central theme in the reaction to positivism/historicism developed in the book – and by later linguists, in particular Louis Hjelmslev (1969) – was that 'The one and only true object of linguistics is the language system (*la langue*) envisaged in itself and for itself' (see Saussure, 1959:14). What that comes to mean in structuralist linguistics is that a science of language becomes more concerned with a virtual, abstract, system of language, than with the institutionally determined meanings involved when people interact with each other. The problem with structuralist linguistics has not been the dichotomy of *langue* and *parole* as such, but the privileging of *langue* over *parole*, that is the privileging of the abstract rule-governed system of language (*langue*) over the actual daily productive uses of language in speech and writing (*parole*). This has been caused chiefly by the eagerness to make the study of language into a science. The problem, therefore, is with the scientificity of structuralism, rather than with its theory of how meanings are made, which in terms of twentieth-century development of thought was a crucially important move away from empiricist/historicist realism. Calling something a science, however, doesn't make its 'scientists' objective and apolitical, though we have, for the most part, been trained to think this way.

It is against this background that the concerns of, and reactions against, a critical movement in literary studies, and an increasing discussion of linguistic structures in literature, might usefully be seen.

Idealization/Actualization

Much of the intellectual activity in the west in the twentieth century has been preoccupied with the need to be explicit. Explicitness is a function of the formal, 'objective' disourse of science. In terms of language this has resulted in a theory that argues that linguistic structures are motivated internally by the principles of grammar, or externally by social and cultural forces. The first is a psychological orientation – language as a mental structure. The second is a sociological orientation – language as a social structure. Ferdinand de Saussure, in attempting to be explicit about the nature of signification and to develop a science of signs (semiology), based his work on the classic relationship in most western philosophies between presence and absence, that is the distinction between virtual worlds and real worlds. For Saussure, this basic distinction was treated, in language, as a relation between *langue* (the system of language) and *parole* (the production of language). The consequences of this formulation, and the emphasis on *synchronic* approaches, effectively argue for the autonomy of the linguistic system (*langue*). Historical context has little or no place here.

Language, as an object of knowledge, is considered to have a binary character, based on the arbitrary nature of the sign, which comprises the signifier and the signified. Language is understood by the way the signifiers are organized in terms of a *paradigmatic* axis of *selection* and a *syntagmatic* axis of *combination*. Thus, in constructing a sentence (*the cat sat on the mat*) *cat* and *mat* or, indeed a range of items would be alternative paradigmatic vocabulary choices; *sat* on the other hand, is more restrictively constrained to be a verb since it follows a subject noun or noun phrase. The ways in which the syntagms and paradigms are organized constitute the structures of language. Thus linguistic signs do not have meaning because there is a one-to-one correspondence between the sign and an object or idea in the world; they have meaning by virtue of their relationship with other signs in the system. So, for example, *cat* only has 'meaning' as a word because it is differentiated in the language system from a word such as *bat* or *pat*. Its meaning is, according to a structuralist linguist such as Saussure, wholly differential, made as a result of differential contrasts with other words.

Langue is Saussure's virtual world and *parole* is his real world. People do, however, live and talk in real worlds – real in the sense that they are socially, culturally and institutionally determined. (Whenever I write about 'real worlds' I always mean a range of realities that are socially, culturally, ideologically, and institutionally determined.) In order, therefore, to be able to talk about how meanings are produced in such a system, a theory of actualization has to be determined, that is, a theory that allows the 'passage' from a state of being absent to a state of being present. Absence/ virtual systems are considered to be stable and constant, whilst presence/real systems are considered unstable and variable. The advantage of developing a 'science' of language that, in practice if not in intent, confined its activities to the discussion of the virtual system of *langue* was that, theoretically, you would be working with a stable, unchanging system rather than with the unpredictable activities of a real system like discourse.

This is the theory of *idealization* and this philosophy underpins most systems of thought and science in the west. 'Ideal' does not mean perfect here; it signals stability, assuming that in a given situation nothing will change. For example, there is a 'law' of physics that states that the relation between the pressure and volume of a gas remains constant if the temperature of the gas remains constant. This is an ideal situation – a virtual situation. In practice, changes in the volume and pressure of the gas will change the temperature, but to include this variability is to shift from a system closed to change to a system open to change, and, hence, to deny the possibility of being formally explicit. In language theories, this distinction was formalized as a structural relation between *-emic* systems and *-etic* system: if you discuss sound systems *phonemically* then you are talking about ideal sound systems; if you talk about sound systems *phonetically*, you are talking about the sounds that people really use. The suffix *-emic* signifies *langue* and *-etic* signifies *parole*. What this means, therefore, is that with *langue* we have the potential to produce the sounds describable in *parole*, but we also need a theory of actualization that allows for the realization of those sounds from one system into the other. The theory therefore must address the way in which the form of language (which belongs to virtual systems) is realized, that is, becomes the substance of language (what people actually say to each other): 'real' discourses.

The linguistics that began to develop during this century, was concerned with designing and building models of virtual systems to understand *langue*. It was not principally (and often still isn't) concerned with *parole*. It was therefore preoccupied with the form (the structures) of language, and is now generally known as *structuralist* linguistics.

These structures of language are structures of virtual systems (not of actual systems – it is crucial to understand this point). These structures are not those of the words on the page, of the utterances of speech. They are the structures of a system that gives the *potential* for the words on the page or the utterances of speech to exist. They belong to the *-emic* world, not to the *-etic* world. Understand this principle (in many ways it goes against our common sense notions of how the world works, which is why it is usually so confusing) and you will understand part of the fundamental philosophy of structuralism and its consequences for twentieth-century thought.

The more complex the structures, the more complex the meanings involved – this is a theory of signification based on the combinatory principle. Structuralist linguistics and much literary theory are based on this principle. Simple structures build (combine) into complex structures; increased complexity of structure signifies increased complexity of meaning. It is a theory, together with the theory of selection, that is, the possibility of substituting one structure for another, that is central to an ideology that privileges complexity over simplicity. The important thing to realize about such theories is that they are not, contrary to the way they sometimes appear, absolute truths.

Scientific fictions

The following points are a simplified summing up of the Saussurean/Hjelmslevian theory of language:

1 This theory of language is not principally concerned with the actual practice of language, but with meaning as relations of difference in an ideal (virtual) system.

2 Certain structures are innocent of meaning.

3 The more complex the relations, the more complex the meaning.

4 The analysis of language is based on a series of binary oppositions within a self-contained, enclosed system.

5 Language is a thing in itself.

The theory assumes that structural relations can be understood by the concept of *difference* – a concept fundamental to western philosophy. According to this theory, you only recognize something as having meaning because you recognize it as not being something else: a verb is a verb, not because it demands intrinsically to be a verb, but because it isn't a noun; the sound [p] is [p] because it isn't [b]. In other words, meaning is a system of classification based on opposition, on dichotomy. This is essentially a relation of contradiction, which is a basic tenet of western thinking, and identifies it as quite different from other systems of thought in the world (see Birch, 1988/89; Hasan, 1984).

What Saussure was basically interested in, then, was creating a science of signs. He was not specifically interested in creating a theory of language. Language, for Saussure, was just one instance of a system of signs. The general principle was, andd is, that if you understand the virtual system, then you will come to understand the real system. The influence of this theory during the course of the twentieth century has been enormous.

Structures and meanings

At the base of the structuralist position is an assumption that certain structures are innocent of meaning. Meaning is determined by the differences between the structures, not the structures themselves. This is a crucial point, and a useful place, I think, to bring in an illustration. Ruqaiya Hasan worked some years ago (Hasan, 1971) on W.B. Yeats's 'The Old Men Admiring Themselves in the Water' and published her analysis in what came to be a very influential paper on stylistics (the application of linguistics to the analysis of literary texts).

The Old Men *Admiring* Themselves in the Water

I *heard* the old, old men *say*
'Everything *alters*,
And one by one we *drop away.*'
They *had* hands like claws, and their knees
Were twisted like the old thorn-trees
By the waters. I *heard* the old, old men *say*
'All *that's* beautiful *drifts away*
Like the waters.'

Hasan was interested in a wide range of linguistic structures in the poem. Here I want to concentrate on her work on the analysis of the verbal processes (these are italicized in the text). Her interest is not in the structures for their own sake, but for what they might contribute to an interpretation of the meaning of the poem. She uses them to highlight the lack of causation in the poem. The subjects of the verbal processes, she argues, are all affected phenomena, not actors. In other words, the subjects (for example, 'we', 'they', 'the old, old, men') have things done to them; they do not initiate the action. This observation allows Hasan to suggest linguistic reasons for what she had intuitively recognized as a 'lack of voluntary action' in the poem, and to interpret the poem as being about the old men having no control over their own lives. The human agents of these verbal processes are not the old men. They are someone else. They are, if you like, deleted from the text, which seems to underline the helplessness of the old men, since they are controlled by some unknown agency.

A similar analysis of agency is undertaken by Samuel Jay Keyser. He examines Wallace Stevens's 'The Death of a Soldier' (Keyser, 1980) and constructs an argument about the relationship between the suppression of agency and 'the meaning' of the poem.

Life contracts and death is expected,
As in a season of autumn.
The soldier falls.

He does not become a three-days personage,
Imposing his separation,
Calling for pomp.

Death is an absolute and without memorial,
As in a season of autumn,
When the wind stops.

When the wind stops and, over the heavens,
the clouds go, nevertheless,
In their direction.

The verbal processes can be divided into those that have agents and those that don't. In this text, according to Keyser's analysis, all but two of the verbs (italicized above) are without agents. Some of these verbs can never have agents, (for example, 'is' 'become') whereas other agentless verbs in the text can (for example, 'contract', 'stop', 'go'). 'Fall', in its sense here, is a verb that cannot take an agent, Keyser argues that in the line 'The soldier falls', the soldier has no choice 'falls' is used like 'die' or 'lives'. In other words, the soldier is not the agent of the action; someone else is. An agent other than the soldier is responsible for the soldier falling/dying in war. The whole text, he argues, is basically representative of a world without human agency;

It is both free from and impervious to human intervention. . . .
Death is like this world, and Stevens has ordered the syntactic and semantic parameters . . . so as to make the form of his poem reflect its content, which is, ultimately, that death is

inevitable and timeless; in a word, absolute. (Keyser, 1980:263)

The approach taken by both Ruqaiya Hasan and Samuel Jay Keyser is one that asks the question 'What does this text mean?' and attempts to answer it using a close analysis of the language of the text. This approach was cause for concern to American critic Stanley Fish, who demanded to know not 'What does a text mean?' but 'What does a text do?' (Fish, 1980).[1] This is an important distinction, for it is central to a structuralist awareness of grammatical structures like verbal processes. Fish's position, a propos the Keyser and Hasan argument (though he only refers to Keyser) is that you cannot separate linguistic structures like agency deletion from meaning. Therefore, agency deletion, like any linguistic structure or phenomenon, does not exist on a separate plane, divorced from the literary meanings that can be assigned to the poem by readers or analysts; it is an integral part of those meanings. In other words there is *no* distinction between grammatical meaning and literary meaning. This is an important theoretical point, because there is a view within intrinsic criticism that understanding language, and that includes specific grammatical structures, is a preliminary process in interpretation, which *leads* to understanding the literary style of the text, which in turn *leads* to a reader formulating an appropriate literary response to a text. The process therefore suggests that readers move *from* grammatical meaning *to* literary meaning. The point that Fish is making here, and which is made increasingly within contemporary discourse analysis, is that there is no 'from/to' movement involved – what a text means in grammatical terms is the same as its meaning in literary terms. The linguistic form of the text in intrinsic literary criticism is usually considered as a separate entity from the meaning of the text, whereas for many linguists and critics, form and meaning are considered inseparable. Meaning is therefore most appropriately seen in terms of pragmatic functions (i.e. what does the text *do*).

Analysts like Keyser and Hasan who use structuralist linguistics with traditional literary theories were often given very short shrift by traditional critics. Walter Nash, writing about D. H. Lawrence's 'Odour of Chrysanthemums' (Nash, 1982), received a stinging critique from Peter Barry, who argued that 'The linguistic scalpel, in a word, is often blunt, and the cuts merely optimistic or clumsy'

(Barry, 1984:51). As a result, he claimed, the work of the stylistician is usually impressionistic and lacking in literary sensitivity.

Central to Barry's argument is a belief that literary meaning and linguistic structure (grammar in particular) are quite separate entities. It is this belief that is behind his criticism of Nash. For example, Nash discusses the part of the text when, at the beginning of the story, the mother breaks off a twig which had three or four flowers on it and holds it against her face. The story continues:

> When mother and son reached the yard her hand hesitated, and instead of laying the flower aside, she pushed it in her apronband.

Nash argues that in the phrase 'her hand hesitated' there is a shift of agency from the woman as a whole, to the hand as a part, which he says 'expresses in a very telling way her division against herself, her alternations of voluntary act and involuntary response' (Nash, 1982:109). He is making a linguistic observation that assumes that the structure of grammar actually means something. Barry objects to this and says 'This is fancifully impressionistic and betrays a misunderstanding of the way language actually works' (Barry, 1984:56). Barry's argument is that the shift of agency exists only in the grammar (Barry, 1984:56). What Nash has done, he says, is to confuse grammar and meaning.

In other words, for Barry, grammar has no meaning. It is simply an innocent structure, a transparent framework, a vehicle in which to carry meaning.[2] Like Keyser's theory of language, Barry's is a theory where the structures of language are meaningless representations of meaning. Fish, on the other hand, argues that the structures of language constitute meaning.

Barry's argument is one based on the philosophy of John Locke, which posits the existence of reality outside language. Language is effectively seen as a tool or instrument of expression and communication – a very widespread perception in certain theories of the sign (see the discussion in Gauker, 1987).[3] Of particular importance in a Lockeian, instrumentalist view of language is the view that ideas are perceived cleanly and neatly – a considerable attraction to a scientistic approach to language. An alternative, non-instrumentalist view, for example, might be that ideas are perceived in a confused, chaotic way.[4] Fish's argument is one that posits a reality constructed by language.[5]

To summarize so far, then:

1 Formal analysis of text has developed mainly as a means by which humanities scholarship could claim the status of a science.

2 This has created a preoccupation with a scientificity in textual analysis and theory, resulting in a privileging of the formal, abstract, virtual world of the ideal (for example, Saussure's notion of *langue*) and a marginalization of socially and institutionally determined worlds of real, *actual* discourses.

3 Structuralist linguistics developed this scientificity to such an extent that discursive meanings were usually ignored because they were considered too messy and indeterminate for explicit statements to be made about the formal, virtual, system of language.

4 Analysis of text is therefore carried out not with the intention of saying anything about the text or its context as such, but as a means to understand the system of language (*langue*). Discourse has obviously little place in this practice.

5 Such a preoccupation with the idealized system means a preoccupation with 'objectivity', suggesting therefore that analysts are neutral, innocent, and disinterested observers of phenomena, rather than politically, socially and institutionally motivated – biased – people.

6 The concern for the objective created a concern with 'blackboard linguistics', not with naturally occurring discourse. In order to exemplify points about the language system linguists constructed texts rather than collected them from actual situations.

7 The ideal world of most sciences is an ordered, neat world. Actual worlds are messy, noisy and full of uncertainty and indeterminacy. The ideal world is inevitably more suited to a scientific approach; the actual world invites the search for an understanding of socially determined realities.

8 Meaning, in an approach that prioritises the ideal, virtual world of the scientific, is considered to operate on a separate plane, with structures like phonemes, morphemes, words and syntax considered as neutral carriers of this meaning. Meaning is therefore considered as if it exists separately from linguistic structures.

9 Analysis of text is therefore carried out as if texts exist in, for, and by themselves, not as part of larger discursive formations.

This type of text analysis has been done, and is being done, according to an abstract model of language, in which meaning (the signified) is often thought to be hidden, or encoded, in a text, and what can be seen (the signifier) is simply a vehicle, innocent of all meaning. Such an analysis has as its central ideology the idea of contradiction/opposition, and it is not principally concerned with the mess and indeterminacies – the fuzzy edges – of socially determined realities. It appears as ahistorical, apolitical, objective, and scientific, and its practitioners assume the same. Analysis of text, therefore, is a discovery procedure to find hidden meanings, it does not aim to say anything about the text, its contexts, its readings and its institutional determinations, but simply to use the text to say something about the system that made the text possible. That system is not language-specific; it is a system of signification that goes beyond language. It is a system that stands independent from its use; an autonomous, autotelic system: ' . . . it cannot indulge in making judgements concerning the nature of the objects it analyses' (Greimas and Courtés, 1979).

This is the extraodinary basis for most of the practices and theories that have been involved, in one way or another, with the analysis of text in the twentieth century.

3 Reading literary texts: traditions, assumptions, practices

> It were as wise to cast a violet into a crucible that you might discover the formal principle of its colour and odour, as seek to transfuse from one language into another the creations of a poet. (Shelley, *Defence of Poetry*, p. 230)

Literature as moral discipline

Concentration on the idea and practice of language is a crucial means by which people have sought an identity that distinguishes them from the rest of the animal world. The more articulate – eloquent – people are, the more they have felt able to distance themselves from that world. A view of an inarticulate and ineloquent person has been, therefore, a view that has placed them 'lower down the order', closer to the animals. In a word, they are considered 'brutish'. If this is an uncomfortable and insidious idea for many in the 1980s it is only so as a reaction against its widespread acceptance (and against the ideologies and practices of which this view formed a major part) in earlier decades. The increasing conservatism and dominance of New Rightism in the present decade might, unfortunately, suggest that my optimism about that reaction is somewhat naive. Whatever the situation, it is nevertheless certain that now, as then, those who have an articulate control of language have potentially more control over other people than do those who are perceived to be less articulate.

The crucial word here is 'articulate': who determines the rules and recognition criteria for levels of articulateness? In England, prior to the First World War (as a convenient, though unreliable, historical 'moment'), the situation was determined for the most part by those who had status and/or property and wealth. The class system unquestioningly assumed that those at the top of the pile were the most articulate and eloquent, and that those on the bottom were the least. This was certainly the view held by many in the universities who, of course, just happened to be sitting on the top of the pile. Consider this from the poet Stephane Mallarmé:

> Language, in the hands of the mob, leads to the same facility and directness as does money; but in the Poet's hands, it is turned above all, to dream and song; and, by the constituent virtue and necessity of an art which lives on fiction, it achieves its full efficacy. (Cited in Quinn, 1982:32.)

or this from Sir Walter Raleigh, Professor of Literature at Oxford until the outbreak of the First World War:

> . . . words carry with them all the meanings they have worn, and the writer shall be judged by those that he [*sic*] selects for prominence in the train of his [*sic*] thought. A slight technical implication, a faint tinge of archaism, in the common turn of speech that you employ, and in a moment you have shaken off the mob that scours the rutted highway, and are addressing a select audience of ticket-holders within closed doors. (Cited in Quinn, 1982:30.)

But by the time Raleigh wrote this, the days of leaving the uneducated in the fields had long gone, and with them the certainty that 'God was in heaven and all was well with the world.' (See Hawkes, 1985, 1986; see also the discussion in Parrinder, 1977, in particular pp. 102–72.) All was *not* well with the world prior to the First World War: religion was not maintaining the 'order' and those at the middle and bottom of the pile, were, for the most part, expressing considerable dissatisfaction. George Gordon, Professor of English Literature at Oxford University, wrote:

> England is sick, and . . . English literature must save it. The Churches (as I understand) having failed, and social remedies being slow, English literature has now a triple function: still, I suppose, to delight and instruct us, but also, and above all, to save our souls and heal the State. (Cited in Eagleton, 1983:23.)

English literature ' . . . would rehearse the masses in the habits of pluralistic thought and feeling, persuading them to acknowledge that more than one viewpoint than theirs existed – namely, that of their masters' (Eagleton, 1983:25).

The development of English literature (as a discipline) for the masses, and later for those at the universities, was effectively ar attempt to find a cure for the ills of England. This pious hope faded (in character at least) with the senselessness of the First World War. Before long, a group of middle class academics at Cambridge – in particular, F. R. Leavis and I. A. Richards – and a little later American critics like John Crowe Ransom, Cleanth Brooks and W. K. Wimsatt argued powerfully and persistently for the 'independent' status of literature, that is, that literature is not 'just' different from other uses of language, it is ontologically different. As a consequence, criticism should be able to distinguish between 'genuine', 'pure' poetry, for example, and mere versifying. Consider, for example, Donald Davie (a critic very much influenced by this sort of thinking) discussing the poetry of Percy Bysshe Shelley in his book *Purity of Diction in English Verse*. He considers 'To Jane: the Invitation' to be 'one of Shelley's greatest achievements' (Davie, 1967:145).

To Jane – The Invitation

Radiant Sister of the Day,
Awake! arise! and come away!
To the wild woods and the plains,
And the pools where winter rains   50
Image all their roof of leaves,
Where the pine its garland weaves
Of sapless green and ivy dun
Round stems that never kiss the sun;
Where the lawns and pastures be,

And the sandhills of the sea; –
Where the melting hoar-frost wets
The daisy-star that never sets,
And wind-flowers, and violets,
Which yet join not scent to hue,   60
Crown the pale year weak and new;
When the night is left behind
In the deep east, dun and blind,
And the blue noon is over us,
And the multitudinous
Billows murmur at our feet,
Where the earth and ocean meet,
And all things seem only one
In the universal sun.

Davie writes:

It maintains the familiar tone, though in highly figured language, and contrives to be urbane about feelings novel and remote. . . . It is an achievement of urbanity to move with such ease from financial and social entanglements to elated sympathy with a natural process; just as it is a mark of civilization to be able to hold these things together in one unflurried attitude. (Davie, 1967:146)

The poem, for Davie, is not just an achievement of writing in a 'highly figured language' for its own sake; it is an achievement of language that marks out the writer as highly civilized (for a classic example of this sort of analysis, see Auerbach, 1946). The accomplishment of the poet is not simply one of being able to put 'proper words in proper order', it is the accomplishment of 'genuine' poetry signalled as sophisticated and worthy to be considered 'high culture'. Such a commentary on the text is not disinterested; it represents a moral and political position on the status of certain varieties of language, certain poetry, and certain writers. Davie writes: 'The poet I have considered here is a poet of poise and good breeding. Shelley was the only English Romantic poet with the birth and breeding of a gentleman, and that cannot be irrelevant' (Davie, 1967:146).

Of course, the ways in which Shelley's status as a gentleman are relevant, are relative to particular ideologies. Davie's view (written in 1967, remember, not 1867 or earlier) represents an elitist ideology anxious to keep poetry and diction 'pure' – and the way you do that in breeding, of course, is to keep the mongrels away from the purebreds.

Traditional literary/practical criticism as we know it in most schools and colleges today is based on many of the assumptions at the heart of Davie's thinking, albeit tempered by a radical reaction to the view of English literature that saw it as a useful, though essentially impotent, means to an imperialist end (for example, Wetherill, 1974). This radicalism was developed by a few Cambridge academics after the First World War, who argued very effectively that literature was an essential relevance. Literature was considered to be 'the spiritual essence of the social formation' (Eagleton, 1983:31). This radicalism rejects the old school of Raleigh, but it develops at the same time into what Northrop Frye was later to call 'a mystery religion without a gospel' (Belsey, 1980:21). Understanding this, together with the developing ideas and practices associated with this critical movement both in England and in America, is crucial to understanding the ways in which countless generations of students have been, and still are, taught how to read and analyse literary texts:

> At schools where poetry is handled with tact and under-standing, by teachers who love it and *are able to communicate their love of it*, boys and girls do not develop the traditional hostility to this form of art, and retain an unashamed pleasure in it which grows with them and which they take away with them into adult life. (Strong, 1946:1)

'Tact', 'understanding', 'love', 'art', 'unashamed pleasure', 'grows' – those words signal very specifically a view that sees literature as special, requiring great care in handling because it is highly-strung demanding a sensibility to its aesthetic distinctive-ness. One of the strongest messages of the new critical movement was (and is) that there needed to be rigorous literary discrimination based on literary values and qualities (see Booth, 1961). Only certain texts would qualify for consideration as Literature. 'Good' literature represents the expression of individuals who are able to control their experiences, compared with the offerings of other people who wander aimlessly in a world of uncontrolled experiences, pulp novels, mass advertising, and celebrations of the mediocre. This tended to mean that the sort of text prioritized by many critics was complex, 'opaque', even seeming 'to turn its back on a reader' (Brown, 1978:125).

Seen in this light Literature becomes an object – an artefact – separated from both writer and reader. It is reified and requires specialized individuals to teach it – to *nurture* it – so that the students themselves can be nurtured and improved *as* individuals for the good of society. Imperialist ideologies might have waned, but elitist celebrations of the 'individual' had not. Literature might not now be the saviour of the basically defunct empire, but it was certainly expected to save the decline of cultured 'civilization' and to reorder the developing populist social chaos.[1] T. S. Eliot, in a characteristically reactionary statement, considered the experiences of ordinary people to be 'chaotic, irregular and fragmentary' (cited in Quinn, 1982:33). The poet's mind, for Eliot, was not.

In 1948 James Reeves wrote a book that was very widely used in schools and reprinted many times. Following Matthew Arnold, he claimed that 'The study of poetry is a training of the emotions – that is, a training for life' (Reeves, 1956:v) because, he asserts, 'Poetry is concerned . . . with the truth about life' (Reeves, 1956:

xxxv). Furthermore, following Shelley, he says, 'Although we may say, then, that poems are made of words, it is really truer to say that they are made of life' (Reeves, 1956: *xviii*), because 'Words are the means by which we think about everything in life and about life itself' (Reeves, 1956: *xviii*). A not uncommon view, then and now. Iris Murdoch, novelist and Oxford philosopher considered, in 1977, that 'bad art is a lie about the world' (cited in Belsey, 1980:13).

Controlling words – language – is therefore seen as a powerful way of controlling life. Signalling that certain words, like literary ones, are accessible only to a few adds to that power, and adds to the privileging of the few over the many. However, with a good Victorian work ethic to help them, the underprivileged (deprivileged), then and now, might be able to pull themselves up a little:

> If poetry is regarded as a relaxation from harder studies, it will not be respected. Most good poetry demands study, and interpretation; it costs its makers much effort of thought and imagination and feeling, and it is worthy of corresponding efforts by its readers. (Reeves, 1956: *v*)

and he continued: ' . . . you should not expect the reading of poetry to be easy; if you want to get all you can from it, you should be prepared to think hard when occasion demands' (Reeves, 1956: *xxii*), particularly as poetry ' . . . is the product of an acute and sensitive mind' (Reeves, 1956: 1).

F. R. Leavis, a leading figure in the new critical movement, wrote in 1943:

> The essential discipline of an English School is the literary-critical; it is a true discipline, only in an English School if anywhere will it be fostered, and it is irreplaceable. It trains, in a way no other discipline can, intelligence and sensibility together, cultivating sensitiveness and precision of response and a delicate integrity of intelligence – intelligence that integrates as well as analyzes and must have pertinacity and staying power as well as delicacy . . . (Cited in Widdowson, 1975:72–3.)

In 1975, at the end of a long career in university English teaching, during which he became a leading figure in Anglo-American new criticism, F. R. Leavis published *The Living Principle*. Its subtitle,

'English' as a Discipline of Thought, effectively sums up Leavis's position on the place of English studies in critical practice and education. The reading of literature should be carried out by disciplined minds, because 'worthwhile' literature is produced by disciplined minds. He wrote:

> Intelligent thought about the nature of thought and the criteria of good thinking is impossible apart from intelligence about the nature of language and the necessary intelligence about language involves an intimate acquaintance with a subtle language with its fullest use. (Leavis, 1975:13)

He considers that 'In major literary works we have the fullest use of language' (Leavis, 1975:44); it is 'the supreme creative act of language' (Leavis, 1975:51) – and this he considers to be a 'truth'.

The concept of truth is important here. Literature is perceived as special, the language used in literature is considered special, and the people involved in producing literature (and literary criticism) are considered special (see the discussion in Wetherill, 1974:253f). Critics who think along these lines create a priesthood; they become guardians of 'poetic truth' and of the meanings they determine for the texts they study. Such critics follow in the nineteenth-century tradition of Matthew Arnold for whom poetry was a substitute for religion and for whom in an ever more secular world poetry came to represent an essentially spiritual 'religious truth'. Such a position accords to poetry a deeper significance and seriousness than that which regards poetry in terms of its aesthetic worth or value. The main outcome, however, is an anti-rational criticism which believes that there is a 'right' way of doing criticism and 'right' meanings to discover.

Literature as traditional orthodoxy

The products of 'acute and sensitive' minds – poetry, for the most part, in the new critical movement – required similarly acute and sensitive ways of reading them. The diverse methods that developed to do this I shall weave together in the rest of this chapter and create something of a convenient fiction under the heading of 'intrinsic criticism'. This fiction ignores a great many of the differences that grew up between some of the critics, but I think it important to get some sense of the ways in which many of their ideas have been appropriated and developed in classroom practices, for the most part under the generalizing rubric of literary/ practical criticism.

Reeves's arguments are, in many ways, representative of that generalization. In order to enjoy and *appreciate* (a crucial term in intrinsic criticism) literature, critics (students) have to recognize quality in the text. Judgements are therefore made on the 'worth' of the text as an artefact of literature, and consequently on the 'worth' of the people writing. Similarly, people will recognize quality in the students by making value judgements on their 'worth' as people. Literary appreciation – practical criticism – is as much about developing criteria for recognising integrity in people as it is about recognizing integrity in text. But this is not done subjectively. The setting of standards is, according to James Reeves in his book *The Critical Sense*, 'independent of personal enthusiasm and preference' (Reeves, 1956:11). The literary criticism that developed is logocentric because its ideology is logocentric. That logocentrism is not an innocent interest in words and language, but an important way of establishing certain ideologies. Established humanist/empiricist thinking – which is at the base of intrinsic criticism, with its celebration of the individual – is simply one of the many realizations in society of classist ideology. *Individuation* (that is, the ideology of the progression of the individual) is considered to reach a peak in human beings, but only, of course, certain human beings. The notion of the individual is therefore vital to understand, because it is fundamental to intrinsic approaches to reading literary texts.

L. A. G. Strong (cited above) actually talks in his paper about teachers who are 'unfit' to teach literature because they don't have the right sensibilities – a view that is very dominant in intrinsic criticism. Alan Rodway in *Truths of Fiction*, talking about the role of the literary critic, says:

> For analysis he [*sic passim*] needs a refined and trained sensibility (to see more than his readers), a combination of common sense and imagination (to convey the precise flavour of what is there, and to refrain from finding what really isn't) . . . and he needs a terminology to convey with as little ambiguity as possible what he has seen and sensed. (Rodway, 1970:223)

What Rodway is talking about here is the distinction between the 'objective' text and the experiences of a text. The argument is that how you decide what is there or not 'in' a text is determined only by some sense of what, objectively, the text is. This refers to T. S. Eliot's concept of the 'objective correlative', which is a term designed to explain the theory that actual experiences are correlatives (equivalents) of emotions. This is an empiricist view, which states that knowledge is the product of experience (Robey, 1982:70). The literary text, if it is successful, presents an actual experience that is the objective correlative of the emotion it attempts to effect in the reader. In intrinsic criticism, the objective text is, for the most part considered to be a unified whole, impossible to break up or fragment. Diverse readings rather than a single 'right' meaning effectively suggest a text that is not a unified whole. And this is where some of the critical tensions have arisen in the last thirty years or so. When John Sinclair, Professor of Modern English Language at the University of Birmingham, produced a paper entitled 'Taking a poem to pieces' (Sinclair, 1966), it focused attention on a developing debate, that, in many places, still continues today. The text as a unified whole *cannot*, the argument went (and goes), be taken apart and put back together again, though its details can be analysed in close reading. John Sinclair, as a linguist, had upset one of intrinsic criticism's most important principles, organic unity, by using a poem as a site – a data base – for making statements about language *not* about the text in itself.

Text-in-itself relevance

Although Coleridge is thought of primarily as a poet his theorizing of literature is of central importance to the way in which criticism has developed. He was particularly concerned with countering the development of eighteenth-century rationalism, which threatened, by its emphasis on science and reason, the traditional Anglican orthodoxy of divine creation and intervention, the traditional idea that the world is a 'manifestation of a single law' (Cornwell, 1962:68). The development of modern science effectively altered the orthodox view of a purposeful universe created by a divine being. Coleridge (and others) were intent on retaining this orthodoxy, on maintaining values that they considered were no longer operating in the world around them. In so doing, they created a rift between literature and science that is still dominant today. Their world is effectively seen as guided by a single being, a single principle, and is therefore considered to be whole, a unity, much like the growing plant, which begins with a small seed; from *within* that seed comes everything that is needed for the plant to develop. It is an organic unity, in which the whole is greater than the parts, and the form shaped from within. Literature, like the world, like the plant, was considered to be an organic whole, containing *within itself* all that was needed to constitute it as literature. The theory of organic unity – 'text-in-itself-relevance' – does not permit speculation or discussion on anything other than the meaning 'inherent' in the text. In its most reactionary form, it is context-free literary criticism, where all that the critic needs to talk about, with regard to the 'total meaning' of the text, is contained within the text. Meaning is therefore immanent, and this apprach mirrors the structuralist enterprise, which sees language as a self-contained, unique, coherent system, summed up by Antoine Meillet, a French linguist, as 'tout se tient' (see Pulgram, 1967:83).

This theory led to a criticism based on close readings, in which very careful attention was paid to very particular details in the text. This method of analysis was developed mainly by I. A. Richards and William Empson, and, though T. S. Eliot accused Empson of 'lemon-squeezer' criticism, close reading became a dominant feature of criticism on both sides of the Atlantic. Richards has been very influential – and still is – in close reading of text, mainly through his ideas on practical criticism (see Richards, 1929) and his method of reading a literary text by concentrating, for the most part, on sense, feeling, intention, tone, rhythm, and metre, that is, on the psychological effects within the text that enable a reader to understand the 'essence' of the text by treating it as 'an embodiment of the author's consciousness . . . of which the unifying essence is the author's mind' (Eagleton, 1983:59). For this method of reading, the reader does not need to know about the situations in which the text was produced, the historical/economic contexts, or the biographical contexts of the writer. It is basically a criticism that produces an interpretation free of any contextual influences that might deflect from understanding the deepest reaches of the author's mind. These depths surface in the text as literary effects. The object of analysis, therefore, is not the specific text, but rather the phenomenon of subjectivity – that which marks us as human. Such criticism is, therefore, a science of subjectivity (Eagleton, 1983:58). A good critic (scientist), Richards argues (1924:87),

1 'must be adept at experiencing, without eccentricities, the state of mind relevant to the work of art being judged';

2 'must be able to distinguish experiences from one another as regards their less superficial features';

3 'must be a sound judge of value'.

In talking about the importance of effects (Richards, 1924:13), Richards is adopting a formal methodological view that is essentially structured on a psychological understanding of immediate experience. This effectively distinguishes his position from that of critics who recognize the social function of experience, and from those of the 'pure' phenomenological critics who attempt to go beyond language in order to find the essence, if you like, of meaning before it 'became overlaid by our everyday conceptions' (Mays, 1970:3). (See for example, the philosophy, of J. L. Austin, 1961, 1962.)

His argument, like Austin's in many respects, is that criticism needs to go beyond the effect of the immediate experience to see what special features of the text create the effect. In principle, this is a development from the philosophy of Emmanuel Kant. Richards talks of the technical and the critical as Kant talked about the knowing subject and the known object. The critical part of criticism describes the value of the experience and the technical part describes the object, that is, what caused the effect. The 'critical' side of criticism is necessarily about making value judgements. This is a view that still requires the total concentration of meaning to reside within the text, but understanding the effects created in an experience of a text is a means, in effect, of re-creating the experience the poet had in composing the poem and, in so doing, allowing a reader to understand *the* meaning of the poem. This requires a criticism that is also self-contained – not going beyond the text, but using the effects created by the text in order to make judgements about the experiences and worth of the text *as* literature. Richards continues:

The arts are our storehouse of recorded values. They spring from and perpetuate hours in the lives of exceptional people, when their control and command of experience is at its highest, hours when the varying possibilities of existence are most clearly seen and the different activities which may arise are most exquisitely reconciled, hours when habitual narrowness of interests or confused bewilderment are replaced by an intricately wrought composure. (Richards, 1924:22)

And this brings us to a central idea in intrinsic criticism – the theory of valuation. The concept of values (moral not market) that an 'exceptional' individual has 'intricately wrought' into literature, means, for I. A. Richards, being able to answer the question 'What gives the experience of reading a certain poem its value?' (Richards, 1924:1) and being able to judge how this experience might be better than another:

> . . . it is our sense . . . of the poet working alone in his or her poem, which will lend that poem the authenticity which makes us assent to its poetic 'truth', to that clarification of value which an achieved poem ultimately delivers. (Holden, 1986:178–9)

And ultimately what is talked about in intrinsic criticism – from the 1920s to the 1980s – are the sorts of values that are explored in literary texts.

For example, Jonathan Holden, in a chapter entitled 'Style, Authenticity and Poetic Truth' from his book *Style and Authenticity in Post-Modern Poetry* (1986), develops his ideas about value and 'poetic truth' by looking at Nancy Willard's 'Walking Poem'.

Walking Poem

How beautifully the child I carry on my back
teaches me to become a horse.
How quickly I learn to stay
between shafts, blinders, and whips,
bearing the plough

and the wagon loaded with hay,
or to break out of trot and run
till we're flying through cold streams.
He who kicks my commands
knows I am ten times his size

and that I am servant to small hands.
It is in mowed fields I move best,
watching the barn grow toward me,
the child quiet, his sleep piled like hay
on my back as we slip over the dark hill
and I carry the sun away.

According to Holden, this is an 'achieved' short lyric which has 'something to do with the reciprocal bond between mother and child, and with power' (179). The central question is: 'What are the values which the poem explores, and how are these values structured?' (179). The answer:

> 'Walking Poem' contrasts the value of child's play and pretend power, on the one hand, against the value of adult playfulness and of real power and responsibility on the other. The poem celebrates both; but it values the adult perspective more highly than the childhood perspective. It merely circumscribes it, is an enlargement of it. Adults can play *and* be responsible. Indeed, the poem suggests that gracefully dispatched responsibility may be the ultimate adult form of play. Willard's structure is narrative. With the poem's very opening words, 'How beautifully', the poem announces the value of child's play. It then proceeds, more or less continuously, to deepen and intensify that value. It is just when the child falls asleep that the poem leaps into the adult perspective, placing all the preceding description in the richer context of adult knowledge, adult love. (180–1)

The text, in an analysis of this kind, is hypostatized, that is divorced from contexts and sites of production, and turned into an artefact that is supposed to have all of its 'essentiality' contained within itself. It becomes a verbal icon (see Wimsatt, 1954). He talks about what 'the poem' does as if it has a life of its own, rather like some critics talk about characters in texts as if they were real.

According to this line of thinking, it is the poem that explores the values; the poet is simply someone who structures – facilitates – the means by which the poem can exist. Intrinsic criticism therefore tends to 'read with' the text. For example, Christopher Ricks in his book *The Force of Poetry* (1984) discusses a poem by William Empson, 'Note on Local Flora':

Note on Local Flora

There is a tree native in Turkestan,
Or further east towards the Tree of Heaven,
Whose hard cold cones, not being wards to time,
Will leave their mother only for good cause;
Will ripen only in a forest fire;
Wait, to be fathered as was Bacchus once,
Through men's long lives, that image of time's end.
I knew the Phoenix was a vegetable.
So Semele desired her deity

As this in Kew thirsts for the Red Dawn.

Christopher Ricks writes:

> The poem is itself a hard cold cone which then miraculously ripens. The buoyant snap of the eighth line – 'I knew the Phoenix was a vegetable' – is that of a ripened conclusion (though it importantly does not conclude the poem); the poem's first sentence had ripened through seven lines to bring this triumphant jauntiness to birth . . . what animates it, what makes it ripen in the mind (ripeness is all) is its relief as it contemplates this apocalyptic begetting. (Ricks, 1984:136)

This is a criticism that assumes the poem to have a life of its own; it 'ripens' and brings 'jauntiness to birth'. It is capable of relief and contemplation. Where is the awareness of a writing process here? Where is the awareness of the text as fiction? Where is the awareness of a construction of meaning? It isn't there because the poem 'is itself', and Ricks, as critic, reads 'with' it.

Similarly, Merle Brown, writing in 1978, is concerned with 'listening' to the poem as a way of interpreting it (cf. Engler, 1982) and looks at several poems, including the last seven lines from Wallace Stevens's 'The Motive for Metaphor' (Brown, 1978).

> The motive for metaphor, shrinking from
> The weight of primary noon,
> The ABC of being,
>
> The ruddy temper, the hammer
> of red and blue, the hard sound –
> Steel against intimation – the sharp flesh,
> The vital, arrogant, fatal, dominant X.

Brown writes:

> The thrust of these lines is all towards forging that motive, that motor force, that leads to the shrinking movement which is metaphor. Without the motive, as the thirteen lines leading up to the last seven make clear, Stevens feels that metaphor is sickly, effete, evasive. Yet the opposite, the motive without the metaphorical shrinking, proves equally intolerable, as a result of which, as Stevens expresses that final line, 'The vital, arrogant, fatal, dominant X', it is evident that he is allowing us to

listen to quintessential poetic listening in metaphorical touch with the expressiveness of that last forged line (Brown, 1978:127).

The structure of the text, the lines, the metaphors are invested here, as they are by Ricks, with human qualities, as if they have a life and force of their own. The analysis of the text is constructed in a way that reads 'with' such structures as if they are at the shoulder of the critic guiding him or her through the labyrinth of the text. Similarly, the poet is invested with a life 'in' the poem, to the extent that the critic reads 'with' the poet, giving opinions on what the poet is doing, what the poet is thinking, what the poet is trying to achieve at certain points, and what we, as readers, are expected to 'get out of' the poem.

And the overall consequences of this way of reading? The critic adopts a neutrality. Critics become vessels into which is poured by some mysterious action the life force of the poem and the poet. They become vehicles, by which to transmit, innocently and objectively, the 'message' and 'meaning' of the poem and the hidden poet, so that, 'Ultimately, we can talk of these texts only insofar as we talk with them' (Carter, 1983:384).

Analysis of text, therefore, has been modelled as if it operates like the structuralist model of language. The critic has no world view, no background, no history, no axe to grind. The critical role is 'simply' and disinterestedly to discover the signifieds hidden in the text. But this comes up against the Portia syndrome: a pound of flesh must be drawn without any blood being spilt. It cannot be done.

Yet it is attempted very often although the theoretical justification for it is flawed. But that is not the only objection. There is a belief, rather like the practice of archaeologists, that the critic must not be seen to alter in any way what is dug up, because to do so would disturb the creative genius of the writer.

John Ruskin developed a theory of unconscious genius that explains quite well the practice of some critics who treat the text in this way. Ruskin wrote:

The artist has done nothing till he [sic passim] has concealed himself; the art is imperfect which is visible. . . . In the reading of a great poem, in the hearing of a noble oration, it is the subject of the writer, and not his skill, his passion, not his power, on which our minds are fixed. We see as he sees, but we see not him. We become part of him, feel with him, judge, behold with him; but we think *of* him as little as of ourselves. . . . The power of the masters is shown by their self-annihilation. . . . The harp of the minstrel is untruly touched, if his own glory is all that it records. Every great writer may be at once known by his guiding the mind far from himself, to the beauty which is not of his creation, and the knowledge which is past his finding out. (Cited in Sawyer, 1985:45.)

The text is therefore seen as a palimpsest, a canvas overwritten to obscure a meaning considered (because it can't be seen) far more interesting, and probably of far greater value, than what can immediately be seen on the surface. It is Alice and the rabbit-hole. Who could resist finding out what the rabbit-hole really signifies? Seen in this way, the text as poem, its writer, and its language are inevitably going to be valorized as having high cultural status, compared to, say, a shopping list.

Literary language, for Richards, though not for many of the American intrinsic critics, particularly T. S. Eliot, is theorized as existing in a way quite different from 'ordinary' language – the sort you would find in a shopping list, for example. This classic formalist argument, developed by Russian Formalism to an extent that Richards would not have adopted (see Fokkema and Kunne-Ibsch, 1978:19–49), maintains that literature belongs to an emotive plane where 'reason had best not meddle for fear of disturbing its fine equilibrium'. (Norris, 1985a:30). Following the lead of T. S. Eliot, American criticism in the hands of W. K. Wimsatt and Monroe Beardsley (see Wimsatt 1954, 1963) developed the idea of the 'effective fallacy', which is exactly the fallacy they claim Richards fell into when he argued for the emotive use of language in literature. Their position, like Eliot's, was that the text was autonomous; the text-in-itself should be the object of the study, not the effects of the text. T. S. Eliot wrote:

We can only say that a poem, in some sense, has its own life; that its parts form something quite different from a body of neatly ordered biographical data; that the feeling, or emotion, or vision, resulting from the poem is something different from the feeling or emotion or vision in the mind of the poet.

And of his own poetry, he said:

. . . I have long aimed, in writing poetry, to write poetry which should be essentially poetry, with nothing poetic about it, poetry standing naked in its bare bones, or poetry so transparent that we should not see the poetry, but that which we are meant to see through the poetry, poetry so transparent that in reading it we are intent on what the poem *points* at, and not on the poetry, this seems to me the thing to try for. To get *beyond poetry*, as Beethoven, in his later works, strove to get *beyond music*. (Eliot, 1920: x)

Wallace Stevens, in a poem called 'Man Carrying Thing', put it like this:

The poem must resist the intelligence
Almost successfully. Illustration:

A brune figure in winter evening resists
Identity. The thing he carries resists

The most necessitous sense. Accept them, then,
As secondary (parts not quite perceived . . .

(Stevens, 1955:350)

Meaning, according to this sort of thinking, is considered to be unchanging. The meaning of the text is always and irrevocably the same, regardless of when it is read, how it is read, and who reads it. In other words the text belongs neither to reader nor to writer. The text just is – and intrinsic critical activity is designed to show this by demonstrating the 'internal consistency' of the text (Daiches, 1956:167).

Internal consistency, what Pierre Macherey calls 'the myth of interiority' (Macherey, 1978:142), is based on a philosophy, developed from the work of John Locke, which is concerned with knowledge as meanings located in the interior of texts, not on a philosophy (developed, in the main, from the work of Bishop Berkeley) that contextualizes knowledge. Interiorization is, of course, the basis of Saussurean ideology. This contrast accounts for the major differences between some intrinsic and extrinsic analysis of text.

The result of intrinsic analysis, whether you read the text from a position of its effects on the reader, or whether you read it as a text sufficient unto itself, is still an impressionistic anti-rational criticism that privileges the critic as being someone who has probably far greater insights into the meaning of a text than anyone else, because he or she is able to recognize the interiorized meanings. Intrinsic analysis assumes that if readers of such criticism are unable to work out for themselves where in that interior the critic's reading has come from, then their own development as thinking, aesthetically aware, sensitive readers is at fault, not the theory, the text, or the critic.

Cleanth Brooks is a good example of a critic obsessed with the idea of internal consistency and text-in-itself ideology. He argues in his 1963 paper 'The Uses of Literature' (Brooks, 1971:1–16) that there are three main types of criticism: reader-oriented, writer-oriented and writing-oriented. His, like that of many critics, is writing-oriented. It is concerned with a text ' . . . as a structure of meanings, as a piece of artistic craft, as a verbal context . . .' (Brooks, 1971: xiii). As Brooks writes (though he is in the process arguing against it), the critic ' . . . would seem to be trapped in a cell without windows or door, staring through a reading glass at his [sic] literary text, effectively cut off from all the activities of the world outside' (Brooks, 1971: xi). As an example Brooks, in a 1959 paper entitled 'The criticism of fiction: the role of close analysis' (1971:143–65), examines William Faulkner's 'An Odor of Verbena':

> 'An Odor of Verbena' is a very rich and subtle story. In some respects it is as finely textured as a poem. It is filled with brilliant description and the description is not mere external decoration, but has its part in shaping the total meaning. Much of the action is internal action, mental action. Even particular metaphors are invested with special meaning. (Brooks, 1971:145)

Very little, except an ability to construct a text based on literary critical cliches, is demonstrated here. If a reader of this text is unable to recognize *in what ways* the description contributes to the 'total meaning' and *how* 'particular metaphors are invested with special meaning', then that reader is presumably insensitive to the privileged insights that Brooks has had. And this, I would argue, is representative of a considerable amount of writing-oriented criticism and forms the basis, still, of many school, college and perhaps (or I am being too pessimistic?) university courses in literary text analysis. Its weakness – which is considered a strength by its practitioners – is that it cannot cope with disagreement, with alternative readings, with unstable meaning. Brooks in his 1968 paper 'Faulkner as a Poet' (1971:247–69), discusses these lines from 'The Marble Faun':

> Beside (a) hushed pool where lean
> His own face and the bending sky

In shivering soundless amity

and writes

> These lines constitute no mean achievement, but how much more brilliant is Faulkner's account of how the idiot found 'a brown creep of moisture in a clump of alder and beech' and scooped out a basin for it 'which now at each return of light stood full and clear and leaf by leaf repeating until (the cow and the idiot) lean and interrupt the green reflections and with their own drinking faces break each mirroring face to its own shattered image wedded and annealed'. (Brooks, 1971;264)

This is a classic example of a critic expecting a series of quotations to function as critical comment. F. W. Bateson, somewhat more rigorous in his approach to analysis, complains bitterly in *English Poetry. A Critical Introduction* (1950)

> . . . that it is now possible to get high marks in most school and university examinations in English literature without being either right or wrong. All that is required in the students is the ability to reproduce a muzzy impression of what they have been reading and to quote indiscriminately. (Bateson, 1950:198)

The point is a useful one for my purposes here. *How* do the lines suggest to Brooks that they are 'no mean achievement'? In *what ways* are the lines he quotes after these three lines 'more brilliant'? There are no answers, because this type of intrinsic criticism demands that the critic's 'sensitivities' are as self-contained as the meanings they suppose exist intrinsically in the interior of the text. Literature will only 'yield up' its primary meaning to the sensitive critic. Bateson goes further, however:

> It is towards the creation and consolidation of a . . . class of common readers today that the energies of the friends of English poetry should be directed. The first step, in my opinion, must be the conscious stimulation of a poetry-reading elite, who can be the missionaries of poetry in a world of prose. (Bateson, 1950:201)

Prose, of course, is considered to be considerably more functional than poetry, and its interiorization of meaning considerably less advanced – the contrast is a little like Donald Davie's idea of civilized and uncivilized people. This is why the elite can be recognized by their ability to 'read' poetry. James Reeves, discussing John Keats's 'Ode to Autumn', writes:

The versification is smooth without monotony, the verbal 'music' is exquisite. The magic by which this enhances the pictorial and other imagery and expresses the harmony and contentment of the poet's mood is beyond analysis. (Reeves, 1956:115)

And this is the crux of the matter, really. Good literature, following a similar argument developed by the Oxford philosopher Ludwig Wittgenstein, will always be seen as *transcending analysis*; defying definition (see Watson, 1969). It has to be seen thus, really, when addressed by a form of criticism whose basic philosophy cannot cope with textual analysis. After all is said and done, texts belong to the messy world of discourse and the philosophy of intrinsic criticism doesn't. So regardless of what is said in any analysis, the text will always remain unsullied and untouched by the 'crudities' of criticism because meaning exists in a virtual world.

Susan Sontag, in her essay 'Against Interpretation', claimed that criticism is 'an infatuation' and can never actually say anything about 'the work of art' (Sontag, 1961). Her argument is that 'in most modern instances, interpretation amounts to the philistine refusal to leave the work of art alone' (Sontag, 1961:8). The irony here is that her move away from the eighteenth- and nineteenth-century impressionism of essayists like William Hazlitt, and from the historicism of philologists like Henry Sweet, towards 'the doctrine of clear precise images' (Ong, 1976:150) ultimately fails. And it does so because English empiricist criticism is so hostile to engaging with actual experience. It replaces it with neat, clear, precise images, all of which can unproblematically contribute a single unique textual meaning (Nuttall, 1974:23) – the sort of meaning demanded in most scientific approaches. The impressionistic appearance of intrinsic analysis, in any or all of its guises, should not lure you into thinking it an unscientific approach, despite all of the protestations against science made by many of the critics. Its philosophical and ideological base is scientistic. James Reeves put it like this:

The poem isolates itself, so to speak, from its context in ordinary experience to take on a separate, unique and indestructible existence of its own – independent not only of our ordinary experience, but also of its own separate constituents of sense and sound. (Reeves, 1956:94)

This is a classic scientistic statement of idealization.

'Reading with' the text

To summarize, then, Literature is considered to 'speak its own truth'. And that, in a roundabout argument, effectively means that the 'truths' of literature cannot be expressed in any way other than literature (cf. Gelven, 1982:314). This point is at the very heart of intrinsic criticism. The text is supposed to have its own way with us, it will reveal itself to the sensitive critic because poetry, as insightful, total reflection of a truth, is quite unlike any other discourse. This is a critical position, developed, for the most part, from the empiricist philosophy presented by John Locke, which argues that ' ... "things themselves" if approached without "preconceived notions will show us in what way they are to be understood" ' (Hill, 1984:140). Locke's position is that we have no direct knowledge of anything except the ideas we have of things. This means that, as individuals, we have a private bank of knowledge. If these private thoughts and insights into the world are expressed textually, then criticism involves the discovery of these otherwise inaccessible thoughts. T. S. Eliot puts it this way: 'All significant truths are private truths' (Eliot, 1920). Reality exists in an 'inner world' and the language of literature acts as a bridge between the reality of the inner world and the outer world of ideas. Criticism based on this notion privileges the status of literature above all other texts, and maintains the myth of the sensitive individual achieving a 'civilized' status. If you, the student/reader, can recognize what critics mean, then you will be considered sensitive, cultured, and civilized, and can join the ranks of the privileged.

Donald Davie's interpretation of the first stanza of Shelley's 'The Cloud' should prove a useful illustration at this point.

The Cloud

Sublime on the towers of my skiey bowers,
    Lightning my pilot sits;
In a cavern under is fettered the thunder,
    It struggles and howls at fits;
Over earth and ocean, with gentle motion,
    This pilot is guiding me.
Lured by the love of the genii that move
    In the depths of the purple sea;
Over the rills, and the crags, and the hills,
    Over the lakes and the plains,

> Wherever he dream, under mountain or stream,
>> The Spirit he loves remains;
> And I all the while bask in Heaven's blue smile,
>> Whilst he is dissolving in rains.

Davie opens with the following point: 'The image is audacious to begin with. There is no reason in natural philosophy to give a basis in logic to the notion that a cloud is directed by electric charges' (1967:135). The image depends entirely on association, which is not easy, but is made easier 'by the elaboration which makes the thunder a prisoner in the dungeons of the cloud' (135). *How* it is made easier is not explained.

There is a problem with the 'he' that appears three times in the last six lines: 'Is this "he" the lightning, the actual cloud, or the idea of the cloud which is always present even in a cloudless sky?' (135–6). Davie asserts that the 'he' is the lightning, but at the same time he says that this is an impossibility because of the last two lines of the poem, which he quotes to support his argument:

> Shelley means to say, I think, that the ideal cloud continues to bask while the actual cloud dissolves in rains; but in fact he says that the cloud, ideal or actual, rides high, while the lightning dissolves. And this is lunacy. (136)

The fault of the 'he', he explains 'lies in the conduct and development of a metaphor, not, in the first place, in choice of language' (136), though the 'metaphor only comes to grief on the loose use of a personal pronoun' (136). *How* this happens is not explained.

Davie then looks at similar 'problems' of language in the rest of the poem, for example: 'The grotesque "and these" is an affront to all prosaic discipline in:

> Like strips of the sky fallen through me on high
> Are each paved with the moon and these.'

Though *why* this is so he doesn't say.

In

> From cape to cape, with a bridge-like shape,
>> Over a torrent sea,
> Sunbeam-proof, I hang like a roof, –
>> The mountains its columns be.

he considers that 'the language is quite indiscriminate; the adjectival "torrent" is a Latinate urbanity, "sunbeam-proof" is an audacious coining, and "The mountains . . . be" is a naivete' (137).

He offers a final comment: 'The poem offers compensations. But all the same, when the barbarities are so brutal and the carelessness so consistent, it may be doubted whether we can let them pass on any understanding' (137) but he concludes that ' "The Cloud" remains a poem splendid in conception but ruined by licentious phrasing' (137).

Text analysis here rests for the most part on judging the poem according to a standard of purity. The rules of that judging are not stated specifically, but are mainly based on models of style developed over generations and dating back to English Renaissance revivals of classic Greek theories of rhetoric: high style, the model for courtiers and governors; middle style for people 'in trade'; and low style for the peasantry. Writing poetry in any of the styles was common. The problem of 'The Cloud' for Davie is that he believes Shelley has not been consistent, and this upsets Davie's sensibilities about what is appropriate for this poem. 'The Cloud' is therefore being judged by an implicit understanding of the ideal style for a text. When the language is judged as moving away from the ideal, it is considered barbaric, careless, audacious, licentious, grotesque, and brutal – epithets used patronizingly and domineeringly for generations, in classist oppressive discourse about people 'of the lower orders' (sic) and the language, style, and cultural practices associated with them. Language, in these terms, is conceived as having its own life, thereby allowing the poet to remain well bred, saved from the barbaric, low-style language of the poem by his poetic invention, which Davie argues is 'the characteristic virtue of the sublime' (134) and presumably the property of 'gentlemen'. The text is therefore used in this sort of critical practice as a model against which individuals can 'realize' themselves morally (cf. Babb, 1972:62, see also Spoerri, 1944). And when a valorized writer seems to be going astray, analysis becomes an exercise in excuse, mainly centred on phrases like '[they] cannot mean what [they] seem to say' (Davie, 1967:185).

A further example might be useful here:

Richard Webster conducts an analysis similar to Davie's on Ted Hughes's 'The Thought-Fox' (Webster, 1984).

The Thought-Fox

I imagine this midnight moment's forest:
Something else is alive
Beside the clock's loneliness
And this blank page where my fingers move.

Through the window I see no star:
Something more near
Though deeper within darkness
Is entering the loneliness:

Cold, delicately as the dark snow,
A fox's nose touches twig, leaf;
Two eyes serve a movement, that now
And again now, and now, and now

Sets neat prints into the snow
Between trees, and warily a lame
Shadow lags by stump and in hollow
Of a body that is bold to come

Across clearings, an eye,
A widening deepening greenness,
Brilliantly, concentratedly,
Coming about its own business

Till, with a sudden sharp hot stink of fox
It enters the dark hole of the head.
The window is starless still; the clock ticks,
The page is printed.

The purpose of Webster's analysis is to examine 'the underlying puritanism of Hughes's poetic vision [and] the conflict between violence and tenderness which seems to be directly engendered by this puritanism' (Webster, 1984:35). This is not simply a product of this one particular poem but, Webster argues, an aspect of Hughes's poetry generally. Webster's position can be outlined as follows.

'The Thought-Fox' is a poem about writing a poem (35). There is a disturbance in the night. Night is a metaphor for 'the intimate darkness of the poet's imagination in whose depths an idea is mysteriously stirring' (36). At first the idea is 'seen but not felt' (36), and 'The poet's task is to coax it out of formlessness and into fuller consciousness by the sensitivity of his language' (36).

These remote stirrings are compared to the stirrings of a fox invisible in the undergrowth. Gradually the fox appears until it and the image it represents – a poem – are complete.

The emergence of the fox in the course of the poem is mirrored in the rhythm, rhyme scheme, sound patterns, and punctuation. These structures 'mime' the 'nervous, unpredictable movement of the fox', whose tracks are 'duplicated' by the sounds and rhythm. 'The first three short words of "Sets neat prints into the snow" are internal half-rhymes, as neat, as identical and as sharply outlined as the fox's paw-marks, and these words press down gently but distinctly into the soft open vowel of "snow" (37). At the end of the stanza the words 'bold to come' are left suspended – as though the fox is pausing at the outer edge of some trees' (37); 'the gap between the stanzas is itself the clearing which the fox, after hesitating warily, suddenly shoots across' (37) before it 'enters the dark hole of the head'.

This is not the party-trick magic of poetry referred to by Sagar (1979:19) but 'is more like the sublime and awesome magic which is contained in the myth of creation, where God creates living beings out of nothingness by the mere *fiat* of his imagination' (38).

Webster continues, 'The studied and beautifully "final" nature of the poem indicates that we are not in the presence of any untrained spontaneity, any primitive or naive vision' (38). Like D. H. Lawrence's, Hughes's 'poetic vision' attacks 'extreme scientific rationalism' and exhibits a 'puritanical rationalism' that reflects a 'feminine sensitivity' that 'can be incorporated into the identity only to the extent that it has been purified by, or subordinated to, a tough, rational, artistic will' (40). This occurs as the poem progresses, and it reaches its climax with the tough 'manly posturing' of poet resisting 'feminine weakness' by pitting himself against the fox – in the final stanza. The poem is therefore about conflict of sensibilities.

Seen as 'formless stirrings' by Richard Webster, the fox needs to find 'form'. It does so by means of the language, structure, and style of the poem. But this is not a statement based on an analysis of the relation between linguistic form and literary content in order 'just' to explain the meaning of the poem. It engenders a textual analysis designed to make judgements about the intellectual sensibilities of the poet. Just as the fox emerges metaphorically from the undergrowth and gains recognition as a poem, so the judgement of Hughes as poet emerges as simile to the poem. The moral judgement being made about Hughes's 'puritanical rationalism' emerges from an interpretation of the poem that sees it as being about the conflict and confrontation of the tough male intellect (poet) involved in the feminine weakness of creating a poem (fox). Analysing this text, therefore, is a means by which to make judgements about the value and 'accuracy' (38) of a poetry reflecting the sensibilities of the poet Ted Hughes.

This is a view of critical practice which found its fullest philosophical statement in the aesthetics of Benedetto Croce, who maintained that a reader could re-experience the creative process that is 'captured' in the text. Richard Webster doesn't go this far, but he does attempt to rebuild that creative process in order to judge the success of Hughes's creativity through his writing. Webster demonstrates that Hughes has an intellectual sensibility that is not 'primitive' or indicative of a 'naive vision'. He is 'able to explore and express the internalized violence of the rationalist sensibility with more imagination than any other modern poet (44), creating, as he does so, 'one of the most completely realized and artistically satisfying' poems in his collection *The Hawk in the Rain* (35). In other words, he stands apart fom the 'primitive' and 'naive' because of his creative sensitivities.

Centres of text and fixed points of meaning

Detailed discussion of parts of a poem, for example the metaphors or the noun phrases, is considered very often in the sort of analysis carried out by Donald Davie and Richard Webster to say little or nothing about the text as a literary whole. The literary whole needs to be understood in terms of a single, unifying principle. This principle, for the most part, is expressed as a conflict of opposites – meaning created by the bringing together, the reconciling of tensions; Eagleton's phrase is 'a delicate equipoise of contending attitudes' (Eagleton, 1983:50). The vocabulary developed, in the main by the American intrinsic critics, reflects this idea: *irony, paradox, tension*. A useful example can perhaps be taken from Simon Stuart's *New Phoenix Wings. Reparation in Literature*, in which, talking of the following passage from Shakespeare's *Much Ado About Nothing*:

> The God of love that sits above, and knowes mee, and knowes me, how pittifull I deserve. I meane in singing, but in loving,

Leander the good swimmer, Troilus the first emploier of pandars, and a whole booke full of these quondam carpetmongers, whose names yet runne smoothly in the even rode of a blancke verse, why they were never so truly turned over and over as my poor self in love.

he writes

The syntax demands attention, for it finds the essence of the character. There is a principle of spontaneity and a principle of sobriety creating a tension which gives the period a unique and unforgettable thisness. (Stuart, 1979:173)

A centre for the text is located out of two forces in tension, 'sobriety' and 'spontaneity'; I don't know what 'thisness' signifies, but the notion of the 'centre' is a very important one in intrinsic criticism.

T. S. Eliot developed the idea of talking about the 'still point' – a moment of energy, a *centre* – where 'all opposites are reconciled – the complete vision perceived, complete reality experienced and complete being attained' (Cornwell, 1962:4). This 'centre' effectively locates the single, unified, interiorized meaning of a text. And in so doing it closes off all possibility of other meanings, other readings. Literature – the literary text – becomes the frame in which diverse meanings are reduced to a single meaning (what Roland Barthes was to call *a-symbolia*). In his book *Principles of Literary Criticism* I. A. Richards talks about this literary fixedness of meaning when he writes:

A single word by itself, let us say night, will raise almost as many different thoughts and feelings as there are persons who hear it. The range of variety with a single word is very little restricted. But put it into a sentence and the variation is narrowed; put it into the context of a whole passage, and it is still further fixed, and let it occur in such an intricate whole as a poem and the responses of competent readers may have a similarity which only its occurrence in such a whole can secure. (Richards, 1924:4)

As we have seen in the first chapter (pp. 7–10), it is against this closure of the text to other readings and meanings by creating a centre of meaning for the text that Jacques Derrida and others have argued so persuasively in recent years. Eliot's 'still point' – the object of the search for a centre – echoes the 'ecstatic moment' Coleridge talked of, and it has been developed in numerous ways by many twentieth-century critics. Marshall McLuhan, for example, possibly more well known for his pronouncements on the media than for his literary criticism, proposed the notion of the 'interior landscape'. This term, like Eliot's 'still point', Coleridge's 'ecstatic moment', and Bateson's 'aesthetic moment', is a way of finding a fixed point of stability in what appears to be a chaos of possible meanings. Allowing a 'free play' of these possible meanings is considered too unsettling a way of approaching interpretations; it is too uncertain, too unscientific and imprecise

In a paper reacting against the work of Jacques Derrida and Roland Barthes, both of whom have argued spiritedly against the idea of 'stable' meanings, closed texts, and the primacy of the author, Bernard Dauenhauer develops a 1980s defence of the intrinsic position on fixed points of meaning. His argument is 'that every interpretation requires discernible points of control' (Dauenhauer, 1982:138) and he uses, as an example, a production of *A Midsummer Night's Dream* at the University of Georgia in October/November 1980. The points of control, the fixed points of the text, are, he argues, the Penguin script, the characters Theseus and Hippolyta – because 'Shakespeare obviously intends these characters to call to mind the stories told in mythology' (Dauenhauer, 1982:139); the contrast between the mortals' world and the fairy world, so that the fixed differences between them allowed a production to present the differences between them theatrically; the Georgia interpretation, that is, the way the people involved in this production developed an interpretation that remained a 'stable object' (140) – a fixed point of reference – throughout the production. Each performance, in turn, became a fixed point with which to compare subsequent performances, and finally, the relationship between the interpret- ation and the choice of costume, lighting, space, set, etc., also became a fixed point. Without access to these fixed points, Dauenhauer argues, interpretation is impossible. This is a classic intrinsic conception of how the act of interpretation can be carried out through an analysis that does everything it can to militate against interpretation. More importantly, perhaps, it demonstrates how to determine, theoretically, that a text is closed. His definition of what constitutes a text is that:

It is a history of fixed points together with what Husserl would call the motivated, and not merely empty, possibilities for subsequent fixings. These possibilities are motivated by the experience of the previously established fixed points. A text, then, is closed in the sense that only some motivatedly possible fixings are genuine possibilities. (Dauenhauer, 1982:144)

Authors, he says, fix points and audiences receive them (Dauenhauer, 1982:145). This is a view that protects the 'property' of the text as being the property of someone or something. Literature and literary criticism, seen in this way, are therefore a means of defending and making a stand against encroachments upon property – upon orthodoxy, upon established views – by the unqualified and uninitiated. This practice is, in short, capitalist.

Marshall McLuhan is a good example of a 'capitalist' critic. In his paper 'Aesthetic Pattern in Keats' Odes' (reprinted in McNamara, 1969) McLuhan is anxious to portray Keats as a poet concerned with showing the development of 'natural growth' in his poetry, where the ideal and the actual (the real and the virtual) are unified in a 'world of rich organic and tactual awareness' (McNamara, 1969:113). Keats is seen as a poet who resolves conflict. This is important because it is central to the polemic against seeing the world as unstable. Intrinsic literary criticism posits writers as people who resolve conflict, order tensions, and make stable the unstable. The poet – like the divine figure – is a steadying influence in the world. The poet's world is a world of the total, that is, the poet seeks to express, through writing, the totality of his or her own experience. McLuhan argues that Keats rejects anything less than a total view of his experience. When faced with that critical assertion, the analyst is left only with attempting to analyse the *whole*. And, for the most part, this attempt at articulating the total meaning has been, and continues to be for many, the raison d'être of intrinsic criticism.

To summarize this type of criticism, then:

1 Only certain texts 'qualify' as literature. The criteria for entry to 'the sacred wood' are based on specific literary values and qualities determined, for the most part, by a view of the writers as sensitive people with greater insights into the world than the rest of us.

2 This inevitably concentrates literary criticism on the idea of the individual. Literature is therefore the expression of certain

individuals able to have and control distinctive experiences.

3 The resultant texts are therefore likely to be complex and opaque, because the experiences they describe and elicit in the reader are considered, necessarily, to be complex and deep.

4 Literature thus takes on the mantle of the icon – it is determined to be special, sensitive, having an aura of the distinctive, non-ordinary about it. It is distinguished as high culture, not popular culture. A canon of 'appropriate' literature is therefore established, isolating certain texts and writers as special, and relegating most writers and texts to the insignificant.

5 This inevitably suggests a view of literary language as being non-ordinary. Literature is considered to be the expression of language at its fullest use – a use given only to a few special individuals.

6 Meaning is located, not within the context and situation of the text and the institutions that determined its production and reception, but within the text itself – located at the centre of the text. Analysis of the text is therefore a process of recovering this meaning, put there by the sensitive writer.

7 Because of this, the text is seen as a self-contained system, in which meanings are closed off; they are fixed and determined as changeless over time, regardless of the range of different readers.

8 The text is therefore hypostasized; closed off from contexts and variation in meanings and readings.

9 The critic is therefore someone who determines what the fixed meanings for the texts are; the critic is privileged, considered to be as sensitive as the writers of 'good' literature.

10 Analysis of text becomes a matter of analysing meanings 'put into' the text by the writer – a sort of literary archaeology.

All readings represent the cultural and ideological values of the systems and theories 'behind' the readings. For intrinsic criticism those values tend to be 'exactness, sensitivity to shades of feeling, the need to see pattern and order, the effort to shut out from consciousness one's own life-situation while reading the poem,

and to pry the words loose from their social origins. . . '
(Ohmann, 1970:130).

The consequences of this approach have been extreme, and
no more clearly so than in the attitudes of intrinsic criticism to
the study of language in texts. Language, for the most part is
marginalized because, as F. W. Bateson makes clear in his essay
'Linguistics and literary criticism', many critics believe native
speaker knowledge of a language sufficient to make comments
about language in literature unnecessary (Bateson, 1972:70).
This is true for many critics, but by no means all, as will be seen
in Chapter 4.

4 Reading texts closely: language, style and the 'buried life of words'

> Reading a poem is like walking on silence – on volcanic silence. We feel the historical ground; the buried life of words. Like fallen gods, like visions of the night, words are erectile.
> (Hartman, *Beyond Formalism*: 341–2)

Language-aware analysis

Though he might not have put it quite this way, William Empson's position in *Seven Types of Ambiguity* (1930) and *The Complex Structure of Words* (1951a), suggests that as readers we are able to engage with choices of meaning in a text, recognition of which comes from our linguistic and literary competences. Such engagement requires a skill with understanding grammatical structures, a skill with words, a skill with literary effects, a skill with meanings, and a skill with language analysis. And whilst such skills may not account for 'total' meaning in a text (a requirement of other critics), for Empson they go a long way towards explaining why a reader reacts in a particular way to a text. More significantly, perhaps, such skills give readers a vocabulary in which to discuss their intuitions about a text – something that became increasingly important for Empson in the wake of his objections to most of the new critical practice examined in the previous chapter.

This approach requires skill and training, a knowledge of linguistic and literary structures, and a recognition, above all, of the crucial importance of language in literary texts.

An illustration of a simple analysis that recognizes this importance might be a useful way of introducing this approach. It is a close reading stripped bare, so to speak, and – as a method of close reading – it is often considered a useful, and gentle initiation into textual analysis. N. F. Blake, Professor of English Language at Sheffield University, offered such an approach to a group of students when he lectured in 1983 in South Korea on the language and style of the British poet Philip Larkin. He was

principally concerned with 'Lines on a Young Lady's Photograph
Album' by Philip Larkin, from *The Less Received* (1955).

Lines on a Young Lady's Photograph Album

At last you yielded up the album, which,
Once open, sent me distracted. All your ages
Matt and glossy on the thick black pages!
Too much confectionery, too rich:
I choke on such nutritious images.

My swivel eye hungers from pose to pose –
In pigtails, clutching a reluctant cat;
Or furred yourself, a sweet girl-graduate;
Or lifting a heavy-headed rose
Beneath a trellis, or in a trilby hat

Faintly disturbing, that, in several ways) –
From every side you strike at my control,
Not least through these disquieting chaps who loll
At ease about your earlier days:
Not quite your class, I'd say, dear, on the whole.

But o, photography! as no art is,
Faithful and disappointing! that records
Dull days as dull, and hold-it smiles as frauds,
And will not censor blemishes
Like washing-lines, and Halls-Distemper boards.

But shows the cat as disinclined, and shades
A chin as doubled when it is, what grace
Your candour thus confers upon her face!
How overwhelmingly persuades
That this is a real girl in a real place,

In every sense empirically true!
Or is it just *the past*? Those flowers, that gate,
These misty parks and motors, lacerate
Simply by being over; you
Contract my heart by looking out of date.

Yes, true; but in the end, surely, we cry
Not only at exclusion, but because
It leaves us free to cry. We know *what was*
Won't call on us to justify
Our grief, however hard we yowl across

The gap from *eye* to page. So I am left
To mourn (without a chance of consequence)
You, balanced on a bike against a fence;
To wonder if you'd spot the theft
Of this one of you bathing; to condense,

In short, a past that no one now can share,
No matter whose your future; calm and dry,
It holds you like a heaven, and you lie
Unvariably lovely there,
Smaller and clearer as the years go by.

According to Blake's explication of the text (1983:342–50)
Larkin avoids treating his subjects romantically or sentimentally
by using a negative vocabulary – usually words with negative
prefixes or suffixes, for example, *disturbing, disquieting*, and so
forth, which, together with negative particles (*not least, not quite*)
and words suggesting imperfection (*blemish, frauds*), creates a
'neutral tone' that is 'reinforced by many words which imply a
taking away or holding back', for example, *reluctant, censor,
exclusion, condense*.

Larkin's use of words like *faintly disturbing* and *I'd say* gives a
colloquial feel to the poem, though there are also poetic uses,
like *misty parks* and *heavy-headed rose*. The result is a mixed
style 'which creates a language different from that of ordinary
speech but which is not so poetic that it becomes mawkish' (342).

Another feature of Larkin's style is verbal repetition, which is
supported by 'other kinds of poetic echo', for example, variation
of determiners: *the* past, *those* flowers, *that* gate and the repetition
of *-ing* 'which helps to reinforce the link among the negative
words in the third and fourth stanzas.' Alliteration – the repetition
of initial consonants – and the repetition of adverbials that occur
at the beginning of every line in the third stanza allow Larkin to
'sidle into his poem, as it were, with a less prominent part of
speech' (344).

Adverbials also occur in the poem as intensifiers, for example
faintly disturbing, invariably loved, these 'provide a suggestion of
social exaggeration and pretension which is undercut by the
contexts in which they occur' (344). The language of the poem
is 'flat' and this is 'assisted by the absence of much metaphor
or imagery' (345), so that the poem can be read in a fairly
straightforward manner – the only typically poetic images are the
idea of the photograph album as a rich diet and the association

of the observer's eye with the camera through the word *swivel*. The active/dynamic verbs refer to the poet and the stative ones refer to the pictures, which 'have an anthropomorphic quality which can affect all who look upon them, for the reminders of a youth that is past wound us all' (346). The verbs, for the most part, are in the simple present, which 'implies something that is continually true, because many of the verbs refer to the pictures and what they portray' (346). The opening stanza, however, begins with a verb in the past tense, and therefore 'what had started out as a single event expressed in the past (*yielded up*) is transmuted at this stage into something which has a present effect but which is also perenially true' (346). The fact that all the verbs are in the active mood 'refers to the poet and indicates the way in which he is the victim of events rather than the originator of them' (346). The participles and other parts of the syntax 'reinforce the impression created by the simple verbs' (347).

The analysis continues along these lines, looking at details of syntax and cohesion before concluding that the 'moral centre' of the poem rests with the reference to *exclusion* in stanza seven, where

> it is the poet's reaction to the past and our human reaction to the whole question of life that is in question, for the poem here turns from an *I* to the *we* . . . (349–50)
>
> However hard we try, we cannot make past and present one. . . . That is why there is no chance of consequence. The poet is left on his own. . . . The adverbials are thrown into prominence. Past and future are set in opposition. . . . The grief of the present cannot alter the past. (350)

This sort of analysis is simple, straightforward, and rests on the main principle that the analyst must examine closely the linguistic choices that have been made for literary reasons by the poet. Analysis involves a knowledge of traditional ways of classifying language according to a system of grammar that has its beginnings in classical Greek. At stake are both a discussion of the 'meaning' of the poem, and, relatedly, a detailed description of what constitutes the language and style of the writer as literary. Language and style, in analyses such as this, are effectively labels for the more traditional concept of diction: *what* writers write – and the linguistic choices they make – are as important as the 'meaning' of the text (for detailed analyses of diction see Groom, 1955).

The choices the critic makes are equally important. N. F. Blake is well aware of alternative models of linguistic analysis. The choice he makes for a given analysis is as expedient as it is political. And the choices he makes for teaching students whose first language is not English and those he makes for teaching students whose first language is English may well be different – though they may well be the same. Either way, the choice is not innocent; it is an 'interested' one that locates both the critic and the analysis at a particular site of interest. The difference between the sort of textual analysis carried out by N. F. Blake, and that carried out by other, more literary-minded critics is that Blake's principal aim is to discuss the language, not the literary meaning. (See Latre, 1983, for a similar stylistic analysis of two Larkin poems, 'Reasons for Attendance' and 'Here'.)

Literary paradigms

I. A. Richards had certain hopes for linguistics, and so too had Empson. His theorizing of language in *The Structure of Complex Words* is his own contribution to linguistic theory, but it is barely recognized. Ronald Carter's recent book on vocabulary (Carter, 1987) relegates Empson's contribution to a single disparaging footnote, for example. But Empson, like Richards, was considerably closer in spirit to the work of literary linguists and stylisticians than is often realized. Certain literary critics were profoundly convinced of the importance of language analysis and the development of linguistic/literary theory, and Empson and Richards were amongst them.

William Empson was an intellectual aware of literary and linguistic developments in Europe and America. This awareness defines to a large extent his own critical practice. He worked in the traditional/realist world of diction and rhetoric, and *The Structure of Complex Words* (Empson, 1951a) demonstrates more clearly than anything else his distrust of a view of critical practice that valorized aspects of the text by conceptualizing them (a mark of scientific intellectual practice) as devices like paradox, irony and tension, or understanding them as instances of emotive or even 'pure emotive' language. This tendency manifests a traditional formalist concern with looking for universals, though it is not always recognized as such and it is one of the ways in which traditional positions show themselves to be, like most intellectual activity in the twentieth century, 'scientifically' based.

The blurb on the jacket of Christopher Ricks's *The Force of Poetry* (1984) gives a good indication of the sorts of concepts that have been, and still are, valorized and treated as universal ways of determining literary meaning through the defining of 'good' literature. The book is about ' . . . aspects, features, resources of the language manifested in poetry'; these resources are, it says, 'diction, figures of speech, sound and sense, dead metaphors, line-endings, prepositions, puns, rhythm, images, bathos, tone and punctuation' – in other words a traditional paradigm of what constitutes literary forms and resources in language. F. R. Leavis on William Wordsworth's 'Upon Westminster Bridge' (Leavis, 1975:116–121) amply demonstrates the use of these concepts in analysis of a text.

Upon Westminster Bridge

Earth has not anything to show more fair:
    Dull would he be of soul who could pass by
    A sight so touching in its majesty:
This city now doth like a garment wear
The beauty of the morning; silent, bare,
    Ships, towers, domes, theatres and temples lie
    Open unto the fields, and to the sky;
All bright and glittering in the smokeless air.
Never did sun more beautifully steep
    In his first splendour valley, rock, or hill;
Ne'er saw I, never felt, a calm so deep!
    The river glideth at his own sweet will:
Dear God! the very houses seem asleep;
    And all that mighty heart is lying still!

Leavis uses his analysis of this poem to establish the weakness of 'Calais Beach' ('It is a beauteous Evening, calm and free') – a sonnet, he says, 'which must be judged to be, in an unfavourable sense, wholly general.' (Leavis, 1975:116)

Calais Beach

It is a beauteous Evening, calm and free;
The holy time is quiet as a Nun
Breathless with adoration; the broad sun
Is sinking down in its tranquility;
The gentleness of heaven is on the Sea:
Listen! the mighty Being is awake

And doth with his eternal motion make
A sound like thunder – everlastingly.
Dear Child! dear Girl! that walkest with me here,
If thou appear'st untouched by solemn thought,
Thy nature is not therefore less divine:
Thou liest in Abraham's bosom all the year;
And worshipp'st at the Temple's inner shrine,
God being with thee when we know it not.

Leavis writes that the opening of 'Upon Westminster Bridge' looks 'uncompromisingly like' that of 'Calais Beach'; the 'key words . . . 'fair', 'soul', 'touching' and 'majesty' suggest the same kind of solemn unction' (117). The closing lines seem to confirm it. The simile of the city and the garment is very 'loose' (117), and was probably arrived at because of the need to find a rhyme for 'fair'.

By the time a reader has arrived at the eighth line of the poem, 'we should by now be aware of a decided superiority in this sonnet which makes it a poem of some interest' (118). How do 'we' know this? Because of a ' "clue" . . . in the unobtrusive adjective "smokeless" ':

> Though unobtrusive, it is far from otiose; obvious as it looks, it does more than it says. It conveys, in fact, both its direct force and the opposite, and gives us locally in its working the structure of the poem. (118)

On reaching 'smokeless', 'we' are able to realize that the simile 'like a garment . . . has, after all, a felicity', because it keeps both the city and the beauty of the morning distinct and any chance that 'smokeless' could now cover the 'ships, towers, domes, theatres and temples' and thus remove the force of the simile, is now gone because of the word 'bare' and the carry over (*enjambement*) of 'lie open'. This 'fact is made present as a realized state in the reader's consciousness by an expressive use of the carry-over (the "lying open" is enacted) and by a good rime which, picking up the resonance of "lie" with an effect of leaving us where we were, enhances the suggestion of a state': of being 'silent, bare'. The suggestion is 'further enhanced by the unenergetic leisureliness and lack of tension of "Open unto the fields, and to the sky".' Then 'comes the key adjective "smoke-less" – revealing the duality of consciousness out of which this sonnet is organized.'

Ships, towers, domes, theatres, and temples are associated

with the Wordsworthian images of valleys, rocks and hills; 'calm hasn't the obvious ambivalence of "smokeless" but beyond question the stillness of the "mighty heart" is touching because of the thought of all the traffic that will later pour over the bridge.'

The structure is not complex. 'Calais Beach', however, has no structure, 'but is just a simple one-way flow of standard sentiment'. There is 'refinement' and 'particularity' in 'Upon Westminster Bridge' where there is none in 'Calais Beach'.

So what does Leavis's analysis achieve? It makes a value judgement on the worth of a text, and, as an integral part of that judging process, it creates a disciplined critical practice that requires a student to recognize the intrinsic worth of a text by recognizing the intrinsic value of a commentary on that text. And as I think Leavis ably demonstrates, the process is not expected to be an easy one (for a similar analysis examining Wordsworth see Gilham, 1980), for quite how a reader should be aware of the 'superiority' of the poem, and quite what is being explained in the discussion of 'smokeless' are never detailed. Quite how 'facts' are made present, how phrases are 'enacted', and how suggestions are enhanced by certain words, and quite how ' "smokeless" reveals a duality of consciousness out of which this sonnet is organized' are never addressed. Most readers of Leavis, of any of this type of critical practice, are effectively being oppressed (disciplined) by an expectation that they will, if they are sensitive readers, recognize the worth of the interpretation. The nature of the 'discipline' does not lie in linguistic rigour or scientific explanation, it lies in training a mind to determine meanings through ambiguities. To 'explain' those meanings by detail is to reduce criticism to absurdity (Leavis, 1975:102). Consequently, to detail *where* and *how* a reading is arrived at would reduce the disciplinary nature of the practice. It would be like explaining to soldiers in the First World War – any war – why they should have to 'go over the top'. The explanation would reduce to absurdity any order, no matter how well phrased.

'Entering' the text

Empson's objections were directed at the sort of view that argues that the text and its language should become transparent to its referents in order to establish as unwavering truth the literary value of a text, or (as I. A. Richards argues) to establish a separate emotive language that defined literary value. Literature was thus being defined as a special, unique process of knowledge, for this view argues that literature, because of its forms like paradox and irony, shifts a normal, 'ordinary' perception away from its usual everyday meaning into a new, unique perception. And this, more than anything else in intrinsic practice, is formalism at its highest. In this, above all, lay the grounds for Empson's fears that rational and methodical approaches to criticism and knowledge were being swept away by the neo-Christianity of the Anglo-American New Critics and were being replaced by irrational formalist theories of literature and language that drilled students into 'an attitude of religious or political orthodoxy' as a means, it would seem, of preventing all the students from becoming communists (Norris, 1985a:37) – which was a not unlikely possibility in Cambridge in the 1930s.

What this effectively meant, for Empson, was that 'doctrinal and political distortion' (Norris, 1985a:38) of the texts closed off many options of meaning in order to serve the 'pious orthodox creeds' of critics like Leavis, Richards, and, in particular, T. S. Eliot. F. W. Bateson, in accusing Eliot, amongst others, of 'critical barbarism' by misreading literature, recommends a greater emphasis on studying literary history as 'It disinfects the sensibility' (Bateson, 1972:102). Bateson, like Empson, recognized that the supposed neutrality and 'innocence' of Anglo-American New Criticism was, in fact, orthodox revisionism. The texts of the traditional literary canon, for example, are all preoccupied with morality of one sort or another, if the contents of F. R. Leavis's *The Great Tradition* (1954) are anything to go by. Empson believed in according pride of place to intuition in his critical practice, but his intuitions were based on an open mind, deeply distrustful of Christianity and the sort of moralizing some critics played out in their work. His analysis is set firmly in what might be called a methodist tradition (in its sense both of adherence to a method of analysis and of non-conformity), which viewed language in more or less the same light as had the eighteenth-century rationalist grammars. This view of language sees literature as being realized, for the most part, through its diction. A good knowledge of traditional grammar (based mostly on the Latin taught at schools – a requirement for university entrance in Empson's time) and a good dictionary were basically all the analytic tools needed.

Leo Spitzer, another critic important for his emphasis on the importance of language in analysing literary text, had related, yet somewhat different, priorities. He wrote in 1948

> . . . the best document of the soul of a nation is its literature, and since the latter is nothing but its language as this is written down by elect speakers, can we perhaps not hope to grasp the spirit of a nation in the language of its outstanding works of literature. (Spitzer, 1948:10)

This contains a familiar elitist approach to the relationship of literature and the spirit of the nation, but it places a quite different emphasis on the role of language. To say, in 1948 (to say it now to many people) that literature was 'nothing but its language' was a heresy of the worst kind. But what Spitzer did here was to 'replace the casual, impressionistic remarks of literary critics' (11) with something much more 'objective', something much more 'scientific'. He advocated a position contrary to much of the positivist/historicist criticism of the 'timeless, placeless philology of the older school (14) that dominated university literary studies. His answer was to develop a critical practice that suggested that critics should treat a text *synchronically*, by working from the surface of a text to its 'inward life-centre' (15) and then, on 'arrival' at the centre (a not unfamiliar term in critical thinking) to integrate the details of analysis into 'the creative principle which may have been present in the soul of the artist' (15). Once this is done, you then make the return trip to the surface of the text. This process he called the 'philological circle'.

There is no formal schema to this, though; there cannot be, because the first step has already been made, Spitzer argues, by the reader being 'struck' by a detail, which is followed 'by a conviction that this detail is connected basically with the work of art' (27). This means that the analysis begins on an intuitive 'observation', which in turn raises a question about textual meaning that then requires an answer. But, as Spitzer points out, there is no way to guarantee 'either the impression or the conviction just described: they are the results of talent, experience and faith' (27). This crucially militates against the scientistic linguistics at the time, which argued for the primacy of *la langue*. Leo Spitzer, in ways not generally recognized today, argued that structuralist linguistics should be turned upside down, prioritizing institutionally determined discourse (Spitzer, 1943).

This point is a vital one, and one I shall return to in the next chapter. If discourse had been the focus of an intrinsic linguistics then the entire structuralist apparatus that argues for the 'conventional, arbitrary, non-iconic relationship between sound and meaning' (Gray, 1977:235) would have had to be reoriented, and the tolerance shown by people like Empson for alternative readings would have been far more widespread (cf. Fowler, 1970).

Spitzerian analysis begins, then, with an intuition, an inspiration about the text, usually based on some small detail. This enables analysts to form a relationship with the text.[1] Spitzer speaks of it as a 'click', and when that click occurs it signals that detail and whole have found a common denominator. Years later Geoffrey Hartman described this process of beginning interpretation as being 'like a football game. You spot a hole and you go through' (Hartman, 1970:351) – though, importantly, he also suggests that you might have to 'induce' the opening a little. The argument, therefore, is that for every text the critic needs a separate inspiration in order to 'get a way into' the text, and when 'in' there, you will 'find' the things which are 'meant' to be 'discovered'.[2] In that respect this approach is classically traditional, arguing that there are 'secrets'/'treasures' of literature to be uncovered. But as in all good adventure stories, there's a catch. The treasures cannot be recovered unless the critic is sensitive/violent enough to get the entrance to the 'temple' open. Literature – the writing of the elite (the sacred wood, the temple) – holds secrets that it will give up, but only if you 'prove' yourself worthy. For Spitzer, and for others, to mix my already strained metaphors here, the cavalry is there if you need help. Inspiration is 'light from above' (Spitzer, 1949:28) and the more you rely on that help the more humble you will become, and as a consequence of that increasing humility and 'the accumulation of past enlightenments that encourages a sort of pious confidence' (28) your criticism will go from strength to strength.

> . . . the critic, in order to keep his [*sic passim*] soul ready for his scholarly task, must have already made choices in ordering his life, of what I would call a moral nature; he must have chosen to cleanse his mind from distraction by the inconsequential, from the obsession of everyday small details – to keep it open to the synthetic apprehension of the 'wholes' of life, to the symbolism in nature and art and language. (Spitzer, 1949:29)

He continues:

... all beauty has a mysterious quality which does not appear at first glance. But there is no more reason for dodging the description of the aesthetic phenomenon than of any natural phenomenon. Those who oppose the aesthetic analysis of poetic works seem to affect at times the susceptibility of a sensitive plant: if one is to believe them, it is because they cherish so deeply the works of art, it is because they respect their chastity, that they would not deflower, by means of intellectual formulas, the virginal and ethereal quality of works of art, they would not brush off the shimmering dust from the wings of these poetic butterflies! I would maintain, on the contrary, that to formulate observations by means of words is not to cause the artistic beauty to evaporate in vain intellectualities; rather, it makes for a widening and a deepening of the aesthetic taste. Love, whether it be love for God, love for one's fellow men (sic) or the love of art, can only gain by the effort of the human intellect to search for the reasons of its most sublime emotions, and to formulate them. It is only a frivolous love that cannot survive intellectual definition; great love prospers with understanding. (Spitzer, 1949:30)

Here is an impassioned argument that analysis of literary texts by linguistic means is not a brutalizing of a work of art, but a worthwhile intellectual pursuit that sees the text as a series of clues to understanding a significance *beyond* language; beyond what the words of the text mean.

Language, text, context

Winifred Nowottny wrote about the need to shift the analysis of literature away from the context-free, language-free analysis of many of the New Critics towards a more methodically/linguistically aware analysis that recognized what Spitzer had been saying years before, namely, that literature is language. Nowottny, as a teacher and writer in the 1950s and 1960s influenced a great many academics who continue to write about the language(s) of literature. In 1962 she published her most influential work, *The Language Poets Use*. Her concern is with what she calls the 'staple components of language' (Nowottny, 1962:*vii*) and 'the interaction between the corporeality of words (as systematised in poems) and the meanings they bear' (*vii*). Central to this concern is the primacy of metaphor, which she develops from the formalist school as signalling the distinctive, poetic function of literature (see Thompson, 1971). Her approach is Empsonian, using a close *explication de texte* method of reading that marks her out as someone who believed firmly that there needed to be a recognition *within* intrinsic criticism that linguistic analysis of literary text was a necessity and not simply an obstructivist aberration.[3]

Her theorizing of language and style never moves beyond a concentration on the supremacy of words; she believes firmly that these words somehow 'contain' meanings, and she argues for maintaining a formalist distinction between poetic and non-poetic language as a means of defining literature. Style, for Nowottny as for many critics, is effectively language manipulated in ways that signal it as different from 'ordinary' language. She writes:

> . . . the value of examining objective characteristics carefully, before talking at large about the imaginative constructs reared on the foundation of words, is that this results, at least, in a recognition of the part played by the corporeality of words, and by the structures which connect them, not only in determining lesser poetic effects but also in directing the larger mental and imaginative processes activated by the poem; it may well lead, further, to a recognition of the fact that the various elements of poetic language interpenetrate one another with an intimacy which is of first importance in any consideration of how poetry 'works'. (Nowottny, 1962:2)

Understanding *how* poetry works is a quite different theoretical and analytic aim from that of the overall intrinsic critical tradition and this phrase would have signalled Nowottny as someone on the language side of English studies, rather than on the literature side – a powerful system of classification in the politics of university English departments. Nowottny, following in the tradition of British linguistics (Firth in particular), was at some pains to distance herself from analytic modes that foreground one feature of language in particular, and she insisted upon relationships between features as being of prime concern in critical practice. Engaging with Leavis, she points out that the good critic is 'not one who strips the layers off the onion one after another until there is nothing left inside' (Nowottny, 1962:19), but someone who integrates these layers. What integrates the layers for Nowottny is 'poetic structure' conceived, in the main, as metaphor. Her *how* is about context and not just immanent linguistic structures. Reflecting the dominant view of linguistics, which defined itself as concerned only with the sentence and its constituent parts, she writes

> Above the level of the sentence the structure of language itself does not constrain a speaker's choice of the best way to arrange his [*sic passim*] discourse; the arrangement will depend on his situation and purposes, the nature of his material, and his whole past experience of how to utter himself so as to make sense to other people . . . (Nowottny, 1962:73)

This is a view that importantly foregrounds the situation and context of the text (see also Gregory, 1967; Gregory and Carroll, 1978; Hasan, 1980). For Nowottony, as for other socially-oriented functional linguists, it is crucial to discuss the situations in which a text is produced. In other words, the situational meanings as well as the 'internal' meaning are crucial parts of the analysis. This places a focus on meaning which is quite alien to the descriptivist linguistics of highly influential academics like Leonard Bloomfield. His attempts to make language study a science, divorced from the tricky problem of meanings, were considered to be his greatest contribution to the study of language (Bloch, 1949:92). As a consequence, he is responsible, amongst others, for shifting the course of language study away from meaning and discourse.

Werner Winter recognized the problem when, in 1965 he wrote. 'If we want our grammar . . . to account for all that actually occurs in a natural language, we must be content to live with the messiness that goes with it' (Winter, 1965:488). But, like Spitzer before him, his call to turn linguistics upside down never stood a chance. Few were willing to give up the orderliness of the scientific approach that systematized language 'so neatly' (see, however, the work of Bakhtin and Voloshinov, which was generally unknown until translations were made available in the 1970s) particularly if such a move were to place them, academically and politically, in a minority. Institutions like linguistics and literary criticism can be very powerful indeed.

Winifred Nowottny's detailed analysis on Dylan Thomas's, 'There Was A Saviour' (Nowottny, 1962:187–222) demonstrated clearly her view of the functional role of language in a close reading of a text.

There Was a Saviour

There was a saviour
Rarer than radium
Commoner than water, crueller than truth;
Children kept from the sun
Assembled at his tongue
To hear the golden note turn in a groove,
Prisoners of wishes locked their eyes
In the jails and studies of his keyless smiles.

The voice of children says
From a lost wilderness
There was calm to be done in his safe unrest,
When hindering man hurt
Man, animal, or bird
We hid our fears in that murdering breath,
Silence, silence to do, when earth grew loud,
In lairs and asylums of the tremendous shout.

There was glory to hear
In the churches of his tears
Under his downy arm you sighed as he struck,
O you who could not cry
On to the ground when a man died
Put a tear for joy in the unearthly flood
And laid your cheek against a cloud-formed shell:
Now in the dark there is only yourself and myself.

Two proud, blacked brothers cry,
Winter-locked side by side,
To this inhospitable hollow year.
O we who could not stir
One lean sigh when we heard
Greed on man beating near and fire neighbour
But wailed and nested in the sky-blue wall
Now break a giant tear for the little known fall,

For the drooping of homes
That did not nurse our bones,
Brave deaths of only ones but never found,
Now see, alone in us,

> Our own true strangers' dust
> Ride through the doors of our unentered house.
> Exiled in us we arouse the soft,
> Unclenched, armless, silk and rough love that breaks all rocks.

According to Nowottny, the poem presents considerable difficulty. The syntax is difficult and the pronouns and tenses are 'peculiar'. It begins in an unplaced past and gradually moves into the present, with the final stanza speaking 'in a kind of eternal Now' (189). The pronouns shift quite dramatically: 'It would be a reasonable inference from this series of changes that "we" and "you" are somehow the same and somehow different' (189). A more detailed analysis of each pronoun reveals 'that it is being forced upon our notice that this is a poem about continuous identities with a changing outlook' (190). The pronouns and the tenses carry the most important thing in the structure of the poem: 'its beginning with children taught about a saviour and its moving on through their lives to death and the redefinition of salvation' (191). All contrasts in the diction of the poem are related to the process expressed through these changing pronouns and tenses.

The poem seems to 'turn on the line "Now in the dark there is only yourself and myself"' (191). 'Now' begins two other lines in the poem, which indicates that these lines 'act as nodal points in the system of contrasts . . . running through the poem'. Everything possible is done (including changes in rhyme scheme, lineation, layout, etc.) to emphasize that at the word 'now' a new development takes place, and a new stage in the argument of the poem gets under way (192). There are three 'hinges': the first has to do with the vanishing of the saviour; the second has to do with expression of human compassion; and the third has to do with the entry of sexual love.

Formal patterns at the level of diction help to explain the poem, for example, equivalence:

In the	jails and studies	of his	keyless smiles
In	lairs and asylums	of the	tremendous shout
In the	churches	of his	tears

The sense of the poem 'declares itself through a persistent verbal pattern suggesting persistent analogy' (194). The constant elements in the poem are 'buildings' and 'expressions of human feeling', resulting in a pattern for the poem of:

[something human] [in the buildings of] [something human]

The patterns and language of the poem have led us to a point where certain parts of the poem are foregrounded, says Nowottny. But these need to be interpreted. Freudian analysis should help:

The cult of the saviour as presented in the poem, reflects something radically unlike the nature of the saviour himself; man (*sic*) remakes the saviour in his (*sic*) own image by distorting him to correspond with the distorted views and institutions that dominate society. The fourth and fifth stanzas offer the 'cure' or solution to this: compassion and the release of sexual love as a liberated and liberating force. (200).

Written in May 1940:

the poet in a time of war examines the religious and cultural symbols that have themselves in great measure shaped the intelligence and feeling that turn to question the meaning of their world. He traces, within the sustained figure of the poem – human–building–human – that people are but children of a larger growth. This might represent itself as the stages of a child moving through adolescence, or the stages of religion (wonder, experience, devotional practice), or the social and cultural relations involved in school, peer group activities, and adult awareness of social ritual and beauty. These are best understood in terms of repression, masochism and sexuality.

The climax is the end of the poem, which 'gathers all that went before it' and allows sexual love to transcend everything. 'In order to leade up to the shattering and endless reverberation at the end of the poem the poet has had to devise a diction that does not so much say what it means as allow all the range of meaning involved in the poem to fit into a peculiar phrasing.

Like Spitzer, Nowottny needed an entrance into the poem, in order to try and understand its complexities. That entrance she found with its language – and just a small part of its language: the pronouns and tenses. From this she builds up a complicated, and enormously detailed analysis of the structure of the poem, which she argues rests on a figure, a pattern, of human–building–human. An important part of this type of text analysis, there-fore, is to use the language of the poem to give evidence for making arguments about the formal relations of the poem and its diction in order to determine themes. These themes are what will give you the clue to understanding the poem, but they need to be interpreted. For that, Nowottny argues, you need to go *beyond* the poem. With this poem she uses Freudian analysis, as well as a vast array of intertextual literary allusions that I've not covered here. These, together with an understanding of the situation in which the poem was produced (in this case wartime) will enable an analyst to sort out the complexities of meaning. Central to this method is a system that first and foremost uses language as the 'entrance' to 'what the diction can tell us about itself through characteristics that recur with sufficient frequency and emphasis to suggest that some pressure of meaning has extruded these curious forms' (193).

Her close reading, then, follows a path of trying to understand how situational/contextual features determine the internal organiz-ation of the text – a path that marks, very specifically, a functional linguistic approach. Metaphor – the rhetorical channel – is the mode that, for the more literary-minded Nowottny (but using the words of functional linguist Michael Halliday), 'tends to determine the range of meaning as texture, language in its relevance to the environment' (Halliday, 1978:117). She concentrates in her analysis on what Halliday calls the textual function of language, that is, the way text relates to its environment, by looking at words (lexis), lexical collocation and repetition; she looks on information structure as rhetoric and examines cohesive ties in the rhetoric of the text. What she does, therefore, is to privilege the status of the text and the textual/poetic function that she argues determine the text as literature. As a consequence she privileges the writer, not the reader. The analysis therefore assumes a stability of interpretation – fixed points, set by a higher level *literary* structure determined by the writer, resulting in a higher level semiotic that goes unquestioned. Poetic language is the means by which the 'larger meaning' of the text is discovered.

This emphasis on language is the key to understanding the development of close reading (see Sebeok, 1960; Levin, 1962; Fowler, 1966a; Chatman and Levin, 1967; Babb, 1972). Many hoped that the methods of linguistics would allow literature and literary language to be described in very precise ways (some still do); others were more sceptical: ' . . . the meanings which litera-

ture conveys are of their nature elusive of precise description'
(Widdowson, 1975:116).

Language, text, communication

The linguist and educationist Henry Widdowson was, and still is,
concerned, like Nowottny, with developing a method of criticism
that, as stylistics, would be a middle ground between linguistics
and literary criticism. The result of this approach was, inevitably,
that 'stylistic analysis shades imperceptibly into literary appreciation' (Widdowson, 1975:117). This, for many literary critics at
least, was considered unsatisfactory because the dominant paradigm of 'scientific/objective linguistics' told literary critics that linguists looked at the language of the text 'without troubling about
what it is attempting to convey' (Widdowson, 1975:117). And
for the most part they did. Meanings, when they did arise, as in
the work of people like Widdowson and Nowottny, tended to
be drawn from the intuitive, literary critical side of the analysis.
Linguistics wasn't able (and still isn't in many respects) to cope
with accounting for textual meanings. Naturally, this created problems. When Henry Widdowson published his analysis of Robert
Frost's 'Stopping by Woods on a Snowy Evening', Sydney Bolt
accused him of not understanding the poem properly. This, Bolt
suggested, was probably because Widdowson had let his
linguistic/stylistic analysis lead him away from literary analysis.
More importantly, perhaps, Bolt suggested that stylistic analysis
had lured Widdowson into treating poetry as if it were ordinary
prose. This, for many intrinsic critics, was the major heresy of
applied linguistics and methodist criticism. Non-literary discourse
can be paraphrased, they argued. Literature cannot.

Widdowson does not have this formalist preoccupation with
maintaining the 'integrity' of the text (in practice, neither did most
of the formalist analyses). He is firmly in the tradition of William
Empson in allowing his intuitions full rein, and his analysis, which
was designed to 'give a definite shape to my own intuitive sense
of what the poem is about' (Widdowson, 1975:121), made it
perfectly clear that he did not believe that either linguistics or
literary criticism could make definitive statements about the single
meaning of a text:

> I do not think that . . . there is any sure procedure of evaluating
> interpretations in terms of their relative 'correctness' . . . There

seems to be no way of deciding impartially on the evidence of the poem itself whether 'Stopping by Woods on a Snowy Evening' is about just some human sleep with its release from responsibility or the last long winter sleep when the moment of peace extends for ever. (Widdowson, 1975:123–4)

Bolt, amongst others, argued that the poem was about death.

Importantly, Widdowson argues that the poem elicits various responses, and the analysis of the language and style of the text serves, as far as he is concerned, to enable a student/critic to articulate a personal response: ' . . . the meaning of a literary work, intrinsic as it is to the unique use of language, can only be recognized by the individual because once it is expressed in different terms so as to be communicated to others it must inevitably change.' (Widdowson, 1975:75)

This is an argument about recognition by experience – the reader-meets-text theory. An illustration of this, in the form of Michael A. Lofaro's analysis of W. B. Yeats's *Per Amica Silentia Lunae* (Lofaro, 1976), might be useful.

Per Amica Silentia Lunae

When I come home after meeting men who are strange to me, and sometimes even after talking to women, I go over all I have said in gloom and disappointment. Perhaps I have overstated everything from a desire to vex or startle, from hostility that is but fear; or all my natural thoughts have been drowned by an undisciplined sympathy. My fellow-diners have hardly seemed of mixed humanity, and how should I keep my head among images of good and evil, crude allegories?

But when I shut my door and light the candle, I invite a marmorean muse, an art where no thought or emotion has come to mind because another man has thought or felt something different, for now there must be no reaction, action only, and the world must move my heart but to the heart's discovery of itself, and I begin to dream of eyelids that do not quiver before the bayonet: all my thoughts have ease and joy, I am all virtue and confidence. When I come to put in rhyme what I have found, it will be a hard toil, but for a moment I believe that I have found myself and not my anti-self. It is only the shrinking from the toil, perhaps, that convinces me that I have been no more myself than is the cat the medicinal grass it is eating in the garden.

Lafaro's explication runs as follows, again in summary:

The prose is not complex or intricate. The narration is first person, mostly, and the syntax and diction are straightforward. What is unusual is the simplicity in the choice of words: almost 75 per cent are one-syllable words.

But there is an 'indefiniteness' about the text, that seems to go against the simple, direct style; the progression of time and the sense of space are elusive. This contributes to the lack of focus in the narrative, compounded by a preference for intransitive verbs, auxiliary forms and the passive mood.

The repetition of abstract nouns lures the reader, who is bombarded with 23 first-person pronouns and is lulled into suspending disbelief. This repetition, both actual and implied, in the syntax, grammar, and lexis of the passage, allows Yeats to express 'states of being in flux rather than particular finite action' (55). The question, of course, is why? The text is a reverie, but there are dangers in the language of this genre – dangers that might lead to sentimentality or the false notion that art is a vision of reality. The lack of spatial and temporal definition in the text therefore acts as a protection against these possible pitfalls of the genre. The non-action of the language of the text is a mirror of Yeats's uncertain relationship with art. The closing line of the second paragraph, with its distorted syntax and tense and mood shifts, prevents either Yeats or the reader from concluding (closing off) the indecision of the two paragraphs. It is therefore an anti-climactic analogy 'for Yeats's poetic hopes and endeavours'.

In *Per Amica*, Yeats continually diminishes the authority of his statements. He is hiding behind a mask of rhetorical indecision that fails, like the metaphor of the cat. 'In his self-pitying non-action, Yeats seems to prefer the life of the saint who can renounce experience itself, to that of the poet' (59) who can't. Yeats is 'weary, unsure, and waiting' (59).

This is an example of a textual analysis that uses quite detailed linguistic analysis, based on a number of linguistic methodologies, together with a close literary reading technique. Lofaro has one main aim in the analysis: to find an empirical foundation for critical judgements on the text. But he makes a number of assumptions in this analysis, most of which do not get questioned. Principally, the analysis of two paragraphs of text is considered a sufficient basis on which to construct statements about the whole work. Furthermore, the work is seen as a mirror of the writer – not as a constructed fiction, but as a representation analogous to the writer's own thoughts and situation. Lofaro builds a case (supported by tables and statistics in a series of appendices) for the linguistic base of the literary genre of *reverie*. (It has to be said that it is not a very convincing case.) He then uses that base to go beyond the text and its genre, not, as Nowottny did, to a series of attempts to try to understand 'the text', but to an analysis of the writer. The text under analysis is therefore the writer – and the entrance to that text is the writer's language.

Lofaro is following the method of criticism established by Ian Watt in his analysis of the first paragraph of Henry James's *The Ambassadors* (Watt, 1964). He is concerned, in particular, to find an empirical means by which to justify any critical pronouncement on a text, but regardless of its use of linguistic terminology and apparently rigorous methodology, this approach is still very firmly rooted in a 'New Critical' approach to the analysis of text.

Widdowson's Empsonian argument against such an approach, and against Leavisite criticism in particular, is that it teaches critical orthodoxy in a formalist way by creating a universal 'set of ready-made judgements for rote learning, rather than strategies of understanding' (Widdowson, 1975:75). Widdowson argues that students need guidance, they need to be taught strategies, they need a vocabulary. This is a particularly important statement because it brought methodist criticism into *applied* linguistics and had great significance in the light of the enormous growth of applied linguistics in communicative approaches to language teaching, whether that language was being taught as a first, second or foreign language. One of the most important researchers in this area is Ronald Carter, who, in the tradition of Empson and with the insights of contemporary applied linguistics, addresses the difficult question of *how* readers arrive, linguistically, at the impressions and responses they have to literary texts. Working effectively within the close reading tradition of I. A. Richards, he attempts to work out ways and means of theorizing literary response through linguistic analysis (Carter, 1982a:42), not as an end in itself, but as a means of developing a classroom practice and pedagogical awareness of the importance of close, linguistically informed, reading of text (see Carter, 1982d, 1982e, 1987).

Because of the work being done in linguistics, the study of language seems, therefore, to offer many critics a means of being empirical about a subject whose own critical practices militated against such rigour. It offers a method of criticism that does not simply privilege the sensitivity of the critic. This has created considerable tension amongst some literary critics and linguists (see the debates in Youngren, 1970; Barry, 1980; Fowler, 1983; Norris, 1983; Thurley, 1983), but it has also created some mediators who argue for a method of analysis and criticism that is not polarized as an either/or (linguistics or literary studies) debate. One such mediator is Geoffrey Leech. He argues, like Henry Widdowson, for a stylistics that draws together the linguistic and literary levels of analysis, which he says 'should provide purely formal criteria for identifying features which are likely to have aesthetic implication' (Leech, 1977:9; see also Leech and Short, 1981). But unlike Widdowson, he has considerably greater faith in what linguistics can achieve in the analysis of literary text. He examines an analysis by F. R. Leavis on Keats's 'Ode to a Nightingale' (Leavis, 1936) and demonstrates how, by using the methods of linguistics, impressionistic statements about the 'fine organization' of a text can be made much more explicit – showing, for example, how, and in what ways, the structures of the text contribute to a literary impression that a text has a 'fine organisation'. Linguistics (contra Youngren, 1970) does have explanatory capabilities, Leech argues (Leech, 1977:20),[4] and he uses phonology (including metre) and syntax to demonstrate this. He is still, however, working within the intrinsic constraints of literary criticism, framing his analysis on the twin concepts of *tension* and *resolution* (Leech, 1977:18).[5]

Literary language and literariness

One of the reasons for the widespread suspicion of a close reading that does attempt to be linguistically analytic, for either linguistic or literary reasons, is the concern for the 'sanctity' of literary language. Paul Sawyer, in his book *Ruskin's Poetic Argument* (1985), is interested in understanding that sanctity in a way that would allow him to argue for the contributions that John Ruskin, as art critic, has made to literature. In order to do that, he appropriates a critical practice that he thinks suitable. The extract he looks at is from Ruskin's *Modern Painters 1*, describing a painting by William Turner.

That sky . . . parting and melting through the chasms in the long fields of snow-white, flaked, slow-moving vapour . . . to the islanded rest of the Euganean hills. Do we dream, or does the white forked sail drift nearer, and nearer yet, diminishing the blue sea between us with the fullness of its wings? It pauses now; but the quivering of its bright reflection troubles the shadows of the sea, those azure, fathomless depths of crystal mystery, on which the swiftness of the poised gondola floats double, its black beak lifted like the crest of a dark ocean bird, its scarlet draperies flashed back from the kindling surface, and its bent oar breaking the radiant water into a dust of gold. Dreamlike and dim, but glorious, the unnumbered palaces lift their shafts out of the hollow sea, – pale ranks of motionless flame, – their mighty towers sent up to heaven like tongues of more eager fire, – their grey domes looming vast and dark, like eclipsed worlds, – their sculptured arabesques and purple marble fading farther and fainter, league beyond league, lost in the light of distance. (Cited in Sawyer, 1985:50–1.)

The question to ask here is where does art criticism stop and literature begin? That's certainly the question Paul Sawyer is asking, and it's one that raises very interesting questions about *literariness*, that is, what decides whether a text is literary or not. So, for example in his article on Larkin, N. F. Blake assumed an understanding of literariness when he talked about the difference between poetic imagery and 'flat' language. Ronald Carter and Walter Nash address this issue very thoroughly in a paper called 'Language and literariness' (see Carter and Nash, 1983), arguing that to polarize language as either literary or non-literary leads to the assigning of values to particular kinds of language, valorizing the literary against the non-literary (Carter and Nash, 1983:123–4). An alternative to this, they suggest, is that language should be seen in terms of a gradation or 'cline', which makes it possible to find elements of literariness in languages which would usually be defined as ordinary/non-literary. Terry Eagleton, in his book *Literary Theory*, suggests that if someone comes up to you at the bus stop and murmurs 'Thou still unravished bride of quietness', you are in the presence of the literary (Eagleton, 1983:2) – *if*, that is, your theory of literature is defined in the formalist terms of a language functioning 'in excess of its abstractable meaning' (2). I would suggest you were in the presence of something far more sinister than literature! But the point is that one of the major means of defining what constitutes literature is based on defining a particular variety of language as literary/ poetic.

The argument receives its fullest statement in the scientificity of Russian Formalism and Prague School linguistics, mainly through Roman Jakobson and Jan Mukařovský. Literariness (*literaturnost*) is considered to be the object of the science of literature, and not the text, writer, reader, genre, or literature generally. The *forms* of literature, therefore – its devices – are prioritized, whereas the content itself is not. Form its considered to condition content. This approach receives its most trivializing Formalist statement in Edmund Epstein's *Language and Style* (1978), which was rightly condemned by Peter Barry (1980:134). In discussing W. B. Yeats' 'Who Goes With Fergus?' Epstein writes: '. . . it contains a great many repetitions of sound and stress, many more than would occur in casual speech. This, when noted by the reader, identifies it as a poem' (Epstein, 1978:14).

Mukařovský and others argued that literary language is 'an aesthetically purposeful distortion of standard language' (Mukařovský, 1970) such that literature *foregrounds* its language, that is, it calls attention to itself, through its *forms*, as language.[6]

Paul Sawyer uses this to his advantage. He says that Ruskin, instead of describing 'mere' objects in ordinary language, describes them in terms of 'energies'. The boat 'drifts, pauses, quivers, poises, lifts, flashes and so on'. This

> superflux of energy is counterbalanced by an even greater stress on essence, which Ruskin conveys by the characteristic grammatical device of linking indefinite nouns with definite adjectives in prepositional phrases: thus, not light or wings but 'fullness of light', 'fullness of wings'; not mysterious crystal but 'crystal mystery'; not the gondola floating but the 'poised swiftness' floating; not islands and hills but 'islanded rest of the Euganean hills'. (Sawyer, 1985:51)

A case is being made here for literature to be defined by a specific literary language – a language, in the main, defined by its supposed deviation from a norm (the norm being 'ordinary' language). This is Roman Jackobson's argument and, to a lesser extent, I. A. Richards': that literary language functions on a different – emotive/poetic – plane, and it is being used here to 'elevate' a text into the ranks of the literary.[7]

The language of this passage, and of the book as a whole, owes more to Shelley, finally, than to Wordsworth. The description of Venice is suffused with Shelleyan diction – 'liquid', 'snow-white', 'flaked', 'azure', 'crystal', 'dim', 'flamed', 'fading' are examples – and its sustained ecstasy of beholding imitates the protean energy of Shelley's 'spontaneous gladness'. This is the language the Wordsworthian child might speak if he (*sic*) wrote poetry, and the broad project of Ruskin's sermonic style, touching as it does on ode, psalm, and apparently thoughtless inspiration, may be usefully understood as absorbing the child's hunger of delight into a disciplined seeing capable of renewing the energies of the adult too long buried beneath a weight of custom. (Sawyer, 1985:53–4)

Sawyer is basically calling upon expressive form as a marker of Ruskin's literariness. The 'fallacy of expressive form' holds that 'merely to verbalize an idea is to give it sufficient artistic form' (Presley, 1979:4). This, for many critics, was considered to be something that only 'weaker' writers did. The point is that there has developed over many years a view of literature based on a theory that literature was a different language from the one we ordinarily write and speak, and that there is a special relationship between the *form* of that language and its *meaning*. That form can take many different directions, and I will illustrate this with an example of an analysis by Geoffrey Hartman on line 540 of Milton's *Paradise Lost* (Hartman, 1970:337–55). It follows, in part, the sort of close reading of texts developed by Jacques Derrida (see also Hartman, 1981 for a further development of his technique).

Sonorous metal blowing martial sounds

Hartman writes:

This is a line balanced by two adjective–noun phrases either side of the 'pivotal' verb. This syntactic pattern can be written 1212. This pattern is 'counterpointed' by the alliteration of the [s] sounds and the [m] sounds, but in a *chiastic* pattern, 1221.

'Sonorous' and 'sounds' are separated by 'metal blowing martial'. This has the effect of keeping 'sonorous' and 'sounds' apart for a while – it delays their coming together. But when they are together there is redundancy in the phrase. Similarly 'blowing' keeps 'metal' and 'martial' apart for a while, but when they come together, the phrase has a certain amount of redundancy too.

'Metal' and 'martial' and 'blowing' are therefore filling a breach in the sentence. This breach, or 'juncture', distances the immediacy of the redundancy of 'sonorous sounds', and as 'juncture' has zero-value phonetically, but in terms of what it achieves in a literary way, it has considerable meaning. It splits the key phrase and creates a *tension* which could not be expressed in words. The silence of the 'juncture' is therefore its literary meaning.

The analysis of this text is initially concerned with familiar structures of language, but not from a linguistic point of view. Geoffrey Hartman is concerned with developing an awareness of the importance of language and structures in literary texts from a contemporary theoretical perspective that is more concerned with literature as a site of ideological and philosophical struggles than it is with the personality, ideas, or beliefs of an author. The text is therefore a springboard to develop a theoretical position about a particular literary phenomenon. It is not designed, primarily, to say anything specific about this text, or about Milton.

Hartman uses as a frame for his ideas here a phrase from a lost play by Sophocles, recorded by Aristotle in the *Poetics*. The play was about Tereus and Philomela. Tereus raped Philomela; to prevent her telling anyone, he cut out her tongue. Philomela, however, wove her story into a tapestry. This Sophocles calls 'the voice of the shuttle' – a powerful image. Hartman uses this image to theorize a feature of literary texts that he calls 'juncture'. The 'power' of Sophocles' phrase comes from the tension created between the phrase and what it represents, that is, the whole story. The phrase effectively represents the whole story (is *metonymic* of the whole story). What Hartman is arguing, from the Milton text, is that the space occupied by the words 'metal blowing martial' creates a similar tension. The tension has no words to signal what it means, but it does have literary meaning. Hartman argues that in 'any crucial arrangement of words, a small change goes a long way' (341). The key word here is 'crucial'. Literature is not, for Hartman (and many others, critics and linguists alike) the same as any other discourse. It 'draws attention to itself' (352). How it draws attention to itself is what makes a literary text a 'crucial arrangement of words'. What Hartman is doing in this analysis is finding a vocabulary, in literary terms, for *how* literature is literature. And he constructs a critical practice – a hermeneutics – using the sounds *and* silences of the text to create a vocabulary for understanding literary texts in literary ways. In the process, he defines literature through analysis of literary language using, like other analysts discussed in this chapter, a method of close reading.

This type of criticism can be summarized as follows:

1 The emphasis is on close reading of text.

2 This foregrounds the importance of language and linguistic structures.

3 Analysis of text therefore requires skill in language, linguistics, rhetoric, and diction. It is effectively analysis of literary texts by linguistic means.

4 Although with analyses on language rather than on literary effects and devices, the view of language is still one that sees language as essentially transparent, an innocent vehicle that 'carries' meaning.

5 The critic is therefore also considered to be innocent and disinterested, working in a supposedly objective, unbiased way and allowing the formalities of the close reading technique to highlight the meaning of the text encoded into it by the writer, rather than examining the institutionally determined readings of the text.

6 This is, however, carried out with a much more sensitive awareness of the context and situation of the production of the text (though rarely of its readings) than intrinsic non-linguistic approaches to analysis.

7 The consequence of an increased awareness of the importance of language and context in text analysis is an increased recognition that analysis is concerned not just with *what* a text means, but *how* a text 'works'.

8 With a greater emphasis on the language of the text comes a more detailed and formally rigorous argument about the 'special' character of literary/poetic language, because language within literature is considered to 'draw attention to itself'.

The concentration on language organization and on the distinctive characteristics of literary/poetic language developed critical practice beyond the narrower confines of close reading with its relatively unsystematic emphasis on rhetoric and diction. Some linguists and critics achieved awareness of the importance of context as well as of the potential pedagogical relevance of linguistically-informed readings of texts. Others, however, saw analysis as a means of developing greater understanding of the system (*langue*) of language, rather than developing a specific interest in and awareness of literature and discourse. The consequences for the analysis of texts were far-reaching, emphasizing and prioritizing in particular the preoccupation for the 'scientific' character of twentieth-century structuralism. Chapter 5 examines this work more closely.

5 The linguistics of text: structures and strictures

Magnolias, for instance, when in bud
Are right in doing anything they can think of;
Free by predestination in the blood,
Saved by their own sap, shed for themselves,
Their texture can impose their architecture;
Their sapient matter is always already informed.

(Empson, 'Letter', 1928)

Stimulus, response, function

I. A. Richards decided that literary criticism was effectively a branch of behaviourist psychology, and as a consequence he was less interested in the aesthetics of criticism, which could never attain explicitness, than in a psychologically oriented close reading that perhaps could. For him analysing text was, therefore, in accordance with the philosophy of A. J. Ayer (Ayer, 1936), an exercise in evaluating the different kinds of formal complexity in the text that control the reader's response.

Behaviourism argues for 'a science of the observable'. What that means in practice is that it effectively rules out scientific discussion of what is going on 'in the mind', because that is not observable. For Richards, this basically means that the critic must concentrate on what is observable in a literary text: literary expression. More importantly, perhaps, this view also focuses attention on the reception of the text. The behaviour of the reader, in attempting to understand the message of the writer, becomes crucial, and can result in a scientific approach that uses subjective responses in an analysis of objective stimuli. The response comes about because of a stimulus 'encoded' in the text by the writer. Because these stimuli and responses are observable, they can also be used as bits of information and hence form part of a behaviourist theory of predictable information. Predictability, according to behaviourist theory, is there-fore 'measurable'.

If a behaviourist approach depends upon the observable, then it follows that if language is involved, it is the expression of language that becomes important, rather than interiorized relations hidden away in a virtual world somewhere. This approach is therefore discourse-based. Empson's work is dis-course-based for humanist/rationalist reasons; Richards's work is also discourse-based, but for behaviourist reasons. Yet both are concerned with language and close reading of literary text, both are interested in the implications of their work for linguistic and literary theory alike, and both are highly influential in a develop-ing critical practice that is concerned with text, 'real' language and 'real' people. However, the nature of the response, in a behaviourist theory applied to text analysis, is determined by cultural, social, and experiential forces, different for each indi-vidual, rather than by the relations of structures in *langue*. Analysis of text, along these lines, would therefore involve analysis of the encoded stimuli, which, in effect, is what happens in analyses by Richards.

The consequences, then, of developing a theory for literary criticism, or for linguistic analysis, that de-privileges *langue*, at a time when it was the focus of the most dominant paradigm, were far-reaching. To a certain extent, this is what Richards attempted, but, as the French/American theorist Michael Riffaterre was to discover there were powerful objections to any theory that looked remotely as if it might shift the ground away from idealization. Richards, together with C. K. Ogden, attempted just such a shift in *The Meaning of Meaning* (Ogden and Richards, 1923), as did Empson in his *The Structure of Complex Words*. But the power of linguistics as a discipline was too strong to allow their work (which was much too empiricist in its orientation anyway) to gain any ground at all. In the 1960s, with the work of the American linguist Noam Chomsky it was to become stronger, more powerful, more protective, and even more 'scientific' than it had been so far. Arguments from people like Spitzer, Whorf, Winter, Empson, and Richards about a discourse-oriented linguistics were easily crushed and relegated to the backwaters of literary criticism or to the history books.

Michael Riffaterre offered a more coherent and theoretically rigorous approach than Richards had managed, probably because Richards had had to temper his position with pedagogic and institutional restraints. Adopting a similar psychologically oriented position, Riffaterre claimed that 'the literary phenomenon is a dialectic between text and reader' (Riffaterre, 1978:1) and since the late 1950s he has argued consistently for a reader-response approach to the analysis of literary text (see Riffaterre, 1959, 1960, 1966; and for a development of his work see Fish, 1972, 1980).[1]

Riffaterre's early work, for the most part, represented a reaction against the formalism of linguists like Roman Jakobson, who, in the analysis of literary text, was principally interested in what made a verbal message a work of art (Jakobson, 1960;350).[2] Developing on the work both of the Russian Formalists and of Charles Bally (one of the first advocates of Saussurean structuralism), Jakobson was principally concerned with understanding how a particular function of language is determined linguistically. For literature, he argued, the function is poetic focusing on the message for its own sake (Jakobson, 1960:356). This type of analysis requires a model of signification that accounts, in ways that Saussure's didn't, for the *situation* in which the message occurs. For this, Jakobson turned to the semiotics of the American philosopher Charles Peirce, who developed a theory of signification along the lines of Saussure's, in that it included a signifier and a signified, but he added a third component – the *interpretant*. This initiated a shift away from the closed world of Saussure's sign because the interpretant signals that the sign is actually involved in some sort of interactive process.[3]

This enabled Jakobson to argue that the functions of language involve relationships between the message and the context in which the message occurs. In other words, Jakobson is dealing with *parole*, not *langue*. Unlike some structuralists, he was prepared to get involved with situationally determined meanings in the analysis of text, because he was interested in how language functions in context. This resulted in an emphasis on multiple meanings rather than on single meanings, because meanings change as the function of the message changes in a given context. Like Empson, then, Jakobson is concerned with language that is *polysemic*, capable of multiple meanings. So far, so good – except that Jakobson applied this theory to all functions of language *except* the poetic function. For literary messages he determined that situation did not influence meaning: the linguistic structures involved are autonomous; the message is not understood in terms of a context, but in terms of itself. The point that is being made here is that the literary text *always* draws attention to itself as poetic. The meaning of the message in literature, therefore, is not determined by the situation, it is determined by the poetic code in *langue* (see Holenstein, 1976; Taylor, 1980:42–62).[4]

For Jakobson 'the essence of poetry lies precisely in the poetic transformation of verbal material and in the coupling of its phonetic and semantic aspects' (Jakobson and Rudy, 1980:97). This effectively results in a detailed analysis of the structures and patterns of text. The classic example of this is an analysis by Jakobson and Jones (1970) of Shakespeare's 'Sonnet 129'. In this analysis they determine formal, structural, patterns for how the sonnet functions *poetically*, based on an attempt to undertake a *total* analysis of the phonemic/metrical, semantic, and syntactic levels. Roger Fowler was to call this an 'ultra-structuralist' analysis in his detailed refutation of the method (Fowler, 1975a:81), and Paul Werth described it as 'seamless' analysis in his even more detailed refutation (Werth, 1976:54).[5]

Sonnet 129

Th'expense of Spirit in a waste of shame
Is lust in action, and till action, lust
Is perjur'd, murd'rous, bloody full of blame,
Savage, extreme, rude, cruel, not to trust,
Enjoy'd no sooner but despised straight,
Past reason hated as a swallowed bayt,
On purpose laid to make the taker mad.
Mad in pursuit and in possession so,
Had, having, and in quest to have, extreme,
A bliss in proof and proud and very woe,
Before a joy propos'd behind a dream,
    All this world well knows yet none knows well,
    To shun the heaven that leads men to this hell.

The analysis of the text 'does not merely re-arrange the poem as a catalogue of linguistic observations. It uses these observations to figure the poem as a set of diagrammatic structures, allegedly simultaneously perceived' (Fowler, 1975a:83). These structures are based on binary oppositions – for example odd/even, outer/inner – giving rise to an analysis of text that finds correspondences between these oppositions and the language/structures of the poem. So, for example, the opposition between 'terminal/non-terminal' results in an analysis that states that the terminal couplet has no adjectives, participles, indefinites or copulas, whereas the non-terminal quatrains are rich in these elements. Using evidence like this, they argue that the sonnet has two topics, the lust and the luster:

> The first strophe characterises lust in itself; the second launches a set of passive participles with a hint to the yet unnamed *dramatis personae* and finishes by referring to the *taker* of the *bayt*; the third strophe uses active participles to depict the taker's behaviour and brings forward images of lust as objects of his (*sic*) strivings. . . . The final line seems to allude to the ultimate persona, the celestial condemner of mankind. (Jakobson and Jones, 1970:27)

Werth (1976:33–4) deliberately parodies this structuralist *reductio ad absurdum* as follows.

i Create divisions (strophes) in the text based on the rhyme scheme and syntactic structure.
ii Analyse in great detail the metre, syntax, phonology, morphology, and lexis of the text.
iii Analyse the rhetorical figures of the text.
iv Make as many permutations based on binary correspondence as possible among the strophes of the text.
v If possible, make semantic generalizations for these binary permutations, that is, assign meanings to them.

And there you have it: a detailed, exhaustive analysis of text based on the structuralist concepts of opposition and actualization and on the formalist/structuralist concept of function.[6] All of these work to enable statements to be made not about the text, but about literarity, that is, that which determines language to be literary/poetic.

Most critics, linguistic and literary, agree that this close formalist structuration of text is likely to be of little value in critical practice, but – and this needs to be emphasized – it is not meant to demonstrate *what* or *how* a text means in *parole*.[7] It is designed to contribute to the theory of literarity and poetic function in *langue*. With this sort of analysis we are back in a virtual world again, but the criticisms are made from a 'real world' perspective, and this is where some of the difficulties lie. The answer, of course, is to concentrate on a theory and practice based on discourse as many now do. (See Bakhtin/Voloshinov, 1930, 1968, 1973, 1981; Kress and Hodge, 1979; Pêcheux, 1975a,

1975b; Fowler, 1981, 1986; Frow, 1984; Hodge and Kress, 1988.)

Structural relations of meaning

Roman Jakobson's concerns were theoretical, driven by a linguistic perspective derived from Russian Formalism, Saussurean structuralism and Prague School linguistics.[8] His background was not that of a literary critic, and his priorities were not those of the realist, intrinsic or counter-intrinsic critic cutting out a path for close reading of text in university English departments as Empson and Richards were. This can be seen in his work (in collaboration with Claude Lévi-Strauss) on Charles Baudelaire's 'Les Chats', which is described by Eagleton as having been carried out with 'toothcombing tenacity' (Eagleton, 1983:116).[9] This work, like the later analyses, was enormously detailed, and came under considerable criticism (see Riffaterre, 1966), but it did serve to focus literary studies onto the structuralist enterprise more than they had been up to this point (Jakobson and Lévi-Strauss, 1962).

It is significant that Jakobson and Lévi-Strauss published their analysis of a poem by Baudelaire in an anthropology journal. Claude Lévi-Strauss was a French anthropologist whose work has been of enormous influence in twentieth-century thought (Lévi-Strauss, 1955, 1958a, 1962, 1969). He was principally interested in the analysis of myth according to an argument that states that though there are countless myths in the world, they are ordered by a finite number of universal structures. Each myth can be understood in terms of these structures, and the analysis of text can be reduced to a single formula:

$$Fx\ (a) : Fy\ (b) : : Fx\ (b) : Fa^{-1}\ (y)$$

Nowhere does Lévi-Strauss explain this formula in detail, but it is based on the relational concept of homology, which is a way of making statements about relationships between equivalent structures[10] and Lévi-Strauss asserts that he has 'never ceased to be guided by it' (Sperber, 1979:20–1). As Dan Sperber points out, most commentators 'have wisely pretended that it does not exist' (Sperber, 1979:21), and I certainly make no claims to understand it. What is clear, though, is that analysis of text (whatever that text might be, poem or tribal society) is, for Lévi-Strauss, a matter of analysing the myths in order to build a 'grammar' of the universal structures. That grammar, like Saussure's *langue*, is an idealization; a system of stable, unchanging order. As in Saussure, meaning is ultimately to be understood in this idealized world. It is located in structural relations, not in the individual rational consciousness, that is, the subject, or in the messy, 'noisy' world of discourse. The aim, as in all structuralist endeavour, is to 'arrive at a certain level of abstraction' (Fokkema and Kunne-Ibsch, 1978:30), and some of the abstractions Lévi-Strauss arrived at were, like the oppositions Jakobson and Jones found in the sonnet analysis, fairly basic: raw/cooked (Lévi-Strauss, 1970); sister/wife (Lévi-Strauss, 1969); and so on (see Leach, 1973:48; Mepham, 1973; Sperber, 1979).

An opposition like raw/cooked could therefore be considered as a universal metaphor for nature/culture. The assumption is that it is a universally accepted idea that the use of fire for cooking distinguishes people from animals, and as people are interested in what makes them people, an opposition like raw/cooked is a universal way of thinking about nature (raw) and culture (cooked). This is based on Saussure's classic principle, which argues that the 'most precise characteristic' of elements of a system – any system – 'is being what others are not' (Saussure, 1959:117). The relations between the elements are what matter. To understand orchestral music, for example, the relations between the players must be understood, not just a single musician's playing in isolation.

Lévi-Strauss, in other words, modelled the world as if it worked like a structuralist model of language. His thinking along these lines, influenced particularly by Roman Jakobson, had far-reaching effects on the analysis of literary text, mainly in the development of narrative theory.[11]

Roland Barthes, in an influential study of the writings of Racine (Barthes, 1963), developed some of the structuralist thinking of Lévi-Strauss, arguing that Racine was best understood in terms of the relationship between desire and authority (following Lévi-Straussian ideas of desire and authority as a means of describing tribal communities). Barthes uses the idea of binary oppositions to rewrite (remodel) Racine's writing, categorizing relations like light/shade, monologue/dialogue, power/weakness in the plays in order to create a *meta-text* that conceptualizes the writing. The result was a categorization of Racine's plays based on a pattern:

A has full power over B
A loves B who does not love A

                    (Barthes, 1963:35 cited in Pettit, 1977:44)

In his work on a wide range of discourses, *Mythologies* (1957) and *Elements of Semiology* (1965), Barthes attempted to understand discourse through structuralist principles, that is, he looked at a system of signs and treated them as if they operated like a structuralist model of language (see for example, his analysis of fashion (Barthes, 1967)). When he looked specifically at narrative, he formulated structural categories (Barthes, 1966) in order to understand their relations with other categories in the text (as all good structuralists would), but he also engaged with much larger issues. From his very first book, he was politically committed to an ideologically motivated understanding of literature and literary history (Barthes, 1953) and to countering much of the intrinsic critical practice that saw single meanings in texts and that assumed that its approach was disinterested and objective, innocent of any ideology (see Sturrock, 1979a). In an important defence of his work on Racine, Barthes produced a book which made it clear that criticism was not, as many intrinsic critics maintain, a more articulate and sensitive form of reading (Barthes, 1966). Literature for Barthes, as for Empson, is about the plurality of meanings. In structuralist terms, this means that the signifier is emphasized over the signified, and Barthes' insistence on this was an important development in the work in narrative theory (narratology) that he and others, specifically Claude Bremond, Algirdas Julien Greimas, Tzvetan Todorov, and Gerard Genette were to produce (see Greimas, 1966; Todorov, 1969, 1971, 1973a, 1973b; Bremond, 1983; Genette, 1972, 1980; see also Prince, 1973).

Much of the initial impetus for structuralist narratology came from reactions to the work of Vladimir Propp, who analysed the motifs and functions of a corpus of Russian folk-tales and concluded that the functions of a folk-tale, rather than its motifs (as in traditional folklore study), should be the basic unit of the folk-tale (Propp, 1958). In doing this he was working, like structuralist linguists, to assign a hierarchy of structures for the tale, the categories of which are determined by the narrative and by a historical perspective on what the tales traditionally meant. Following Victor Shklovsky's earlier formulations about narrative structure, Michael O'Toole (1975:146) likens his approach to the 'constituent structure grammars' that Chomsky roundly condemned (1957:12).[12] If part of the text (a motif or a function) changes, for example, in a traditional tale, then it effectively changes the meaning of the whole. This is classic synchronic structuralism; narrative texts gain meaning from their parts, which are determined by choices along the paradigmatic and syntagmatic axes of choice. Propp isolated thirty-one functions as signifying structures of folktale. These functions are distributed amongst seven 'spheres of action':

the villain
the donor
the helper
the princess and the father
the dispatcher
the hero
the false hero

(Hawkes, 1977:69)

Depending on the tale, a character may be involved in one or more or none of the spheres of action. Regardless of which characters are involved, there are always seven spheres of action. In other words, they are universal structures of narrative, so narrative analysis consists of mapping the functions into sequences using these seven spheres, resulting in a grammar of the narrative. A. J. Greimas worked on this principle and developed a detailed grammar based on a reordering of Propp's seven spheres of action, and on a theoretical premise that narrative worked in the same way as the model of the structuralist sentence. He proposed a grammar based on universalist categories like:

subject/object (hero and princess)
sender/receiver (father/dispatcher and princess)
helper/opponent (donor/helper and villain/false hero)

What Greimas has done here is transpose Propp's categories into universal oppositional concepts that can produce an idealized (virtual) grammar applicable to all narratives in all languages. He also reduces the thirty-one functions by what Samuel Levin was to call 'coupling', that is the coupling together of equivalent structures at different levels of language, for example, the phonological and semantic levels (Levin, 1962).[13] Analysis of narrative, according to Greimas, would therefore involve the analysis of text according to these conceptual structures: in other words, structures that are <u>meaning-oriented</u> (such as contracts, performatives and movements – Hawkes, 1977:94). But this is done not to produce a grammar of real time narrative, but to produce a grammar of virtual time narrative – a *langue* of literature (Hawkes, 1977:95). An illustration of the consequences of this sort of thinking for text analysis is demonstrated in Eleanor Cotton's work on e e cummings's 'if everything happens that can't be done' (Cotton, 1980):

if everything happens that can't be done

if everything happens that can't be done
(and anything's righter
than books
could plan)
the stupidest teacher will almost guess
(with a run
skip
around we go yes)
there's nothing as something as one
one hasn't a why or because or although
(and buds know better
than books
don't grow)
one's anything old being everything new
(with a what
which
around we come who)
one's everyanythingso

so world is a leaf so tree is a bough
(and birds sing sweeter
than books
tell how)
so here is away and so your is a my
(with a down
up
around again fly)
forever was never till now

now I love you and you love me
(and books are shuter
than books

can be)
and deep in the high that does nothing but fall
(with a shout
each
around we go all)
there's somebody calling who's we

we're anything brighter than even the sun
(we're everything greater
than books
might mean)
we're everyanything more than believe
(with a spin
leap
alive we're alive)
we're wonderful one times one

Eleanor Cotton considers that 'basic to our appreciation of a piece of literature is our perception of its structure' (Cotton, 1980:274), and suggests that this structure occurs as an element of discourse – rhetoric, semantics, syntax and phonology; or as levels of text – stanza, line and word. She argues that the 'basic meaning' of the poem is 'that different elements and entities are joined, not by logic, but by love, giving rise to a new and powerful force' (286). How this happens in the poem is the focus of the analysis.

Each stanza is composed in three different languages (L1, L2 and L3). L1 functions to present the main argument about love, L2 to compare love and logic, and L3 to describe love. L3 is the childish language of delight: 'with a run/skip around we go yes'; L2 is the language of the impertinent youth: 'and anything's righter/than books/could plan'; and L1 is the complex language of the mature speaker: 'if everything happens that can't be done'. Within these three language varieties are parallel structures that can be 'filled' with semantically equivalent elements. This 'multiple equivalence' exists at all levels (textual and discoursal) in the poem, thereby creating a 'design' that actually embodies the meaning of the poem. The meaning of the poem has been determined, at the rhetorical level, to be about the comparison of love and logic, and at every level in the parallel structures this comparison takes place in one form or another. In other words, a structuralist view of the text overrides all other considerations.

Linguistic/structural form is considered to mirror meaning, so what becomes important in a structural analysis like this, then, is not the theme of the text, the writer, or the meanings of the words, but the structural 'facts' that lie behind the 'fusion of form and meaning' (Cotton, 1980:285).[14]

Reading and rereading

Tzvetan Todorov, working on the Henry James stories (Todorov, 1973b), looks for a 'primal plan on which everything else depends, as it appears in each one of his works' (74), picking up on a speech by Vereker, one of the characters in 'The Figure in the Carpet', Todorov's search for that primal plan, leads him to argue that 'James's tales are based on the quest for an absolute and absent cause' (74). This, and its variants is at the base of all the stories – 'the string on which the pearls of the individual stories are strung' (Todorov, 1973b:101).[15] He concludes his analysis by writing:

> . . . criticism . . . is a search for truth, not its revelation – the quest for the treasure rather than the treasure itself, for the treasure can only be absent. Thus, once we have finished this 'reading' of James, we must begin to read him, and throw ourselves into the quest for the sense of his work, though knowing as we do that this sense is nothing other than the quest itself. (Todorov, 1973b:101)

This suggests, therefore, a reading and rereading process (see, for example, the various approaches to 'Sonnet 94' in Easthope, 1983) that received its most systematic application within structuralist theory – but with a quite distinct counter-intrinsic polemic – in Roland Barthes, *S/Z* (1970). Barthes takes a story by Balzac, 'Sarrasine', and systematically analyses it section by section (which he calls *lexies*, that is, units of reading). He divides the text into 561 of these units and analyses them according to five codes: *hermeneutic* which looks for and solves enigmas in the narrative; *actional* which looks at the way particular actions are structured; *semic* and *symbolic*, which look at the way the narrative structure works in terms of characters, situations and events; and *referential*, which looks at the references that are made outside of the story (see Sturrock, 1979a:74). Once analysis of each of the 561 *lexies* has been made, Barthes puts them all back together at the end of the book. The polemic aims to demonstrate the plurality of meanings and to deconstruct the valorized position into which intrinsic critics had placed the writer.

Central to the structuralist enterprise is a rewriting or *remodelling* of a text. The attraction of this approach? An ability to be more explicit about the system of literature. The result? As in structuralist linguistics, a concentration primarily on synchronic studies of literary texts.

Myths, structures and archetypes

As has been seen, scientific objectivity/explicitness is a principal attraction of the structuralist enterprise, and Northrop Frye, in 1957, had offered the beginnings of that quest for the objective with the publication of his book *Anatomy of Criticism* (Frye, 1957a; see also Frye, 1959b, 1970). For Frye, the system of literature was better understood in terms of structures like myth and genre than in the subjectivities and intuitions of intrinsic criticism. He developed a theory of literary modes of comic, romantic, tragic, and ironic, which in effect is a self-generating theory. It argues that a literary text is generated from a closed system of literature, much as Saussure saw *parole* as being generated from *langue*. Literature as a system, then, is not the sum total of the expression of individuals, but a manifestation of the universal functions (archetypes) of a virtual system. This is close to Jackobson's formalist position, but Frye differs in that meaning is not based on relations of opposition and equivalence, as it is for Jakobson and structuralist linguistics, but on knowledge of the 'larger' system of myths and archetypes from which literary texts draw their existence. And in that respect he considers that 'Poetry is a disinterested use of words: it does not address a reader directly.' But larger, mythic systems do, through their exposition in criticism (Frye, 1959b:29–30). This is a very specific type of criticism, though, in that it seeks to develop an explicit understanding of systems of literary myth:

The first step in developing a genuine poetics is to recognize and get rid of meaningless criticism, or talking about literature in a way that cannot help to build up a systematic structure of knowledge. This includes all the sonorous nonsense that we so often find in critical generalities, reflective comments, ideological perorations, and other consequences of taking a large view of an unorganized subject. (Frye, 1957b:41)

Text analysis informed by this sort of theoretical position tends, therefore, to look quite different from either intrinsic or methodist criticism. Frye's work on Milton's *Lycidas* should illustrate this (Frye, 1959a).

Lycidas is a pastoral elegy written to commemorate the death of Edward King, who drowned at sea. Analysing the diction of the poem, Frye suggests, leads nowhere. A conventional analysis becomes 'a scissors and paste collection of allusive tags' (Frye, 1959a:411).

> The absurd quantum formula of criticism, the assertion that the critic should confine himself (*sic*) to 'getting out' of a poem exactly what the poet may vaguely be assumed to have been aware of 'putting in', is one of the many slovenly illiteracies that the absence of systematic criticism allowed to grow up. (Frye, 1957b:40)

What is needed, he argues, is a unifying principle, and in the case of *Lycidas*, that principle is the Adonis myth. Understanding this is crucial to understanding Frye's method, because it is this myth that links *Lycidas* to 'other forms of poetic experience' (Frye, 1959a:411), and that makes the poem what it is. This view is central to Frye's myth criticism, because 'Every poem must be examined as a unity, but no poem is an isolateable unity' (411). For Frye, every poem is connected to other poems *of their kind*, and text analysis, for the most part, consists of recognizing the myths, archetypes, and structures of text that contribute to these genres, which in turn contribute to a total understanding of what constitutes humanity. For Frye, this is the motivation for criticism. Understanding the universal constants (myths and archetypes) of a stable, unchanging humanity – embodied in literature – is the ultimate goal of the work. The rub comes, of course, in the knowledge required by students and critics to recognize these constants, the acquisition of which puts them into a world of specialized knowledges and establishes an elite who are able to read the myths: '. . . the skill developed from constant practice in the direct experience of literature is a special skill, like playing the piano, not the expression of a general attitude to life, like singing in the shower' (Frye, 1957b:50).

There is no escaping the influence of structuralism in Frye's work, but the way in which the world works is not, for Frye, based on arbitrary relations. It is quite clearly governed by categories whose meanings are derived from something much larger than the structures and their relations, or the systems to which they belong: 'just as there is an order of nature behind the natural sciences, so literature is not a piled aggregate of "works", but an order of words' (Frye, 1957b:40). Logocentrism – the centralizing of 'the word' in western philosophy and culture – is not without its moral and religious doctrine, as Frye as a Christian humanist makes perfectly clear. Myths and texts do not exist as autonomous entities; they exist as part of a much larger, universal scheme of things.

Situation and culture-dependent meanings

Frye's archetypal theory of literature argues against close attention to the language of the text – for Frye, literature is not about words. Language is treated as a 'secondary order which merely "imitates" the world of ideas' (Belsey, 1980:25), so that thought is considered to be independent of language, and meaning considered to exist before it is 'expressed' in words. This was (and is) a popular view of language, motivated by a psychological, rather than a sociological, understanding of the world. During the early decades of this century, it was also the dominant view. But anthropologist Bronislaw Malinowski thought otherwise. His work was mainly concerned with Polynesian and, later, American Indian cultures, and the one thing that he kept returning to was the question of translation – linguistic and cultural. If language is a closed system, how, he wanted to know, was translation from one culture to another possible? His argument was that language is not psychologically self-contained, but is culture-dependent and situation-dependent. His view was therefore a sociological one, arguing for the importance of the context, both immediate and general, in the understanding of how language works and how meanings are produced.

Meaning, for Malinowski, is a result of social functions. What people want and need to do produces meanings. Meanings are not 'out there' in the world already, just waiting for a linguistic expression to act as vehicle; nor are they genetically encoded and parcelled up in the mind, just waiting to be selected when needed. Meanings and language structures develop in response to social needs (Malinowski, 1935). As a result of this view, he established a number of macro-functions by which to describe a particular society: these were based on language as a form of action, language as a means of control, and language as a historical record. These categories have had far-reaching consequences in the development of functional theories of language this century. One theory in particular, developed by Michael Halliday and now known as Systemic Functional Linguistics, can trace its origins directly back to the work of Malinowski and the grammarian Benjamin Whorf (see Halliday, 1973, 1975, 1978; Kress, 1976).

Whorf took issue with the structuralist view of language as a self-contained system, and argued, like Malinowski, that language and meaning are determined by culture (Whorf, 1956). His approach, developed from Gestalt psychology (which is concerned with understanding whole structures, not just parts of them), extended Malinowski's discussion of covert categories into an attempt to understand the cognitive as well as social organization of language. He developed what is effectively a functional grammar based on overt and covert categories that distinguish between the surface structure of language (for example, the way a singular noun becomes a plural noun) and deep structures (for example, the way a noun can be recognized as animate without any distinctive surface structure to signal this). With his student Edward Sapir, Whorf developed a theory of language now known as the Sapir–Whorf hypothesis, which argues for a relativist view of language. It states that meanings are determined by the culture, or, to appropriate a more contemporary formulation, that meanings 'arise as a result of the knowledges, preoccupations and hegemonic necessities of specific societies and kinds of societies' (Fowler, 1981:146).[16] According to this theory, certain people, because of their language, see the world in ways that might be different from the ways in which other people, with a different language, see it.

Anthropologists like Lévi-Strauss and Malinowski were always conscious of the importance of recognizing that ways of seeing the world differ from society to society, and that these ways inform and determine the language of these societies. But it tended to be the grammarians and linguists, like Whorf, Sapir and Firth, who shaped these ideas into linguistic methodology and theory (see Sapir, 1921; Firth, 1957). This methodology and theory is, fundamentally, structuralist, despite being sociologically and functionally oriented, particularly for J. R. Firth. He concentrated his attention on the paradigmatic axis of meaning, unlike most structuralist linguists, who concentrated on the syntagmatic. This means talking not just about what is in a text, but about what is not there, too. In other words, by concentrating on paradigmatic relations, Firth emphasized the notion of choice – language as resource. To that extent, then, Firth is much more oriented towards prioritizing *parole*. This is a feature of British structuralist linguistics that, though it did not result in a shift of structuralist theory as a whole, certainly resulted in a greater orientation towards analysis of actual, 'naturally occurring' discourse.

Generativism and textual analysis

The major psychologically oriented theory of language developed in America by Noam Chomsky – Transformational Generative Linguistics (see Chomsky, 1957, 1964, 1965, 1968) – could certainly not be described as having an orientation towards the analysis of actual discourse. Chomsky's theory of language, which has been the most influential theory in the second half of the twentieth century, engages with the linguistics developed out of Saussurean structuralism, most notably in the area of syntax. The philosophy behind it is Cartesian, arguing for a universalist approach to understanding the innate resources of an individual's language. Individuals are considered to generate language from these innate resources. Generativism's main idea, which arose from an attempt to create a computer-generated grammar of English, was initially to account for the creativity of people's use of language, that is, their ability to generate sentences that have never been produced before (like this one). What generativism did, dramatically, was to push language studies into much more formal and theoretical enterprises. Its practice results in a concentration on understanding and describing an individual's ideal grammar (linguistic competence) in order to understand *langue*. In practice – and this is where its theoretical inconsistencies are similar to those of all structuralist theories of language – it concentrates on making contrastive judgements about the grammaticality (the well-formedness) of utterances in an individual's idiolect (his or her personal use of language) relative to an idealized (that is, virtual world) grammar. For example: which of the following utterances is well-formed?

5.1   [The cat sat on the mat.]

5.2   [Cat the sat on the mat?]

In a theory of language that ignores context and situation, you would probably answer (5.1). In a theory of language that includes context and situation you would have to answer, both (5.1) and (5.2), given that (5.2) is well-formed in the context for which it is being used, namely, academic exemplification. The generativist position *always* would reject (5.2), because as a theory and as a practice it is not concerned with situation and context – with *discourse*. It is concerned only with an idealized grammar. As in the gas law mentioned in Chapter 2, once you start including the possible contexts for an utterance, you open the floodgates of variability and instability. In a theory of language that aspires to formal explicitness above all things – particularly in a theory that has as its ultimate aim to produce a grammar of language universals this would have disastrous results. If, however, as a literary critic, you are concerned with understanding literary texts as instances of a literary language that disturbs the 'well-formedness' of ordinary discourse, then generative approaches might seem to offer a useful theoretical foundation for analysing text.

Generativism has changed dramatically since Chomsky's first statements in 1957. Though its dominance in Europe and Australia is now mostly over, it is still the major linguistics paradigm in the United States. A central feature of generativist linguistics is the development of the notion of overt and covert categories into the concepts of surface and deep structure. This has had a marked effect on text analysis, particularly as the generativist approach to covert categories of grammar is determined by a belief that the deep structure of an utterance will unambiguously indicate its meaning. The crucial term here is 'unambiguous'. Central to a generativist approach is the claim that two sentences like

5.3   [The student understood the term.]
5.4   [The term was understood by the student.]

are considered to be derived from the same deep structure, and are therefore considered to be semantically equivalent. The way that the surface structure is derived (transformed) from the deep structure is different in each sentence, but this does not change the central tenet of generativism that these sentences effectively mean the same thing. In this theory, deep structure rather than surface structure is the source of meaning. The difference between the two sentences is therefore considered to be a difference of style, not of meaning. (For a development of this, see Ohmann, 1964, 1966; Christensen, 1969; Newmeyer, 1983; Banfield, 1982.) This theory, of course, is unable to account for stylistic differences in sentences like

[The student understood the term.]
[The student understood the locution.]

which have the same deep structure, but which end on different, though 'synonymous', nouns. This difference is a stylistic one, which cannot be accounted for in standard generative theory (see Fowler, 1972).

In other words, the approach is one that argues that if the surface structure doesn't indicate *the* unambiguous meaning of the utterance, the deep structure will. The way in which the deep structure indicates meaning can be formally represented by rules that transform deep structures into surface structures. The resulting grammar, regardless of how it has changed over the years since Chomsky first outlined it in 1957, is a grammar of linguistic competence, not of linguistic *performance*, that is, it is a grammar not of discourses, but of idealized rules for the generation of sentences. And the danger of this, as Robert Hodge and Gunther Kress point out in a paper entitled 'Transformations, models and processes: towards a more usable linguistics', is that the grammar 'reflects the structures predicated by the grammar itself' (Hodge and Kress, 1974:10).

What Hodge and Kress argue for, very persuasively, is that the transformations be recognized as part of the messy world of discourse, not as some internalized, idealized operation (see also their discussion in Hodge and Kress, 1986). In practice, this is how the transformations have always been seen, but in terms of the theory this is, strictly speaking, not allowed.

Good examples of this lack of fit between the theory and practice of transformational generative linguistics are given in a paper by William A. Bennett, who looks at several literary texts, including William Wordsworth's 'Upon Westminster Bridge' and Ted Hughes's 'The Thought-Fox'. Bennett hypothesizes that

> . . . from a linguistic point of view we might consider it likely that the poet will use the possibilities of immediately apparent surface-structure to lead the reader down through the labyrinthine paths to a deeper, language-universal structure. (Bennett, 1977:35)

If this is so, he argues, then a linguistic analysis of literature should be able to account for both the surface and deep structure of text. But there are problems in a language theory that is concerned with ideal speaker grammar and with a complete 'automaticity' that ensures that the grammar generates *all and only* grammatical (well-formed) sentences. Poets, Bennett argues, are concerned with the performance capabilities of their readers, not their linguistic competence, hence when Wordsworth wrote

> Earth has not anything to show more fair:
> Dull would he be of soul who could pass by
> A sight so touching in its majesty:
> This city now doth, like a garment wear
> The beauty of the morning; silent, bare,
> Ships, towers, domes, theatres, and temples lie
> Open unto the fields, and to the sky;
> All bright and glittering in the smokeless air

he presumably knew that what the reader would have to do to work out a reading for the poem would be quite complex. The deep syntactic structure of the first line might be something like:

> NEGATIVE (Earth has something (Earth shows
> something (Something is fair) (X is not fair)))

The deep structure contains a sentence that does not appear in the surface structure, and its subject (X) is unknowable, yet the 'more' in the surface structure is signalling a negative comparison (more fair than what?). The reader who perceives this needs to find that missing item. Line 2 doesn't offer it, but the noun phrase 'A sight', in a prominent position at the beginning of line 3, might. But a sight of what? The semantics of 'sight' are likely to send the reader looking for a concrete reference to specify what is signalled by 'sight'. The noun phrase at the beginning of line 4 might offer a parallel, 'This city', but line 6 offers a list of particular, concrete references to 'sight'. To understand the surface structure of the first sentence, then, the reader has to understand the deep structure. But if generative grammar can characterize the first sentence as a well-formed sentence, then it also has to account for sentences like 'Mars has not anything to sell more cheap' or 'Sincerity will not have anything to sing more safe'. The only alternative, Bennett argues, is to establish a grammar for each text[17] which he does not favour. Bennett's preferred solution, like that of Hodge and Kress, is to suggest that a linguistic theory that is concerned with idealized grammar is wholly unsuitable for the analysis of actual text. But ultimately the argument is not really important, because, despite the claims of its proponents, generative stylistics never had very much to offer that had not already been better covered elsewhere (see Taylor, 1980:93), from the point of view of a performance/discourse-oriented analysis of text it never even got off the starting blocks.

But the theoretical possibilities of generativism held attractions for both analysts and theorists. Jonathan Culler is one such theorist. His interest, like Stanley Fish's, was not to find out what a text means (see page 53 above), but how readers make meanings. Unlike Fish, Culler wanted to formalize this by formulating explicit rules for the way this happened. To do this he turned to French structuralism and Chomskyan generativism. His basic argument is that the way a reader constructs meaning is not determined by the text itself, which is what the intrinsic critic would argue, but is determined by the reader's literary competence. Competence, in this sense, is drawn from generativist theory. It therefore denotes an idealized system, not an actual, 'real-world' system. Effectively, then, Culler's notions of literary competence are located in a literary *langue*, not in a literary *parole*. In other words, Culler suggests that readers have an internalized grammar of reading conventions that directs them to read texts in certain ways – to generate *all and only* well-formed readings of a text, just as a Chomskyan grammar is designed to generate *all and only* well-formed sentences. The generativist flaw now surfaces, because Culler argues that the principles that determine the way readers will read are to be found in the institutions that teach readers to read – in other words, in real processes: 'Anyone lacking this knowledge, anyone wholly unacquainted with literature and unfamiliar with the conventions by which fictions are read, would, for example, be quite baffled if presented with a poem' (Culler, 1975:114).

In other words, a poem read without an internalized grammar

of how to read a text as literature would be read as any other discourse. Suppose that text were William Blake's 'Ah! Sunflower'

Ah, Sun-flower, weary of time,
Who countest the steps of the Sun,
Seeking after that sweet golden clime
Where the traveller's journey is done:
Where the Youth pined away with desire,
And the pale Virgin shrouded in snow
Arise from their graves, and aspire
Where my Sun-flower wishes to go.

If you read it as 'Blake's dialectical thrust at asceticism is more than adroit. You do not surmount Nature by denying its prime claim of sexuality. Instead you fall utterly into the dull round of its cyclic aspirations'; where does this reading come from? he asks (Culler, 1975:115). It comes from the primary convention of what he calls the 'role of significance', which is a rule that requires a text to be read as though it were 'expressing a significant attitude to some problem concerning man (sic) and/or his (sic) relation to the universe'. There are also the conventions of thematic unity and metaphorical coherence, amongst others – all things that are 'constituents of the institution of literature' (Culler, 1975:116; see also Eagleton, 1981). The institutional argument is a vitally important point, it seems to me, but one that is theoretically weakened because of its grounding in generativist notions of internalized grammars of literary competence.[18] These competences are learnt in and expressed through performance – expressed in real-time processes, not internalized in virtual-time closed systems. But what Culler is interested in is developing a structuralist poetics that is theoretically only interested in the system of literature, and that argues that meanings are produced only in *langue*. The reader Culler is talking about is the ideal reader. But his approach, like so many based on the virtual/real dichotomy, seems in practice unable to operate without the interpretation of individual texts, and hence, the production of meaning in the messy world of discourse. The phantom of the structuralist linguistic opera rides again in its quest to render socially constructed realities explicit, neat, orderly, and stable.

Functionalism and textual analysis

Generativist grammars are not solely the responsibility of Chomskyan linguists. The principle of generativism is central to structuralist linguistics as a whole. Michael Halliday, probably one of the linguists most consistently opposed to Chomskyan grammars, is as generativist as Chomsky. His objections have not arisen from the argument about language generation, for the most part (though see Fish, 1973a, 1973b; Dillon, 1978), they have come about, within linguistics, mainly as a response to the psychological orientation of the theory.[19]

Like Jakobson, Halliday develops a functionally based linguistic theory that argues against the sort of autonomy suggested by generativist theory. To do this he develops three principal language functions: ideational, which is the expression of content; interpersonal, which is the expression of interaction; and textual, which is the expression of situation through coherent text – this is very much in the tradition of Malinowski (see Halliday, 1973, 1978, 1985a, 1985b; Halliday and Hasan, 1985; for their relations to the study of literary text see O'Toole, 1971; Birch and O'Toole, 1988). Linguistic choices made from all three of these functions constitute the text. Like Chomsky, Halliday is concerned principally with sentence grammar, but from a sociological perspective; his field of analysis is 'language as social semiotic' (see Halliday, 1978). He rejects Chomsky's refusal to engage with context as well as the descriptivist approach that refuses to engage with meanings. Communication, he argues, is carried out by text in context. The social system, not the mind, motivates the language code.

His views on the literary text are, however, staunchly intrinsic. Literature has special status as verbal art (Halliday, 1983: vii) and by 'analysing a literary text as a verbal artefact, we are asserting its status as literature' (*viii*). As such it has independent status, such that, unlike other registers it defines the world 'beyond' the text, rather than being defined by its situation (*xiv*; cf. Ure, 1982). Analysis of literature is at its most creative, Halliday asserts, when it is a linguistic analysis (*viii*; cf. Hasan, 1988). That last statement, in particular, places Halliday quite firmly in the structuralist tradition that asserts, quite forcefully, the effectiveness of linguistics as a science (psychological or sociological). He does, however, object strongly to the determinist theory of style as deviation from a norm, and to the concentration within generativist linguistics on the derivational history of sentences and its appropriation for stylistic study by Chomskyan linguistics (cf. Ohmann, 1964, 1966; Christensen, 1969; Hirsch, 1975; McLain, 1976, 1977; 1979), offering the important consideration that the supposed norm is also a part of the stylistic make-up of a text.

Henry Widdowson makes the point that an analysis 'which derives from an interest in deviant sentences adopts an orientation to literature which is essentially different from that of the literary scholar' that is, it approaches literary texts as 'aesthetic objects sufficient unto themselves' (Widdowson, 1972:295). He was reacting, in the main, to the generativist-inspired text analysis that prioritized deviant sentences – expressions that in the linguistics literature would be preceded by *, for example,

* Cat the sat on the mat.

signalling that the expression is not well-formed. What Henry Widdowson wanted to know was, if a grammar accounts for the knowledge speakers have, why is it that speakers know how to interpret ungrammatical sentences (Widdowson, 1972:294)?

What he also wanted to address was the practice, amongst linguists analysing literary text, that attempted to account for every linguistic structure with equal importance (cf. Jakobson and Jones, 1970, who attempted to do this; Roger Fowler's response in Fowler, 1975a; and Werth, 1976). This practice was in many ways the inevitable outcome of most linguists treating literature like any other discourse, with the consequence that each linguistic item was considered to be as important as the next. As Fowler points out, following Riffaterre (1966), 'A complete analysis provides *too much* detail. . . . All characteristics of a text are reduced, by being displayed, to the same level of detailed but banal observation' (Fowler, 1975a:82). What Widdowson suggests is that because there is more to literature than linguistic deviance, the analyst should not be asking the question ' "What are the linguistic peculiarities of this text and how can they be accounted for in grammatical terms?", but rather "What is being communicated in this text and how are the resources of the language being used to bring this communication about?" ' (Widdowson, 1972:299). This might perhaps, seem a very commonsensical question to ask, but in the context of Chomskyan linguistic analysis of text in the early 1970s, this was heresy of the first order.

The question of 'resources' raised by Widdowson is important here, because linguistics under the banner of both Chomsky and Halliday was for the most part a linguistics of the sentence. Widdowson's questions here about resources and social functions go beyond the sentence. What Widdowson is arguing for is that linguists should consider literature as communication. This is a very important point, because a communicative view of language is one of the last considerations in formal, structuralist analyses of text (see the development of these views in Widdowson, 1975; 1978). Ronald Carter, in a detailed linguistic analysis of John Crowe Ransom's 'Janet Walking' and of an extract from Lionel Johnson's 'Oxford' (Carter, 1982d), demonstrates ways in which the integration of language and literature study can take place in an 'English' lesson. His points are straightforward, but still surprisingly necessary: the analysis of linguistic structures, particularly lexis, can be undertaken in systematic, not just impressionistic, ways; communicative/interactional approaches to the study of language in texts are essential; and work on lexis, in particular, can fruitfully take place in a sociolinguistic framework within the language classroom. Importantly, he concludes the paper with a proposed syllabus for integrated language and literature study that aims to develop student awareness of the structural and functional properties of language, to introduce some basic linguistic concepts and terminology, to stimulate sociolinguistic awareness in the production and reception of writing and speech, to enable students to work creatively within a normative language framework, and to increase 'sensitivity of response to the way language works in literature and to raise questions about the nature of the literary artefact' (Carter, 1982d:178).

Carter's position on the integration of literary and linguistic insights into a communicative language teaching syllabus demonstrates how an older, more traditional approach to 'English Studies', which integrated both language and literature concerns, had been filtered out of most educational systems. This had occurred mainly as a result of the polarization of disciplines into literary studies (mostly New Critical analysis) and linguistics. For example, Michael Halliday's analysis of W. B. Yeat's 'Leda and the Swan' in 1964 (Halliday, 1964a; see also Halliday 1964b) demonstrated quite different concerns from his analysis of William Golding's *The Inheritors* in 1971 (Halliday, 1971). In the 1964 paper Halliday indicated that as a linguist his primary interest in the poem was with the description of it as *text*. He was not interested in developing the literary 'message' of the poem. That, he argued, was for literary analysts.

> If it is considered that the meaning of a piece of literature lies between the lines rather than within the lines, it seems likely that linguistics has no message. . . . Linguistics is not and never will be the whole of literary analysis, and only the literary analyst – not the linguist – can determine the place of linguistics in literary studies. But if a text is to be described at all, then it should be described properly; and this means by the theories and methods developed in linguistics, the subject whose task is precisely to show how language works. (Halliday 1964a:70)

Henry Widdowson probed this statement and he suggested that although Halliday's analysis of nominal group structure, for example, points to the fact that this particular linguistic structure is being used in an unusual way in 'Leda and the Swan', it doesn't say *how* this contributes to a literary understanding of the poem (Widdowson, 1975:10).[20] In this respect Halliday is establishing the credentials of linguistics as a discipline that should form part of literary analysis, arguing for a recognition that literature, as Spitzer had argued many years earlier, is made of language.[21]

The problem lies in the supposed objectivity and explicitness of linguistic methodology. John Sinclair concluded his detailed grammatical analysis of Philip Larkin's poem 'First Sight' by writing:

> Grammar deals with contrasts, multiple choices from a great many systems simultaneously, and the meaning of a grammatical statement can only be fully elicited with reference to the total grammatical description. Nevertheless, the exercise shows how some aspects of the meaning of the poem can be described quite independently of evaluation. (Sinclair, 1966:81)

The idea that meaning could be described without evaluation was heresy in many critical quarters, but, like Halliday, Sinclair effectively throws out a challenge to literary critics that basically says, unless you have our detailed and specialized knowledge of language structures, you will not be able to give full interpretations of the texts. It was polemical – and designed to be so, I'm sure, in a situation in which linguistics was carving out a disciplinary niche for itself in much the same way as the Cambridge academics had done (so successfully) for English literature thirty years earlier. Sumner Ives, in an analysis of the grammatical divisions of Andrew Marvell's 'To His Coy Mistress' (Ives, 1962) concluded:

> I do not claim that these results constitute a critical analysis of the poem, but these results display a physical poem on which critical analysis can be performed or interpretations advanced. When I have carried this kind of analysis to its ultimate limits . . . my work as a linguist is complete. (Cited in Hendricks, 1974:6.)

But there was a problem with structuralist linguistics that Sinclair, Halliday, and others were perfectly capable of recognizing, but were not able to solve. In the words of Roger Fowler in 1966, this was that:

> There is no logical step from linguistic criticism to evaluation or interpretation (except on points of detail); but linguistics does provide ways of unfolding and discussing precise textual effects, and may be a means of assuring a sound factual basis for many sorts of critical judgement. (Fowler, 1966a:28)

The terms 'logical', 'precise' and 'sound factual basis' all signal the preoccupation of linguistics with developing as an objective, explicit science of language. Of course there could be no logical step between linguistic criticism and evaluation (though many have tried to formulate one) and the recognition of that within British linguistics, and the critical linguistics developed in the 1970s and 1980s in particular by Roger Fowler, Gunther Kress, and Robert Hodge, is the freer for it.

By the time Michael Halliday turned his attention to William Golding's *The Inheritors* in 1971 he wasn't even looking for that step. He was both theoretically and methodologically more confident. Systemic linguistics was on a much firmer footing and an understanding of its functional component had been established. He used a detailed analysis of passages of *The Inheritors* to demonstrate this.[22] This time his analysis did not illustrate a simple descriptive technique, but showed a linguistic theory and its method of analysis to constitute a powerful means of understanding how texts (and their underlying ideologies) mean.[23] He argues that analysis can 'establish certain regular patterns, on a comparative basis, in the form of differences which appear significant over a broad canvas' (Halliday, 1971:133), and also that the features analysed 'represent . . . a world view, a structuring of experience that is significant because there is no *a priori* reason why the experience should have been structured in this way rather than another' (Halliday, 1971:134).

But there are social and ideological reasons, which Halliday was to explore more fully in Halliday, 1978. He continued:

> In *The Inheritors*, the syntax is part of the story. As readers, we are reacting to the whole of the creative writer's use of 'meaning potential'; and the nature of language is such that he [*Golding*] can convey, in a line of print, a complex of simultaneous themes, reflecting the variety of functions that language is required to serve. And because the elements of the language, the words and phrases and syntactic structures, tend to have multiple values, any one theme may have more than one interpretation. . . . (Halliday, 1971:135)

Although Halliday is concentrating here on meanings encoded into a text by a writer, this analysis makes a shift from the rather balder and bolder statement about linguistics and literature in his 1964 papers.[24]

Chomsky and Halliday have been the leading thinkers in the linguistics of the last thirty years. Their thought and their writings have been powerful and influential, and this in itself has not escaped attention. Robert Hodge and Gunther Kress (as cited earlier) turned their attention to the theory developed by Chomsky, and analysed certain aspects of Chomsky's language to reach the conclusion that generative linguistics had fallen prey to its own rhetoric (see Hodge and Kress, 1974:6–8). A few years later, Michael Hoey similarly turned his attention to Chomsky's writing in a paper entitled 'Persuasive rhetoric in linguistics: a stylistic study of some features of the language of Noam Chomsky' (Hoey, 1984). He concluded that Chomsky uses evaluation 'as a running supportive commentary on his own arguments and as a device for cowing opposition' (Hoey, 1984:28) and that he has a predilection for not supporting his more controversial evaluations by making references to unspecified work, or by considerable syntactic embedding.[25] More recently, Robert Hodge analysed aspects of the language of Michael Halliday to see how the intellectual production of systemic functional linguistics is developed within the language and style of Halliday's own discourse (Hodge, 1988). Similarly, Gunther Kress and Tony Trew undertook a contrastive analysis of selected discourse written from a generative perspective (Smith,

1961), which sees syntax as problematic, and of discourse written from a non-generative, distributionalist position (Hill, 1958), which considers syntax to be relatively unproblematic (Kress and Trew, 1978:31–38). Analyses like these are a demonstration that the discourse of linguists is not the disinterested, objective analysis of the 'scientist'. The authors of these analyses are concerned to show how ideologies are part of the textual structure.[26]

A relationship between the structures of the text and the thinking processes of the writer is assumed. This is both classically rhetorical and hermeneutic; rhetorical in the sense that structures are sought *above* the level of the sentence, and hermeneutic in the sense that the text is demythologized in a detailed close reading – a textual exegesis. Concern for textual analysis of this kind has been a part of intellectual life for a great many years and has been central to literary studies.[27] This has not been the case with contemporary linguistics. Language, in descriptivist, generativist and systemic linguistics, was always theorized in terms of the sentence as the largest structural unit, even when attention turned to the development of 'textgrammars'.

Textlinguistics and discourse

Textgrammars developed in the early 1970s as recognition that linguistics needed to be able to handle whole texts made up of coherent stretches of *connected* sentences, not just isolated sentences. They are associated, for the most part, with a movement amongst German and Dutch linguists that concerned itself with 'textlinguistics' (though cf. Scheglov and Zholkovskii, 1975). It was, like the structuralist linguistics of the sentence, designed to be an explicit, formal means of accounting for the way text worked in *langue*. In effect, this meant that 'text' as a formal unit of language was considered to act like a 'super-sentence' (cf. Hendricks, 1967) and textgrammars became enormously complicated expressions of formal logic. Manfred Bierwisch, a German linguist in the tradition of Chomsky, proposed as early as 1965 to develop a grammar of literary texts (a poetics) based on 'axiomatization and mathematical treatment' (cf. van Dijk, 1971). This would create:

1 an exact characterization of the types of poetic rules and the relationships between them

2 an explication of the necessary types of poetic structural description

3 an algorithm that uniquely assigns to the generated texts

resulting in empirical examinations of text on a very large scale (Bierwisch, 1965:113–4).[28] 'The progress,' Bierwisch wrote, 'of a science does not depend merely upon the amassing of individual insights, but above all upon the formulation of new relationships and the posing of new questions' (Bierwisch, 1965:114). The textlinguists who developed some of these new relationships and questions in the 1970s were attempting to handle a vast array of linguistic phenomena in the description and analysis of text that a sentence grammar couldn't (and still can't) handle; the way new and old information is structured across sentences, how tense and time are handled across sentences, how semantic relations work between sentences, pronominalization, referencing: in short, the way the text becomes coherent – a well-formed text.

That last phrase is important, because textlinguistics drew its theoretical impetus from generative linguistics. It was therefore interested in the way that *all and only* well-formed text was generated, and, like a generative linguistics of the sentence, it was therefore interested only in the system that generated the texts, not in the actual texts themselves (see Rieser, 1978). Teun van Dijk developed what he called the 'macro-structure hypothesis' (van Dijk, 1972, see also Bierwisch, 1965:113): a superstructuralist enterprise to account explicitly and formally for coherent text generation in order to produce an idealized grammar of text that 'should be considered as a more or less abstract account of the ability of native speakers to produce and understand any well-formed and interpretable text of their language' (van Dijk, 1981:4). In effect they wanted a science of text (see Petöfi and Rieser, 1973:2).

In terms of the analysis of literary text, they attempted to demonstrate 'that a certain type of work in the theory of grammar is *especially* acceptable to the study of literature' (Ihwe, 1973:301). Central to textlinguistics, however, was the proposition that there was nothing special about literature – it is conceived 'as a constitutive sub-process within the frame of all language-centred discipline' (Ihwe, 1973:309) and the study of literature is assumed to be 'an empirical and theoretical science' (314). Other textlinguists like Jens Ihwe and Robert de Beaugrande wanted to develop an empirical pragmatics of literature (de Beaugrande, 1978). The study of texts would therefore entail an enormously difficult and involved analysis. It was a programme of frightening proportions, and early analyses were *awe-ful* (as one of my students wrote when I taught a Masters course in textlinguistics).

Central to the literary theoretical enterprise in textlinguistics was Russian Formalism, as it came closest to the model textlinguists aspired to. What textlinguists wanted to do was account for the production and reception of literature, fully and systematically. Poetic language – the signal of literariness – cannot be accounted for in linguistic structures alone. This point is still valid (Ihwe, 1973:336), and, importantly, it raises questions about the 'ideological character of accepted notions of literature' (338): 'we find that verbal utterances within natural languages are very strongly dispersed, and layered, respectively, according to class' (338). The textlinguists, like the Russian Formalists, wanted to find 'organizing principles' for understanding constants in language, but here is the rub:

> It is not the means in themselves, however one will determine them, which determine the 'text-quality' of a verbal utterance, nor is it the ('arbitrary') decisions of persons P. The type-forming (or better, type-characteristic) specificity of a verbal utterance much rather takes effect in the specific manner in which formal (structural) means are organised, which may be encountered in the corresponding specificity of processing actions. (Ihwe, 1973:338)

The spectre of linguistics as a science, concerned with virtual worlds only, is always there, determining directions and informing results:

> An analysis which aims only at objectifiable contents cuts its task short; it must even appear, and especially when it has 'texts' as its objects, as nothing but a technicalised continuation or reproduction of the quasi-scientific interpretive procedures of all language-centred disciplines. It is quite another matter to attempt to build up a unified descriptive language for the language-centred disciplines, and hence to develop a categorical framework (oriented towards an extended standard logic) for the investigation of the principles governing the referential mechanisms in various types of verbal utterances. (Ihwe, 1973:341–2)

And that, in a convoluted nutshell, was the textlinguistic enterprise: the development of a *unified* theory of language in *langue* (cf. Fawcett, 1980) – an enterprise that Roger Fowler described in 1977 as 'a project of unattainable magnitude for the imaginable future' (Fowler, 1977a:66), and no wonder, when 'Its *direct aim* is to describe the knowledge of the "ideal native speaker/listener" concerning the grammatical structuredness of verbal texts, i.e. his [sic] *verbal grammatical competence*' (Petöfi, 1973:206).

The results of this work were 'disappointing', to say the least, for those who had expressed great hope for formal descriptions of text grammars, and after a few years of feverish activity and a great deal of formal logic (see van Dijk, 1973), the super-structuralist enterprise gave way among its proponents to rather more reasoned activity. Just as linguists working with literature had been unable to find the 'logical', that is, formal, step from structuralist linguistics to literary evaluation because the theory itself wouldn't allow it, so textlinguists soon realized that they were approaching the idea of text from a totally inappropriate angle. Instead of treating the text as if it worked like a sentence, they began to think of ways of describing how it *did* work. That involved shifting the unaccommodating generative/structuralist theory to one side to make room for a more suitable one. Van Dijk, who had been the first to publish a major work on textlinguistics, was also the first to problematize what he and others were doing and he argued for a pragmatic approach to text within a theory of action; that is, he argued for treating language as resource, rather than as formal internalized *rules* (see van Dijk, 1977; Schmidt, 1978; see also Green, 1982). This had been the traditional assumption for most British linguists and text analysts (see for example Halliday *et al.* 1964; Ullmann, 1964; Crystal and Davy, 1969; Halliday and Hasan, 1976; Leech and Short, 1981). It had also been the approach of Zellig Harris, whose work on discourse in the 1950s had been the impetus for Noam Chomsky.

Chomsky's work shifted the direction of text analysis as discourse analysis, which was central to Harris (see Harris, 1952a, 1952b), towards a preoccupation with the deep structure of text. This resulted in grammar becoming little more than formal derivational histories of sentences (Kress and Trew, 1978:46). Van Dijk's shift of direction signalled within the dominant generativist paradigm across the world the importance of work carried out on language as a theory of action by philosophers like J. L. Austin

(Austin, 1962) and John Searle (Searle, 1969), and sociolinguists like William Labov (Labov, 1972a, 1972b), and sociologists of interaction like Dell Hymes (Hymes, 1964) and Ervin Goffman (Goffman, 1981), who worked with text as discourse. The interests of text analysts in Britain had always lain in this direction (see, for example Quirk, 1986) and work on the analysis of text as discourse was revitalized in the 1970s as British linguistics returned, as it were, to its *parole*-based/textual roots.[29]

The structuralist linguistic approach to the analysis of text can be summarized as follows:

1 There is emphasis on the need to be formally explicit and rigorous in the analysis of linguistic structures.

2 This explicitness is designed to enable the analysis of texts to exemplify the idealized world of linguistic systems rather than the actual world of real discourses, though with critical linguistics this situation is changing.

3 There are two main approaches to structuralist linguistic analysis of text: the psychological and the sociological. Both are concerned with understanding the system of language, but the sociological is more concerned with situationally determined meanings than is the psychological.

4 The concentration on understanding linguistic systems involves a greater emphasis on universals and codes of language. This type of analysis of literary text is therefore much more about isolating universal linguistic structures, codes, and myths than it is with textual interpretations, explanations of readings, and discussions of intuitions about texts. This is the theoretical base of the structuralist linguistic enterprise, though in practice many literary-based linguists more interested in discourse analysis and textual explication than in developing theoretical arguments and philosophies concentrate on a linguistics that is effectively a language-aware practical criticism. It is therefore important to distinguish between the linguistics-theorists who conduct text analysis for systemic reasons and the applied linguists/critics who conduct text analysis for purposes of evaluation and interpretation.

Linguistic theory claims to offer explanations of the processes of communication, but so far it has done so with scarcely a glance at 'real' interaction between people. The concentration on under-standing the system of language has resulted in a marginalization of discourse analysis, with discursive meanings and formations playing a decidedly minor role in the linguistic analysis of text. The failure of structuralist linguistics to account for how texts mean, and therefore how societies and institutions mean, has been spectacular. This is the legacy of a twentieth-century preoccupation with a scientificity that has demanded explicitness and objectivity in a world that operates, for the most part, as a denial of the explicit and objective. It is therefore a scientificity that seeks to compartmentalize and pigeon-hole the world into categories and classifications – structures and relations – that allow statements to be made about idealized worlds, not actual worlds. This is a scientific, formal convention, the convenience of which has modelled the world as something that it is not – neat, ordered and unproblematic.

Critical linguistics

One of the difficulties with treating the world as neat, ordered and unproblematic is that analysis of the texts that make up that world tends also to be neat, ordered and unproblematic. In a word they tend to be lifeless. This is certainly the criticism that Roger Fowler made in his important introduction to a collection of essays he edited following a one-day conference held at the University of East Anglia in 1972. He writes of such analyses that they are 'distant from the interpretation; the poems become, paradoxically, meaningless when exposed to a technique which is supposed to reveal meaning' (Fowler, 1975b:10). He was writing, in particular, of the more formal and mechanistic analyses, and was concerned that analysis of literature should 're-connect critical interpretation and linguistic analysis . . . based on the assumption that it is legitimate to take account of the reader's response' (Fowler, 1975b:10). This approach does not advocate abandoning the techniques and insights of structuralist linguistic analysis; on the contrary, it proposes to use these techniques and insights to the full within a critical context. Nor does it suggest, as some linguistic analyses of literature had seemed to, that there is no role for any sort of literary criticism in such analyses. The question is rather 'what sort of criticism and what sort of linguistics are to be re-connected?'. For Roger Fowler and others beginning to work in what came to be known as 'new stylistics', and later widened to be known as 'critical linguistics', one crucial issue was clear: structuralist linguistics and intrinsic literary criticism needed to be considerably modified if there was to be a successful inter-face of linguistics and literature. The key to any future success would lie with *interdisciplinary* approaches to analysis. This would mean recognising the restrictions and constraints of single disci-plinary approaches to the subject, i.e. linguistics and literary criti-cism treating a literary text for their own distinct purposes. What was needed was an approach which embraced insights from other disciplines, like sociology, philosophy, history, politics and so on. Fowler wrote:

> An urgent priority for contemporary stylistics is to determine just what additional fields of knowledge are relevant to literary discourse, how they relate to the diversification of language outside of literature and, perhaps most fascinating of all to the linguistics-inclined critic, how these systems of literary know-ledge are coded in the structure of language. (Fowler, 1975b:122)

There are a number of very important points raised in what Fowler had to say here. Raising the issue of what additional fields of knowledge are relevant to literary discourse, also raises the crucial distinction between intrinsic and extrinsic criticism. To consider other fields of knowledge *other than* the text itself, a central feature of intrinsic criticism which we have seen often in the analyses in this book, is to advocate a move towards a more extrinsic form of criticism, and this move towards the more extrinsic is certainly a central tenet of critical linguistics. Moreover, the use of the term 'discourse' in 'literary discourse' is not as arbitrary as it might first appear. The work of many philosophers and social scientists, as we have seen already, had widened the reference of this term to include philosophical, social, economic and ideological contexts. Discourse no longer simply signalled an alternative word for 'text'; it signalled a political commitment to widening the notion of 'literature' by incorporating various fields of knowledge involved in the making and reception of the literary text. And of course, what this means, is that literature becomes associated with other discourses, not normally considered by many critics to be in the same league as literature, and this did (and does) create difficulties for some critics who wish to maintain the distinctiveness of their work, and more importantly, to main-tain strict boundaries marking out their discipline as a distinct discipline, different from someone else's. It is this intellectual protectionism which probably above all else is considered by critical linguists to be the most intransigent obstacle to interdisciplinary, and hence more effective, analysis of texts.

Also crucially important in Fowler's call for determining additional fields of knowledge is the role of language. As I developed in Chapter 1, forms of language are not as freely chosen as we might like to think. We choose according to circumstances, and those circumstances are ideologically and socially determined. Interpretation of those texts is therefore interpretation of socially determined language, and that means being involved as analysts in understanding the processes, functions and meanings of social interaction. This, in turn, means being involved in the politics of interaction. And this involvement is what makes the linguistics *critical* because it assumes that the links amongst people and society are not arbitrary and accidental, but are institutionally determined (see Fowler *et al*, 1979; Kress and Hodge, 1979; Kress, 1988a; Hodge, 1988). The nature of the criticism is therefore to select and deconstruct these links and to understand the patterns of meaning involved in order to understand the nature of language and society; because people categorize the world, and are categorized themselves, through language. This process of selection and deconstruction is not arbitrary either. It is informed by the insights gained from interdisciplinary approaches to understanding the world and applying those insights in a selective and critical way. This necessarily suggests to many critics, suspicious of such approaches, that the selection is subjective, and hence unscientific, and they therefore condemn the approach. But to do this is to miss the point. It is that very process of subjectivity which gives reasons for the analysis because it operates on the principle that the *form* of a text is not the only thing that critics should be concerned with. This was a central issue in the debates that Roger Fowler had with literary critics following the publication in 1966 of his *Essays on Style and Language*, in particular the debate with F. W. Bateson in the journal *Essays in Criticism*. In 'Linguistics, stylistics; criticism?' (reprinted in Fowler, 1971, 32–42) which was first published in 1966, Fowler makes the point that linguistics had reached an impasse because it did not consider criticism as part of its brief for the analysis of literary texts. This, Fowler argued, resulted in a 'blind competence' which 'has produced many a fatuous or useless analysis: technical analysis without thought or sensitivity'

(Fowler, 1971:33). Mere description of texts was not sufficient because it was not critical. It was too thorough in the sense that it could 'lay bare the formal structure of the language in more detail than any critic would want' (Fowler, 1971:38). The point about linguistics was that it was not selective: 'It describes everything, and all data are of equal significance' (Fowler, 1971:39). For *critical* analysis 'one must know (or have some at least marginally positive clue) *why* one is undertaking verbal analysis: and this knowledge will inevitably direct the manner of the analysis' (Fowler, 1971:39). Despite caveats like this, there was considerable hostility expressed by some critics towards any sort of linguistic analysis of literature, to the extent that one reviewer of Fowler's 1966 essays went so far as to say that 'linguists as a species are incapable of treating literature' (Fowler, 1971:44). Such objections were unfounded, but indicative of the protections some non-linguists felt had to be put around themselves and their discipline. Critics of linguistic analysis of literature felt that linguists had to produce revelations about the texts which were gained from formal, 'objective', analysis of the language of the texts, in order to justify their incursions into the literary field. Such revelations weren't evident, and so the analyses were condemned. In his reply to a review by Helen Vendler of his 1966 volume of essays, Roger Fowler made it clear that his position was not that linguistics claimed to have a sensitivity about literature which literary critics did not have, but that the 'closest claim is that the consciousness, concentration and fidelity to text demanded by the act of analysis may help in working out hunches about a work, and may aid in catching effects possibly missed through laziness' (Fowler, 1971:51). The accusation of laziness, amongst other things, was bound to provoke response because it touched on the central issue of language analysis. F. W. Bateson, the editor of *Essays in Criticism*, responded with a view that the problem with linguistic analysis of literature was that it *required* the analysis of language in a text. His position was that 'For the native speaker, except occasionally and superficially, this is simply not true' (Fowler, 1971:62). In other words native speakers of English, for example, knew all there was to know about language without needing linguistics to help them. Bateson was of the opinion that language was a separate activity to literary meaning – a preliminary to understanding the style of a literary text, which in turn was a preliminary to the *literary* response 'in its fullest sense' (Fowler, 1971:79). Linguistics had therefore been disqualified, as Fowler made clear in his response to Bateson, as 'a discipline of relevance to literature' (Fowler, 1971:65). Bateson's position, of course, confuses the distinction between knowing *about* a language, and knowing a language, and it is this 'knowing about' which is a crucial part of defining the notion of critical analysis for Fowler. At the time of his debate with Bateson the 'about' was still mainly concerned with the formal structures of language, but this developed into a more detailed awareness of the social, functional, and ideological meanings involved in language, as we saw in Chapter 1.

There are, as Roger Fowler and Gunther Kress make clear, 'strong and pervasive connections between linguistic structure and social structure' (Fowler and Kress, 1979:185), to the extent that linguistic meaning is inseparable from ideology. This also applies to critical linguistics itself, and, as a consequence, not only should linguistic analysis be aware of the ideologies involved in the construction and reception of discourse, it should also be aware of the theoretical and methodological assumptions which form its own practice. The structures of language cannot be separated from language use; texts are 'the linguistic part of complicated communicative interactions' (Fowler and Kress, 1979:195) which are in turn 'implicated in social processes' (Fowler and Kress, 1979:195). Language, they argue, is 'not just a *reflex* of social processes and structures', but contributes 'instrumentally to the consolidation of existing social structures and material conditions' (Fowler and Kress, 1979:195–6). As Robert Hodge and Gunther Kress make clear in their most recent book, *Social Semiotics*, a theory of language 'has to be seen in the context of a theory of all sign systems as socially constituted, and treated as social practices' (Hodge and Kress, 1988). Interpretation, therefore, 'is the process of recovering the social meanings expressed in discourse by analysing the linguistic structures in the light of their interactional and wider social contexts' (Fowler and Kress, 1979:196). As the contributors to the volume edited by Roger Fowler *et al* entitled *Language and Control* (Fowler *et al*, 1979) make clear, and in the words of Gunther Kress and Robert Hodge, 'Language is an instrument of control as well as of communication' (Kress and Hodge, 1979:6). People can therefore be both informed and manipulated by language, and of course can inform and manipulate others. Theories of language are therefore theories of ideology and as such are organized presentations, in one way or another, of realities (Kress and Hodge, 1979:15). In that respect a critical linguistic approach is not concerned with developing a theory of language which is specific to literary texts only, but attempts to theorize language as ideology with respect to all texts, whether they are poems, Mafia underworld language or liturgical responses. As Kress makes clear 'all texts are subject to the same linguistic and social determinations, so-called literary texts no less than so-called non-literary texts' (Kress, 1988b:127) – a shift in thinking which is characteristic of critical linguistics and which I developed in detail in Chapter 1 of this book.

This shift in direction within critical linguistics and discourse analysis, away from the privileging of literature as a high culture text needing to be treated sensitively, towards an analysis which has the potential of including any text, might suggest a levelling of all texts to a single common denominator. This would be true if the analyses were carried out without rhyme or reason, but they are not. *Why* the analysis is being carried out determines the choice of texts. The 'why', within critical linguistics at least, has tended to be politically motivated, as we saw with several of the analyses in Chapter 1, not least with concerns of class and gender injustices. What this means, of course, is that from an intrinsic critical viewpoint, critical linguistics is concerned with matters usually considered extrinsic to both the text and to literary/linguistic analysis. But it is this very 'extrinsicity' which is, for critical linguists, the crucial focal point, because it is this that determines the 'why' of the analysis. It also importantly suggests that critical linguistic analyses need to be *intertextual*, i.e. aware of other texts and readings which inform the ideological processes involved, and it is with such intertextual approaches that some of the most interesting work is being produced (see Threadgold, 1988; Thibault, 1988; Kress, 1988a, 1988b; Birch, 1986, 1988b). An example of my own work might be a useful way of closing this chapter and indicating what an intertextual approach to the analysis of text looks like.

Critical linguistics: a sample text analysis

Mudrooroo Narogin (Colin Johnson) is an Aboriginal writer (in English) living in Australia. His most recent publication (after four novels) is a collection of poems, *The Song Circle of Jacky and Selected Poems* (Johnson, 1986). There are a number of poems in this collection which I keep returning to as a way of balancing the biased white Australian presentation of Aboriginal issues in the various media, not least at a time when Australia counts the number of Aboriginal deaths in State prisons and police lock-ups in the last ten years in the hundreds, and when the issue of Aboriginal land rights is still a long way from ever being justly resolved. I return in particular to one titled 'Encapsulated' – why I do is the point of the analysis.

Encapsulated

I

Once we wanted bread, you gave us indigestible stone;
Once we wanted bread, collected by our own hands:
Our paradise was in our being,
Our being was our paradise.

II

5 We were shameless,
They came and gave us shame;
We were innocent,
They came and gave us guilt.

III

Once our brains were fluid with thoughts;
10 Once our brains moved with the world;
Once our minds were unbounded as the land,
The sky was our resting place,
Our minds the sky of our brains.
Now we are marked by roads
15 Leading to towns of congealed thought;
Now our brains are laid out neatly;
Now our thoughts cannot wander;
But must keep to the highways which lead
To the imposed capital cities of their states of mind;
20 Even the skyways of our going lead straight on
Surveyed by the unswerving thoughts of their aeroplanes.

IV

Where are the roads we must follow?
Here they are, laid straight out,
Tarred and cemented, sticky with distant goals.
25 Where are those goals we must reach?
Here they are, thickly bound in this book,

Where are our souls which we must lead?
Here, in this church, strong-walled as a prison cell.

I read this as a very powerful political statement about the oppression that has been meted out to the Aboriginal people at the hands of white Australia, though neither Aboriginal people nor white Australia are specifically mentioned. I have formed that particular reading, simple though it is, *extrinsically*, but triggered by intrinsic linguistic structures. I have gone through an interpretive process which has contextualized those triggers, and it is that process of contextualizing – what might be termed a *reading formation* – which forms the focus of the analysis. Why? Because based on my reading of the poem I would then want to make statements about the text as a political statement. I want to draw inferences, based on my reading of this and other texts, about the poem as part of a discourse of aggression against political forces oppressing Aboriginal people in Australia. In order to do that I need to justify my reading process.

In other words, I am not simply involved in an intrinsic practical criticism of the poem in order to articulate its meaning, or to propose that through analysis I can 'access' the intentions of the poet. What I am involved in is understanding and articulating my own reading formation, and this is necessarily an intertextual process.

Issues of power and solidarity form a major part of my reading for 'Encapsulated'. These issues are triggered in the main, for me, by pronouns. Isolated from the rest of the text they read like this:

I

we   you   us
we   our
our   our
our   our

II

we
They   us
We
They   us

III

our
our
our
our
our   our
we
our
our
their
our
their

IV

we
they
we
they
our   we

The opening line establishes the contrast of *we you us*. I want to read this in terms of a time progression and feel that I can, given the prominence of the 'once' adverb. I want to read the opening line as 'Once there was 'we'; then there was 'you'; and then there will be 'us'. Power shifts hands from the original 'we' to the 'you' and then back to the 'us' — not to 'you' and 'us' but to 'us' only. The progression is made all the stronger by the fact that 'you' and 'us' are not used again. What becomes the dominant pronoun system is a contrast between 'we'/'our' and 'they'/'their'. This shift from 'you' to 'they' I think is particularly significant. Moving from second to third person pronouns is not an arbitrary meaningless move signalling different participants — it is a shift in point of view of the same participants. But once made, the move puts a much greater distance between the participants — between the 'we' and the 'you'. The distance is an important part of my reading of this poem, but more than that, it is the dynamics of the move that is made to create that distance which strikes me as even more powerful. To distance yourself from someone or something that you find distasteful, for example, is made much more strikingly if there is a physical movement *away* and not simply a verbal expression of distaste. That physical

movement *away* has been made by the move away from 'we'
and 'you' to 'we' and 'they'.

It is striking, I think, because it is a contrast that relies on
an opposition between *subject* and *owner*. The 'we' and 'they'
pronouns are subject pronouns; the 'our' and 'their' are
possessive pronouns signalling ownership of one form or another.
But who are the subjects of the 'we' pronoun? Who are the
subjects of the 'they' pronoun? Who or what is possessed by the
'our' pronoun? Who or what is possessed by the 'their' pronoun?

Reading other poems in the collection gives me some answers.
The 'they' are the 'people a long way from home' (Song Six,
17) who wreck the land and who 'go on and on without accepting
our land' (Song Six, 17) and who call all Aboriginals 'Jacky':

> They give Jacky rights,
> Like the tiger snake gives rights to its prey;
> They give Jacky rights,
> Like the rifle sights on its target.
> They give Jacky rights,
> Like they give rights to the unborn baby.
> Ripped from the womb by its unloving mother.
> (Song Eight, 19)

They are the 'they' who 'march on Anzac Day morning'; who
'shout on Anzac Day afternoon' and who on Anzac Day evening
'discuss old matches, old campaigns, old seasons and old wars'
(Song Four, 15). They are the 'they' of the popular patriotic
novel of Allan Marshall, *These Are My People* (Marshall, 1944),
who according to the blurb on the dustjacket of the 1972 edition
are the 'ordinary Aussies. The men and women who were
prepared to stand and fight, not for the glories of war or for
plunder, but because they believed that the defence of freedom
and liberty is the right of all mankind [*sic*] and not the right of a
handful of dictators.' Whereas the 'we' is Jacky who 'arrived here
long ago' (Song Fifteen, 26); who 'walks down a street, the street
all white' and who 'sits in a show, the laughter all white' (Song
Fourteen, 25). But who is prepared to shout 'we want our rights!
Our traditional land to be ours for ever' (Song Eleven, 22); who
can demand that compensation be paid 'To those forced off their
lands by alien hands' (Song Eleven, 22). They are the 'we', 'the
poor boong' who has 'tasted the wine, And forgot his culture,
forgot his dancing feet' (Lord Help Us, 86).

This contrast, then, between the 'we' and the 'they' – the

subjects – and the 'ours' and 'theirs' – the owners – is a crucially important one and I read it as supported in several ways by other triggers in the poem. One of these ways is in the *nominalizations*. A nominalization is a phrase which functions like a single noun but which relies for its meaning on a verbal process of some description. For example the phrase 'the imposed capital cities' in line 19 is most effectively understood in terms of a *process* of someone imposing something on someone. Who is the someone that does the imposing? What is the something? Who is the someone that has the something imposed upon them? We can answer only one of those questions with direct evidence from the text and that is that it is 'capital cities' which are imposed by someone upon someone. The *what* is therefore answered intrinsically. The *who* has to be answered extrinsically, though in my reading I would want to suggest that it is the 'they' who do the imposing and the 'we' who are imposed upon. The point of the nominalization is that it leaves these questions unanswered – the *agents* of the action and those *affected* by the action are often hidden from view and therefore require inferences to be made as to identities. This can be of particular significance in situations, for example, where the agent of an action is manipulated out of sight in order to prevent specific participants from being openly identified, as we saw with the analyses by Hasan and Keyser above (pp. 51–53). But there are also other significant ways of constructing meaning with nominalizations, one of which is to demonstrate the power of one participant – the agent – over the other participant – the affected. For example 'the unswerving thoughts of their aeroplanes' (line 21) is a nominalization which suggests to me a process something like 'someone has made the thoughts of their aeroplanes in an unswerving way', in other words there is an agent who is responsible for a mode of travel (and probably more importantly given my reading of the metaphor here, a mode of thought and culture) which is *straight* and unswerving. I understand a word like 'unswerving' in terms of its contrast 'swerving', i.e. a contrast between straight and non-straight. The point of the nominalization, therefore, is to suggest that the agent has created not simply straight modes of travel, or straight modes of thinking, but has created *difference* between the agent and the affected. Again, the adverbs, contrasting 'once' and 'now' suggest this as a *movement* involving *time*. Importantly then, the nominalization involves the power of an agent over an affected, for example 'the skyways of our going' (line 20) involves the creation of skyways by someone – and that someone seems clearly to be the 'they' of the poem' not the 'we' – and they are created to the extent that the 'we' of the poem seems to have no choice but to follow the ways directed by the 'they'. The 'we' is therefore oppressed by the 'they', though this is often seen by the 'they' as the faults and inadequacies of the 'we' and not as a direct result of their oppressive activities, an issue (treated ironically) which does not go unnoticed in the following poem from the same collection:

> Sing sadness, sing sadness over our land;
> Sing sadness, sing sadness throughout our land;
> We have failed ourselves, sing sadness.
> Poor Jacky Jacky tasted the wine,
> And forgot his culture, his ceremonies,
> Sing sadness, sing sadness, English culture,
> Sing sadness, A Dreaming from a faraway land,
> Where the sun does not take revenge, revenging
> Itself on white flesh bared in a black land;
> Revenging itself on a white culture reshaping our land.
>
> (Lord Help Us, 96)

There are roads and goals which have to be followed – roads and goals which are now a different 'Dreaming'. Where once the Aboriginal Dreaming was understood in terms of 'Our paradise was in our being, Our being was our paradise' (lines 3–4) it is now overshadowed by another Dreaming determined by white Australia – a Dreaming created by others so that 'our brains are laid out neatly' (line 16) by who? 'our thoughts cannot wander (line 17) why not? Because the 'once' has been transformed by someone into a 'now' which is straight and foreign compared to a time when people were not constrained by this straightness, when 'our brains moved with the world' (line 10) and 'our brains were unbounded as the land' (line 11). But now 'we are marked by roads' (line 14) built by what agent? I don't have that information directly because the passive 'are marked' has the effect of hiding the agent involved. Similarly in line 11 the passive hides the agent of the process 'our minds were unbounded', by who or what? Again in line 16 'our brains are laid out neatly' by who or what? and in line 23 the roads 'are laid straight out', they are tarred and cemented, they are sticky – again who or what is the agent of these processes?

Of the agents involved in the passives in the text, only two seem to be associated with the 'we' (lines 9, 10) while all the others seem to suggest the 'they'. I put it like this, rather than saying the 'we' is the agent of the process 'were fluid' and 'were unbounded' because I do not read the 'we' as being directly responsible for their own actions in these processes. This is an important part of my reading, because the contrast that I have constructed for this reading is not one between an active 'we' responsible totally for their own actions at one point of time versus an active 'they' who have at a later point of time oppressed these actions, but a 'we' whose actions are *now* controlled by human agency where *once* they were controlled by a non-human agency. In other words the extent of the oppression is not simply that of oppressing a person's own active agency but of oppressing a cultural agency. Consequently where thoughts were once fluid because of this cultural agency, the 'we' is now being led by the straightness of the oppressor into towns (not unbound lands (line 11)) of 'congealed thought' (line 15). Again, the adjectival phrase 'congealed thought' is most effectively understood as a verbal process because an agent is responsible for the act of congealing. The contrast, therefore between straightness and non-straightness is an important one, because it operates very effectively as an image of oppressive change. In 'City Suburban Lines' the image is developed more fully, but is still tied very firmly to the pronoun distinction between 'ours' and 'theirs':

Their roads are straight;
Their streets are straight;
Their fences are straight;
Straight are the bricks
Of their walls,
As straight as the lines
Of their vehicle-minds,
Rushing in straight thoughts
To straight feelings.

Straight is the world they have fashioned;
Straight are the walls of their imprisoning cells;
Straight are the lives we are forced to endure:
Born between straight lines;
Dying between straight lines;
Laid to rest between straight lines,
Buried in rows as straight as supermarket goods;
Our heaven will be straight lines;

Our hell will be all curved lines,
Unable to fit the straightness of our souls. (84)

My reading, therefore is that there are two subjects involved,
a 'we' and a 'they'; that the 'they' is an oppressor of the 'we',
not simply because they have changed the life-styles of the 'we'
but because they have imposed an alien agency upon the culture
and thought-processes of the 'we'. The 'we' are the Aboriginal
people of Australia and the 'they' is the institution of white Australia. More importantly, perhaps, I read the text not simply as
an expression of this oppression, but as a political statement
which requires active involvement by readers to interpret the
agents on both 'sides' of the divide. Frank Roberts in 'Being an
Aboriginal in Australian Society' puts it like this:

> The oppression and depression thrust upon us by the govern-
> ments of Australia and by the people as a whole, force us to
> emerge as a power structure related to politics and culture, and
> to all the directions that can make us a powerful pressure group
> in our confrontations with the Australian nation. (Roberts,
> 1971:19)

and continues:

> No matter in what direction you turn in Australia today you
> will find strong anti-Aboriginal attitudes, expressed in political
> and spiritual discriminations. There will emerge a radical group
> of Aborigines who will confront these attitudes on the ground
> that they cannot tolerate the situation and must take drastic
> steps to remove the blots, curses, blemishes that have so under-
> mined and desecrated them. (Roberts, 1971:19)

And Pearl Gibbs, a 72-year-old speaking in 1972 put it like this:

> There's no white man, or woman, who has that feeling we
> have. They can study us all they like, but we've got them
> studied too. Because this is *our* country – the country of my
> mother's mother – a full-blooded Australian Aborigine. And it
> is *my* country. Always remember this. My Australian Aborigines
> did not go to England and claim it and then leave a whole lot
> of mixed bloods who no-one wants. It is *our* country. It belongs
> to us, it is precious to us. And that is something no white man
> will ever understand. . . . (Gilbert:1973:12)

This requires a participation by the reader or listener which

164 Language, Literature and Critical Practice

involves them in a dynamic process of interpretation. This is true of 'Encapsulated' too. Interpretation therefore means becoming involved in the political world of the poem, in just as active a way as would be required in a street march or rally of opposition. To concentrate on this poem as though it fitted comfortably into a literary mould by emphasizing literary effects and preoccupations would, I think, reduce the reading from a politically radical and dynamic process to a passive, less politically potent reading and to put it on a par with the easy comfortableness of an uncaring white Australia – the sort of thing that one of the characters created by Barry Humphries (known to many as Dame Edna Everage) had to say in a 1962 sketch entitled 'Operation Oz-Image' and spoken by Humphries in the role of a Minister for National Identity developing a super-plan for creating a national Australian identity:

> The Aboriginal population of Australia, it must be admitted, presented us with a big problem at first. We were faced with a choice between a continuance of the accepted program of benevolent neglect or elimination and the creation of the standard Ab-image. In view of their potential as a tourist attraction we decided on the latter course. To make this colourful species conform to an Ab-image presented no difficulty whatsoever since Nature had assisted us by rendering all members of this dusky race absolutely identical to one another in every respect. Consequently work on this phase is now virtually complete. They have all been issued with white knee-length Palaco shirts, we've got the birth rate constant and tourists can now at any time of the day or night visit the new flood-lit Ab-image tribe sites and be guaranteed a good show. A first rate squad of trainers has got them at their bark-carving, cave-painting, boomerang-throwing and bone-pointing and doing the standard corroboree as never before ... (Humphries, 1981:64–65)

This is actually meant to be funny and was published as 'funny' in 1981. Compare Song Fourteen from *The Song Circle of Jacky*:

> It's strange how some people can laugh at rape;
> It's strange how some people can laugh at murder,
> Pain, stupidity, ignorance and last year's losers.
> It's strange how laughter often is a grimace of contempt,
> Directed at what we fear, hate, or want to mistrust. (25)

This appalling Humphries humour and the horrors it really signifies is a major part of the context by which I read 'Encapsulated'. The voice I have constructed for this poem, using the triggers constructed by Mudrooroo Narogin, is uncompromising – relentless in its pursuit of the Aboriginal cause. It has to be in the light of the injustice and oppression which has continued for two hundred years, and continues still. Example: a case brought before the Commission for Community Relations in Perth, Western Australia (Hotel 81/7583) in 1981. A hotel sign which portrayed an Aboriginal on whose distended stomach the week's beer specials were written caused offence to some Aboriginals and a complaint was made. The verdict: dissemination of ideas based on racial superiority or hatred is not unlawful under the Racial Discrimination Act of 1975.

This, then, is also a part of the process involved in my reading formations for this poem. It is a reading which views the poem as demanding its readers to bring about change in an unjust situation. The cause that argues for such change is bigger, more important and certainly more consuming than the more usual concerns analysts tend to get involved in in criticism. My reading of this poem suggests that it is not simply a commentary on the past, or a recognition of the here and now, but an important part of a political discourse demanding political action and change. As a reader I cannot simply assume the role of innocent bystander. My critical position – my analysis – is a political act, as indeed *all* criticism is. What is generally articulated within critical linguistics is that we recognize the political acts we are involved in and make those the reasons why we do the analyses and choose the texts we choose.

Afterword

The critical study of language is a study not just of the structures of language and texts, but of the people and institutions that shape the various ways language means. In a functional theory of language, analysts are not just interested in *what* language is, but *why* language is; not just in *what* language means, but *how* language means. In the critical linguistics that has developed since the mid-1970s, which forms the base of Chapter 1 in this book and against which many of the ideas outlined in the other chapters are problematized, the assumption is that the relationship between the form and content of texts is not arbitrary or conventional, but that it is determined (and constrained) culturally, socially, and ideologically by the power of institutional/discursive formations. The choices and selections that producers of text therefore make from the system of language are principled choices, instituted by social, messy, 'real' worlds of discourse, not by idealized abstract worlds. The structures – the forms – of language do not pre-exist social and cultural processes; they are not encoded in some sort of psychological imprint. The forms, and hence meanings, of language are shaped and determined by institutional forces. Analysis of text, therefore, according to this way of thinking, is analysis of ideologically loaded structures and meanings, not of innocent, arbitrary, random structures. Answering the question of how texts mean therefore answers the question of how institutions mean. This is therefore analysis concerned with discourse as process, not with language as idealized product.

Paul Ricoeur argues that structuralist linguistics excluded too many important aspects of language phenomena, most importantly the *act* of speaking, that is, language as performance (Ricoeur, 1981). Analysis of text that marginalizes language as meaningful activity therefore marginalizes (and, as we have seen, often excludes) the primary aim of language, which is to say something about something to someone, in order to *do* something. Ricoeur's hermeneutics, that is, his theory of linguistic interpretation, is consequently discourse-based, and it is a text-based/discourse-based approach to language that has formed the standpoint of this book. It has done so in order to demonstrate the need for text analysis to focus upon the messy, indeterminate world of meanings, to recognize that discourse is self-referential inasmuch as all language, even a single word, functions as text and refers in some ways or another to its producer, because discourse is realized in 'real' time and is always about something and, as a consequence, 'refers to a world which it claims to describe, to express, to represent' (Ricoeur, 1981:198). Discourse is also about interaction and exchange; about people, institutions, power, and status; about relationships and differences. In such circumstances analysis of text becomes more than just an attempt to recover meanings, 'it is always interpretation always criticism, always, as with Heidegger, a process of understanding 'discourse as projecting a world' (202). Texts have no fixed meanings, no centres of signification, no routes to closure. Analysing text is therefore about interpreting language as meaningful action. It is a process of guessing and construing possible meanings, – possible readings; it is a 'cumulative, holistic process' (213), never right or correct, never completed, never closed:

> . . . understanding has nothing to do with an immediate grasping of a foreign psychic life or with an *emotional* identification with a meaningful intention. Understanding is entirely *mediated* by the whole of explanatory procedures which precede it and accompany it. The counterpart of this personal appropriation is not something which can be *felt*, it is the dynamic meaning released by the explanation . . . its power of disclosing as world. (Ricoeur, 1981:220)

Critical linguists argue that it is through and with language that we classify and therefore make sense of such worlds. We therefore experience the world because of language. We do not relate *directly* to the world except through a mediating system of classifications and categorizations. These classifications differ from group to group, society to society, ideology to ideology. Analysis of the classifications of language is therefore analysis of ideologies. Structuralist linguistics and intrinsic criticism have not, for the most part, been concerned with such things because they have been concerned with idealized worlds, not 'real' worlds of discourse. Roger Fowler made the point some years ago that 'contemporary linguistics cannot be absorbed into criticism without real modification' (Fowler, 1985a:120). That modification rests firmly on a recognition that analysis of text – literary or otherwise – needs to treat text as discourse, needs, in Saussurean terms, to be *parole*-based. The resultant, re-oriented, linguistics needs to recognize that all texts are multi-levelled, multi-layered, multi-meaninged; that these meanings are not the sole property of the speaker/writer but are constructed and produced in communicative interaction; it needs to recognize the importance of 'real' discourse with its messiness and fuzzy edges; to be concerned with language as showing and doing, and not just with language as saying; to recognize that the judgements and choices we make in producing texts and making meanings are not arbitrary, but are institutionally and therefore ideologically determined; and that analysing text is analysing discourse.

Notes

1 How texts mean: reading as critical/political practice

1 See Giles, 1987, for an application of some of Lukács' ideas on the novel to D. H. Lawrence's *St Mawr*.

2 See also Rorty, 1979, where he centres interaction/conversation in a philosophy of language.

3 For a feminist reading of *A Scots Quair*, the trilogy by Lewis Grassic Gibbons, see Burton, 1984.

4 For a fascinating interface of feminist criticism and biblical studies see Collins, 1985; Russell, 1985; Kaiser, 1987.

5 For a study of women's language in prophecy and testimony in pentecostal services in Southern Indiana see Lawless, 1983, and for a similar analysis of masculine language/style see Schwenger, 1984; Sedgwick, 1985.

6 See, for example, Rosenfeld, 1984, for a discussion of the innovative language and style of French writer Monique Wittig.

7 Cf. Selden, 1985:66.7, for a similar, though less formal, experiment.

8 Cf. Irving Massey, who argues that contemporary linguistics is *too* concerned, not innocent enough, and 'condemned to perpetual responsibility' (Massey, 1970:97).

9 Cf. the discussion in St Clair, 1978:50, where he talks about cultural pluralism reducing abuses against minorities, and 1978:53f on the language of oppression; see also St Clair, 1982, for similar issues.

10 See Guback, 1967, for an analysis of the various ways in which a speech by John F. Kennedy was treated on a number of radio and television stations; see also Medhurst, 1987, for a similar analysis of a speech by Dwight D. Eisenhower; see also Moss, 1985, on the rhetoric of defence in the US; Richardson, 1985, on speeches against the peace movement in the UK, and the various papers in Chilton, 1985.

11 For work on the language/discourse of schizophrenics see Rochester and Martin, 1979.

12 For work developing this sort of analysis of newspaper discourse see Hartley and Montgomery, 1985; Cohen and Young, 1973; Ellis, 1982; Hartley, 1982; Trew, 1979; Hodge, 1979.

2 Language, literature and scientific fictions

1 See Toolan, 1984, for a critique of Fish, 1980.
2 Perhaps Barry should have read what he wrote in an earlier critique of linguistics and literary criticism, when he said: 'Can there still be people who believe in the "innocence" of language, or of any other medium?' (Barry, 1980:138; see also Grundy, 1981, for a response.)
3 See Gauker, 1987:56f for just such an account, posited by the philosopher Gottfried Wilhelm von Leibnitz.
4 See Fowler, 1979, for an account of the shift from singular to plural views of language.
5 There are many accounts of structuralist practice and theory; the three I would most recommend, for accounts which do not, as most do, retell the same old story, are Petitt, 1977; Falck, 1986; White, 1974.

3 Reading literary texts: traditions, assumptions, practices

1 See Widdowson, 1982, and Batsleer, et al., 1985; see also Hawkes, 1986; Mulhern, 1979; Durant, 1985; Brumfit and Carter, 1986.

4 Reading texts closely: language, style and 'the buried life of words'

1 See the discussion on the Spanish critic Damaso Alonso in Greenwood, 1965. Alonso argued, like Spitzer, for close readings of texts, initiated by intuition (cf. Carter, 1982a). Greenwood follows this principle in a close stylistic analysis of George Herbert's sonnet 'Prayer'.
2 See Mason, 1982, for an analysis that follows Spitzer's notion of the 'click' in the first four paragraphs of Charles Dickens's Little Dorrit.
3 For later debates on this see Bateson, 1972, and his criticism of Sebeok, 1960; Spencer and Gregory 1964; Fowler, 1966a; see also King, 1980; Norris, 1985b, for similar debates.
4 See also Grundy, 1981, for an analysis of a passage from Thomas Hardy's Tess of the d'Urbervilles in response to Barry, 1980, arguing that linguistics had nothing of value to say for literary studies. But see also Weber, 1982 on a passage from Virginia Woolf's The Waves, suggesting that linguists might have something to learn from literary scholars (in particular mode, tense, and aspect of the English verb); a study by Zelda Boyd on the modal auxiliaries of Jane Austen's Sense and Sensibility (Boyd, 1983), and Toolan, 1983, where he looks at progressive verbs in William Faulkner's Go Down, Moses.
5 See also Cluysenaar, 1976:53–7 for a similar linguistic treatment by

Leavis of a passage from *Paradise Lost*. An interesting comparison could also be made between Carter, 1982a, and Bateson, 1950:167–72, who both analyse closely W. H. Auden's 'Oxford' – Bateson with what Paul de Man has called in another context his 'robust literalism' (de Man, 1979:84), and Carter with a concern for pedagogy. Bateson concentrates on an early version of the poem and Carter on a later one. See also D'haen, 1983, and Birch, 1984a, for collections of papers dealing with the relations of linguistics and literary criticism.

6 For extended discussions of this proposition, including refutations of it, see, for example, Quinn, 1982; Posner, 1982; Werth, 1976; Fowler, 1981; Fish, 1973b. See also the detailed linguistic/structural analysis by John Sinclair on Wordsworth's 'Tintern Abbey', where he argues that there is nothing special about literary languge (Sinclair, 1972b).

7 Cf. Saha, 1968, for a similar approach, following, in the main, Enkvist, 1964 and Spencer and Gregory, 1964 (particularly their analysis of Yeats's 'The Hero, the Girl, and the Fool', 17–21).

5 The linguistics of text: structures and strictures

1 See Rader, 1974a, 1974b, for attacks on Fish; and also Dillon, 1978. See Pratt, 1982/3, for a detailed account of reader-response theory, and also Suleiman and Crossman, 1980; Tompkins, 1980. For a radically different approach to reading see Sharratt, 1982, and for a contemporary version of practical criticism approaches to reading see Kintgen, 1983; Lumsden, 1987.

2 For a contemporary use of Jakobson in an attempt to develop an African semiotic, see Anozie, 1981:126–87 and Ngara, 1982.

3 See Freadman, 1986, and also Kirstein, 1982, for a theoretical application of Peircean concepts to stylistic analysis, though rather oddly Kirstein says that she will not actually conduct a semiotic analysis for fear that 'an unconvincing semiotic interpretation may lead to nothing more than student rejection of semiotics as a method of literary analysis' (Kirstein, 1982:9).

4 For detailed discussion of Jakobson's theory see Michels, 1982, which contains an analysis of selections from James Joyce's *Ulysses* that applies the Jakobsonian adage that 'The poetic function projects the principle of equivalence from the axis of selection into the axis of combination' (Michels, 1982:25).

5 See also Culler, 1975, for an analysis of Sonnet 129 and, for a study that sets out in some ways to add to Jakobson and Jones, see Brinton, 1985. See also Vendler, 1973, for a comparison of the treatment of the sonnet both in Jakobson and Jones and in Richards

1970; see also Ehrlich, 1973; Melchiori, 1976:120–58, Skinner, 1973:199–209; Rosen, 1971.

6 For a similar analysis designed to account for the differences in two versions of Yeats's 'Sorrow of Love' see Jakobson and Rudy, 1980.

7 See Riding and Graves; 1928, Empson, 1930:50–51 for close readings of Sonnet 29, but based on different theoretical assumptions. Riding and Graves wrote a pioneering account of detailed close reading of literary texts and influenced Empson so much that he wrote most of *Seven Types of Ambiguity* as an undergraduate dissertation in *two weeks*. His tutor was I. A. Richards, who later wrote: 'He seemed to have read more English Literature and to have read it more recently and better, so our roles were soon in danger of being reversed.' (Cited in Bradbrook, 1974:4.) For a comparison of analyses of Sonnet 73 by Roger Fowler, Winifred Nowottny, and Anthony Easthope, see Birch, 1988a. For a comparison of different approaches to Sonnet 94, see Easthope, 1983.

8 See Medvedev and Bakhtin, 1978, and Jauss, 1974, for a critique of formalism.

9 See Posner, 1982, for a detailed reaction to Jakobson and Lévi-Strauss, 1962, working through some of the structuralist ideas of Jurij Lotman, 1977; see also Boon, 1972:38–61, for a detailed account of the Jakobson and Lévi-Strauss analysis of 'Les Chats', and Riffaterre, 1966, for a scathing attack on it.

10 This is developed in Lévi-Strauss, 1958, but for a fascinating display of the use of four-term homologies 'within and between four Sunday Express front-page news stories' see Hartley and Montgomery, 1985:241–5.

11 See Kantor *et al.*, 1982, for work that combines linguistics, psychology, narratology, and story grammars in examining children's text; see also Barthes, 1966; Prince, 1973; Ruthrof, 1981. For more particular studies see Jahner, 1983, in which she looks at a Dakota Indian story; Witherspoon, 1980, in which he looks at a Navajo story; and Urban, 1984, for an analysis of a Shokleng story. See also Bliss and MacCormac, 1981, for a contrast with generative approaches and Barthes/Lévi-Straussian approaches using Wallace Stevens's 'The Sense of Sleight of Hand Man'; and Carter, 1982c, 1984; Stubbs, 1983:194–211; and Friberg, 1982, for different analyses of Ernest Hemingway's 'Cat in the Rain'. See also Wilbur *et al.*, 1973, for five different analyses of Robert Lowell's 'Skunk Hour'.

12 For an analysis of Arthur Conan Doyle's 'The Sussex Vampire' following narrative techniques developed by the Russian structuralist poetics movement and the functional linguistics of M. A. K. Halliday, see O'Toole, 1975, and see also O'Toole, 1982 for a development of these practices with some Russian short stories. For a narrative analysis of a passage from Arthur Conan Doyle and J. Dickson

Carr's *The Exploits of Sherlock Holmes* using the transformational generative linguistics of Chomsky, 1957, 1965, see Pavel, 1973; see also Belsey, 1980:109–17.

13 See Levin, 1970, for a detailed account of coupling using Shakespeare's Sonnet 30.

14 For a similar analysis integrating form and meaning in this way see Keyser, 1980, on four Wallace Stevens poems.

15 See also Todorov, 1981.

16 See also Kuhn, 1962 – a very influential book in the last two decades, and one that develops a lot of Whorf's ideas. See also Dillon, 1982, for the development of Whorf's ideas for stylistics.

17 And that is exactly what J. P. Thorne did (Thorne, 1965, 1970). See also some of the analyses of literary text in Closs Traugott and Pratt, 1980, which have been influenced by generative linguistics; see Fodor, 1980, for a general account of meaning in a generativist approach.

18 See Schauber and Spolsky, 1981, 1984, for a development of generative approaches to literary theory and rules of reading.

19 See Barton, 1985, for a discussion, sympathetic to generativist positions (through Schauber and Spolsky, 1981), of Chomsky, Halliday and Fowler as the leading competitors in linguistic interpretation of literary text.

20 For other analyses of 'Leda and the Swan' see Spitzer, 1954, and an account of his in comparison to Halliday's in Robey, 1982:59–63, Widdowson's analysis (1975:7–14), and three analyses from different perspectives, including Halliday's, in Butler, 1984:36–46.

21 See also John Sinclair's analysis of Philip Larkin, 'First Sight' (Sinclair, 1966), Roger Fowler's analysis of the 'Sermo Lupi' (Fowler, 1966c); Geoffrey Leech's analysis of Dylan Thomas, 'This Bread I Break' (Leech, 1965); Archibald Hill's analysis of Gerard Manley Hopkins, 'The Windhover' (Hill, 1955), Seymour Chatman's analysis of Robert Frost, 'Mowing' (Chatman, 1956); Sumner Ives on Andrew Marvell, 'To His Coy Mistress' (Ives, 1962) and Nelson Francis on Dylan Thomas, 'Alterwise by Owl-light' (Francis, 1967).

22 See O'Toole, 1988, on Henry Reed's 'Naming of Parts'; Hasan, 1988, on Anne Sexton's 'Old', and the analyses in general in Hasan, 1985a; Durey, 1988, on *Middlemarch*; Halliday, 1988, on Tennyson's *In Memoriam* and Darwin's *The Origin of Species*; and the various analyses in Cummings and Simmons, 1983, for detailed applications of systemic functional linguistics. For a thorough account of the model see Butler, 1985a, and Halliday, 1985b.

23 See Threadgold, 1988, on Thomas Keneally's *The Chant of Jimmy Blacksmith*; Thibault 1988, on agony column letters in *Cleo* and Thibault, 1986, on a speech by Ronald Reagan; Kress, 1988b, on a Mills and Boon romance and a drug advertisement, and Kress,

1978, on John Donne's 'Nocturnall'; and Toolan, 1988, on fictional dialogue.

24 For analyses using a similar model see also Hasan, 1967, 1971; Sinclair, 1968, on Wordsworth's 'Tintern Abbey', and Sinclair, 1984, on Edwin Thumboo's 'Krishna'; Short, 1972, on T. S. Eliot's 'Prelude I'; Gregory, 1974, on Donne's 'Holy Sonnet XIV' and Gregory, 1978, on Andrew Marvell's 'To His Coy Mistress'; Kennedy, 1982, on passages from Joseph Conrad's *The Secret Agent* and James Joyce's *Two Gallants*; Butt, 1983, on Wallace Stevens's 'Late Hymn from the Myrrh-Mountain', and Butt, 1988, on Wallace Stevens's 'Dry Loaf'; Yap, 1984, on Carl Sandburg's 'Grass'; Butt and O'Toole, 1985, on Graham Greene's 'Jubilee'; for one of the most detailed statements about Hallidayan theory, using as exemplification Thurber's 'The Lover and His Lass', see Halliday, 1977.

25 See Botha, 1973, 1982, and Hoey, 1983. See also Pratt, 1981, on the ideology of speech act theory; Silverman and Torode, 1980, on a range of philosophical discourses; Burton and Carlen, 1982, on official/governmental discourses.

26 See Fowler, *et al.*, 1979; Kress and Hodge, 1979; Fowler, 1977a, 1981, 1986; Pateman, 1975; Fairclough, 1988; Threadgold, 1986, 1988.

27 For studies which bring these two concerns together from a stylistic/ discoursal point of view see the analysis of *Mark* 4, 30–32, by Poythress, 1982, and the analysis of *Hebrews*, 1, 1–4 by Black, 1987.

28 See Birch, 1980a, for a detailed bibliography of stylistics, including statistical accounts of stylistic analysis, and Birch, 1981, 1983, 1984, 1985, for demonstrations of statistical analysis of the language of literary texts; see also Kenny, 1982; Butler, 1985.

29 See Birch, 1982 on the Birmingham school of discourse analysis; see also Sinclair, 1972a; Halliday, 1970b; Hasan, 1967, 1985b; Halliday and Hasan, 1985; Burton, 1980; Stubbs, 1983; and the papers in Hak, *et al.*, 1985.

Bibliography

Abel, E. (ed.) (1982), *Writing and Sexual Difference*, Brighton: Harvester Press.

Adams, H. (1983), *Philosophy and the Literary Symbolic*, Tallehassa: Florida State University Press.

Aers, D., Cook J. and Punter D. (1981), *Romanticism and Ideology, Studies in English Writing, 1765–1830*, London: Routledge & Kegan Paul.

Aers, D. and Kress, G. (1982), 'The politics of style: discourses of law and authority in *Measure for Measure*', *Style*, XVI/1, 22–37.

Alexander, G. (1982), 'Politics of the pronoun in the literature of the English Revolution', in Carter, 1982c, 217–35.

Altieri, C. (1975), 'The poem as act: a way to reconcile presentational and mimetic theories', *Iowa Review*, 6, 103–24.

Altieri, C. (1977), 'The qualities of action: a theory of middles in literature', *Boundary 2*, 5, 323–50; 899–917.

Altieri, C. (1978), 'The hermeneutics of literary indeterminacy: a dissent from the new orthodoxy', *New Literary History*, X/1, 71–99.

Anozie, S. O. (1981), *Structural Models and African Poetics, Towards a Pragmatic Theory of Literature*, London: Routledge & Kegan Paul.

Attridge, D., Bennington, G. and Young, R. (eds) (1987), *Poststructuralism and the Quest of History*, Cambridge: Cambridge University Press.

Atwood, M. (1972), *Power Politics*, Toronto: Anansi.

Auerbach, E. (1946), *Mimesis. The Representation of Reality in Western Literature*, Princeton: Princeton University Press.

Austin, J. L. (1961), *Philosophical Papers*, London: Oxford University Press.

Austin, J. L. (1962), *How to Do Things With Words*, London: Oxford University Press.

Ayer, A. J. (1936), *Language, Truth and Logic*, London: Gollanz.

Babb, H. S. (ed.) (1972), *Essays in Stylistic Analysis*, New York: Harcourt Brace Jovanovich.

Bakhtin, M. (1968), *Rabelais and His World* (trans. Helena Iswolsky), Cambridge, Mass: MIT Press.

Bakhtin, M., (1973), *Problems of Dostoevsky's Poetics* (trans. R. W. Rostsel), Ann Arbor: Ardis.

Bakhtin, M. (1981), *The Dialogic Imagination* (ed. M. Holquist and C. Emerson), Austin: University of Texas Press.

Banfield, A. (1982), *Unspeakable Sentences: Narration and Representation in the Language of Fiction*, London: Routledge & Kegan Paul.

Barrett, M. (1980), *Women's Oppression Today: Problems in Marxist Feminist Analysis*, London: Verso.

Barry, P. (1980) 'Linguistics and literary criticism: a polytheism without gods', *English*, XXIX/133, 133–43.

Barry, P. (1981) 'Is there life after structuralism?', *Critical Quarterly*, 23/3, 72–7.

Barry, P. (1984), 'Stylistics and the logic of intuition; or how not to pick a chrysanthemum', *Critical Quarterly*, 27/4, 51–8.

Barthes, Roland (1953), *Le Degré Zero de L'Ecriture*, Paris: Seuil; trans. as *Writing Degree Zero,* London: Jonathan Cape (1967).

Barthes, R. (1957) *Mythologies*, Paris: Seuil.

Barthes, R. (1963), *Sur Racine*, Paris: Seuil (1964). *On Racine* (trans. Richard Howard), New York: Hill and Wang.

Barthes, R. (1965), 'Eléments de sémiologie', *Communications* 4, Paris; trans. as *Elements of Semiology*, London: Jonathan Cape (1967).

Barthes, R. (1966), 'Introduction á L'Analyse Structurale des Récits', *Communications*, 8, reprinted and translated as 'An Introduction to the Structural Analysis of Narrative' in Heath, 1977, 79–124.

Barthes, R. (1967), *Systéme de la Mode*, Paris: Seuil.

Barthes, R. (1970), *S/Z*, Paris: Seuil; (1974) *S/Z* (trans. Richard Miller), New York: Hill & Wang.

Barthes, R. (1972), 'The death of the author', in Sears and Lord (eds), 1972, 7–12 and Heath (ed.), 1977, 142–8.

Barthes, R. (1975), *The Pleasure of the Text* (trans. Richard Miller), New York: Hill & Wang.

Barthes, R. (1977), 'From work to text' in Heath (ed.), 1977, 155–64.

Barthes, R. (1981) 'Theory of the text' in Young (ed.), 1981, 31–47.

Barthes, R. (1984) *Camera Lucida. Reflections on Photography* (trans. Richard Howard), London: Flamingo.

Barton, E. L. (1985), 'Structure and function in competing models of literary interpretation', *Lingua e Stile*, 20/4, 483–502.

Bateson, F. W. (1950), *English Poetry. A Critical Introduction*, London: Longman.

Bateson, F. W. (1972), *Essays in Critical Dissent*, London: Longman.

Batsleer, J., Davies, T., O'Rourke, R. and Weedon, C. (1985), *Re-Writing English. Cultural Politics of Gender and Class*, London: Methuen.

Beaugrande, R. de (1978), 'Information, expectation, and processing: on classifying poetic texts', *Poetics*, 7, 3–44.

Beaugrande, R. de (1980), *Text, Discourse, and Process,* Norwood, NJ: Ablex.

Beaugrande, R. de and Dressler, (1981), *Introduction to Text Linguistics*, London: Longman.

Beauvoir, S. de (1949), *The Second Sex* (trans. H. M. Parshley), New York: Bantam.

Belsey, C. (1980), *Critical Practice*, London: Methuen.

Belsey, C. (1982), 'Re-reading *The Great Tradition*', in Widdowson (ed.), 1982, 121–35.

Bennett, J. R. (1971a), 'A contextual method for the description of prose style', in Bennett, (ed.), 1971b, 224–31.

Bennett, J. R. (ed.) (1971b), *Prose Style*, San Francisco: Chandler Publishing.

Bennett, T. (1987), 'Texts in history, The determinations of readings and other texts', in Attridge, *et al.*, (eds.), 1987, 63–8.

Bennett, W. A. (1977), 'An applied linguistic view of the function of poetic form', *Journal of Literary Semantics*, 6/1, 29–48.

Berger, P. and Luckmann, T. (1967), *The Social Construction of Reality*, New York: Anchor Doubleday.

Bierwisch, M. (1965), 'Poetics and linguistics' (trans. Peter Salus), in Freeman, 1970, 96–115.

Birch, D. (1980a), 'Style and stylistics – a select bibliography', *Indian Journal of Applied Linguistics*, 6/1, 113–29.

Birch, D. (1980b), 'Varieties of stylistics: linguistics and literary', *Indian Journal of Applied Lingustics*, 6/2, 38–56.

Birch, D. (1981), 'Linguistic style differentials in the English prose of St Thomas More', *Indian Journal of Applied Linguistics*, 7/1–2, 160–86.

Birch, D. (1982), 'The Birmingham School of discourse analysis and communicative approaches to language teaching', *RELC Journal*, 13/2, 98–111.

Birch, D. (1983), 'Statistical rank and the Friedman test as an indication of significance in the preliminary stages of a multi-variable analysis of literary texts', *Studia Neophilologica*, 55, 129–41.

Birch, D. (ed.) (1984a), *Style, Structure and Criticism*, special issue of *Indian Journal of Applied Linguistics*, X/1–2, New Delhi.

Birch, D. (1984b), 'The determination of an optimum sample size for the analysis of linguistic/stylistic features in literary texts', *Poetica*, 17, 58–70.

Birch, D. (1985a), 'The Stylistic Analysis of Large Corpora of Literary Texts', *Association of Literary and Linguistic Computing Journal*, 6/1–2, 33–8.

Birch, D. (1985b), 'Language and understanding in Doris Lessing's later novels', in de Vos, 1985, 281–96.

Birch, D. (1986), 'Cunning beneath the verbs: demythologising Singapore English poetry', in Hyland, 1986, 147–90.

Birch, D. (1988a), 'Expanding semantic options for reading early modern English', in Birch and O'Toole (eds), 1988, 157–68.

Birch, D. (1988b), 'Working effects with words. Whose words? Stylistics and the reader's inter-textuality', in Carter and Simpson (eds), 1988 forthcoming.

Birch, D. (1988/9), 'Re-orienting semiotics: performance philosophy and theory, in Gay McAuley, Tim Fitzpatrick and Gareth Griffiths (eds), *Performance Analysis: Studies from Australia*, forthcoming.

Birch, D. and O Toole, M. (eds) (1988), *Functions of Style*, London: Frances Pinter,

Bisseret, N. (1979), *Education: Class, Language and Ideology*, London: Routledge & Kegan Paul.

Black, D. A. (1987), 'Hebrews 1:1–4: a study in discourse analysis', *Westminster Theological Journal*, 49, 175–94.

Blake, N. F. (1981), *The Use of Non-Standard Language in English Literature*, London: André Deutsch.

Blake, N. F. (1983a), 'Philip Larkin's language and style with reference to "Lines on a Young Lady's Photograph Album" (from *The Less Deceived*)', *The Journal of English Language and Literature*, 29/1, 341–50.

Blake, N. F. (1983b), *Shakespeare's Language. An Introduction*, London: Macmillan.

Bliss, F. W. and MacCormac, E. R. (1981), 'Grammatical and literary structures', *Human Studies*, 4, 67–86.

Bloch, B. (1949), Obituary of Leonard Bloomfield, *Language*, 25, 92–3.

Bloom, Clive (1986), *The 'Occult' Experience and the New Criticism*, Brighton: Harvester Press.

Bloom, H. (1979), 'The breaking of form', in Bloom, *et al.*, 1979, 1–38.

Bloom, H., Man, P. de, Derrida, J., Hartman, G. and Hillis Miller, J. (1979), *Deconstruction and Criticism*, New York: Continuum.

Bloomfield, M. (1970/1), 'Jakobsonian poetics and evaluative criticism', *The University Review*, 38, 165–73.

Bolinger, D. (1980), *Language The Loaded Weapon. The Use and Abuse of Language Today*, London: Longman.

Boon, J. A. (1972), *From Symbolism to Structuralism. Lévi-Strauss in a Literary Tradition*, New York: Harper & Row.

Booth, S. (1969), *An Essay on Shakespeare's Sonnets*, New Haven: Yale University Press.

Booth, W. (1961), *The Rhetoric of Fiction*, Chicago: University of Chicago Press.

Bosinelli, R. M. B. (ed.), (1984), *US Presidential Election 1984. An Interdisciplinary Approach to the Analysis of Political Discourse*, Bologna: Pitagora.

Botha, R. P. (1973), *The Justification of Linguistic Hypothesis*, The Hague: Mouton.

Botha, R. P. (1982), 'On the Galilean style of linguistic inquiry', *Lingua*, 58, 1–50.

Bourdieu, P. (1985), 'The market of symbolic goods', *Poetics*, 14/1–3, 13–44.

Boyd, Z. (1983), 'The language of supposing: modal auxiliaries in *Sense and Sensibility*, in Todd (ed.), 1983, 142–54.

Bradbrook, M. C. (1974), 'The ambiguity of William Empson' in Gill (ed.), 1974, 2–12.

Bremond, C. (1973), *Logique de Récit*, Paris: Seuil.

Brinton, L. J. (1985), 'The iconic role of aspect in Shakespeare's Sonnet 129', *Poetics Today*, 6/3, 447–59.

Brooks, C. (1971), *A Shaping Joy, Studies in the Writer's Craft*, London: Methuen.

Brower, R., Vendler, H. and Hollander, J. (eds) (1973), *I. A. Richards: Essays in His Honor*, New York: Oxford University Press.

Brown, M. (1978), 'Poetic listening', *New Literary History*, 10/1, 125–39.

Brown, R. and Gilman, A. (1960), 'The pronouns of power and solidarity', in Sebeok, 1960, 253–276.

Brumfit, C. and Carter, R. (eds) (1986), *Literature and Language Teaching*, Oxford: Oxford University Press.

Burton, D. (1980, *Dialogue and Discourse: The Sociolinguistics of Modern Drama Dialogue and Naturally Occurring Conversation*, London: Routledge & Kegan Paul.

Burton, D. (1982), 'Through glass darkly: through dark glasses', in Carter (ed.), 1982c, 195–216.

Burton, D. (1984), 'A Feminist Reading of Lewis Grassic Gibbon's *A Scots Quair*', in Hawthorne (ed.), 1984, 34–46.

Burton, T. and Carlen, P. (1979), *Official Discourse. On Discourse Analysis, Government Publications, Ideology and the State*, London: Routledge & Kegan Paul.

Butler, C. (1984), *Interpretation, Deconstruction, and Ideology: An Introduction to Some Current Issues in Theory*, Oxford: Clarendon Press.

Butler, C. S. (1985a), *Systemic Linguistics: Theory and Applications*, London: Batsford.

Butler, C. S. (1985b), *Statistics in Linguistics*, London: Blackwell.

Butt, D. (1983), 'Semantic "drift" in verbal art', *Australian Review of Applied Linguistics*, 6/1, 38–48.

Butt, D. (1988), 'Randomness, order, and the latent patterning of text', in Birch and O'Toole (ed.), 1988, 74–97.

Butt, D. G. and O'Toole, L. M. (1985), 'Discourse structures in literary narrative: examples from Graham Greene's "Jubilee" ' in Hasan (ed.), 1985a, 83–105.

Cameron, D. (1985), *Feminism and Linguistic Theory*, London: Macmillan.

Carter, R. A. (1982a), 'Responses to language in poetry', in Carter and Burton (eds), 1982, 28–56.

Carter, R. A. (1982b), 'Style and Interpretation in Hemingway's "Cat in the Rain" ', in Carter (ed.) 1982c, 65–82.

Carter, R. A. (ed.), (1982c), *Language and Literature: An Introductory Reader in Stylistics*, London: Allen & Unwin.

Carter, R. A. (1982d), 'Sociolinguistics and the integrated English lesson' in Carter (ed.), 1982e, 156–82.

Carter, R. A. (ed.), (1982e), *Linguistics and the Teacher*, London: Routledge & Kegan Paul.

Carter, R. A. (1983), 'Poetry and Conversation: An Essay in Discourse Analysis', *Language and Style*, 16/3, 374–85.

Carter, R. A. (1984), 'The sociolinguistic analysis of narrative', in Birch (ed.), 1984a, 97–106.

Carter, R. A. (1987), *Vocabulary: Applied Linguistic Perspectives*, London: Allen & Unwin.

Carter, R. A. and Burton, E. (eds) (1982), *Literary Text and Language Study*, London: Edward Arnold.

Carter, R. A. and Nash, W. (1983), 'Language and literariness', *Prose Studies*, 6/2, 123–141.

Carter, R. A. and Simpson, P. (eds) (1988 forthcoming), *Language, Discourse and Literature*, London: Unwin Hyman.

Chapman, R. (1973), *Linguistics and Literature: An Introduction to Literary Stylistics*, London: Edward Arnold.

Chapman, R. (1982), *The Language of English Literature*, London: Edward Arnold.

Chatman. S. (1956), 'Robert Frost's "Mowing": an inquiry into prosodic structure', *Kenyon Review*, XVIII, 421–38.

Chatman, S. (1971), *Literary Style: A Symposium*, Oxford: Oxford University Press.

Chatman, S. (ed.) (1973), *Approaches to Poetics: Selected Papers from the English Institute*, 1972, New York: Columbia University Press.

Chatman, S. and Levin, S. R. (eds) (1967) *Essays on the Language of Literature*, Boston: Houghton Mifflin.

Chilton, P. (ed.), (1985), *Language and the Nuclear Arms Debate: Nukespeak Today*, London: Frances Pinter.

Ching, M. K. L., Haley, M. C. and Lunsford, R. F. (eds) (1980), *Linguistic Perspectives on Literature*: London: Routledge & Kegan Paul.

Chomsky, N. (1957), *Syntactic Structures*, The Hague: Mouton.

Chomsky, N. (1964), *Current Issues in Lingustic Theory*, The Hague: Mouton.

Chomsky, N. (1965), *Aspects of the Theory of Syntax*, Cambridge, Mass.: MIT Press.

Chomsky, N. (1968), *Language and Mind*, New York: Harcourt Brace Jovanovich.

Christensen, F. (1969), 'A generative rhetoric of the sentence', in Love and Payne (eds), 1969, 27–36.

Chua, B. H. (1979), 'Describing a national crisis: an exploration in textual analysis', *Human Studies*, 2, 47–61.

Cicourel, A. (1968), *The Social Organization of Juvenile Justice*, New York: John Wiley.

Closs Traugott, E. and Pratt, M. L. (1980), *Linguistics for Students of Literature*, New York: Harcourt Brace Jovanovich.

Cluysenaar, A. (1976), *Introduction to Literary Stylistics*, London: Batsford.

Cohen, R. (ed.) (1974), *New Directions in Literary History*, Baltimore: Johns Hopkins University Press.

Cohen, S. and Young J. (1973), *The Manufacture of News: Deviance, Social Problems and the Mass Media*, London: Constable.

Cole, P. and Morgan J. L. (eds) (1975), *Speech Acts, Syntax and Semantics*, New York: Academic Press.

Collins, A. Y. (ed.) (1985), *Feminist Perspectives on Biblical Scholarship*, Chico, Calif.: Scholars Press.

Corbett, E. J. (1969), 'A method of analyzing prose style with a demonstration analysis of Swift's "A Modest Proposal" ', in Love and Payne (eds), 1969, 81–98.

Cornwell, E. F. (1962), *The Still Point*, New Brunswick: Rutgers University Press.

Cotton, E. (1980), 'Linguistic design in a poem by Cummings', *Style*, XIV/3, 274–86.

Coward, R. and Ellis J. (1977), *Language and Materialism*, London: Routledge & Kegan Paul.

Crystal, D. and Davy, D. (1969), *Investigating English Style*, London: Longman.

Culler, J. (1975), *Structuralist Poetics: Structuralism, Linguistics and the Study of Literature*, Ithaca, New York: Cornell University Press.

Culler, J. (1987), 'Criticism and institutions: the American university', in Attridge *et al.* (eds), 1987, 82–100.

Cummings, M. and Simmons, R. (1983), *The Language of Literature, A Stylistic Introduction to the Study of Literature*, London: Pergamon.

D'Angelo, F. J. (1974), 'Style as Structure', *Style*, VIII/2, 322–64.

D'haen, T. (ed.) (1983), special issue of the *Dutch Quarterly Review of Anglo American Letters*, 13/2.

Daiches, D. (1956), *Critical Approaches to Literature*, Chicago: University of Chicago Press.

Dauenhauer, B. (1982), 'Authors, audiences, and texts', *Human Studies*, 5, 137–46.

Davie, D. (1967), *Purity of Diction in English Verse*, London: Routledge & Kegan Paul.

Dekoven, M. (1983), *A Different Language: Gertrude Stein's Experimental Writing*, Wisconsin: University of Wisconsin Press.

Derrida, J. (1967), *L'Ecriture et la Différence*, trans. as *Writing and Difference* (trans. Alan Bass, London: Routledge & Kegan Paul, 1978), Chicago; Chicago University Press.

Derrida, J. (1970), 'Ousia and gramme: a note to a footnote in *Being and Time*, in Derrida, 1982, 29–68.

Derrida, J. (1973), *Speech and Phenomena, and Other Essays on Husserl's Theory of Signs* (trans. D. B. Allinson, from *La Voix et le Phénomène*, Paris: Presses Universitaires de France), Evanston: Northwestern University Press.

Derrida, J. (1976), *Of Grammatology* (trans. Gayatri Chakravorty Spivak from *De La Grammatologie*, Paris: Minuit, 1967), Baltimore: Johns Hopkins University Press.

Derrida, J. (1979), 'Living on', in Bloom *et al*, 1979, 75–176.

Derrida, J. (1982), *Margins of Philosophy* (trans. Alan Bass from *Marges de la Philosophie*, Paris: Minuit, 1972), Brighton: Harvester Press.

Dillon, G. (1978), *Language Processing and the Reading of Literature: Towards a Model of Comprehension*, Bloomington: Indiana University Press.

Dillon, G. (1982), 'Whorfian stylistics', *Journal of Literary Semantics*, XI/2, 73–7.

Drakakis, J. (ed.) (1985), *Alternative Shakespeares*, London: Methuen.

Dressler, W. (ed.) (1976), *Current Trends in Textlinguistics*, Berlin: de Gruyter.

Durant, A. (1985), 'Modern literary theory in the teaching of literature', *Prose Studies*, 8/1, 58–78.

Durey, J. (1988), ' "Middlemarch": the role of the functional triad in the portrayal of hero and heroine', in Birch and O'Toole (eds), 1988, 234–48.

Eagleton, T. (1976a), *Marxism and Literary Criticism*, London: Methuen.

Eagleton, T. (1976b), *Criticism and Ideology: A Study in Marxist Literary Theory*, London: Verso.

Eagleton, T. (1981), 'The End of Criticism', *Southern Review*, 14/2, 99–106.

Eagleton, T. (1983), *Literary Theory: An Introduction*, Oxford: Basil Blackwell.

Eagleton, T., Bennett, T., King, N., Hunter, I., Hulme, P., Belsey, C. and Frow, J. (1984), 'The "Text in Itself", Symposium', *Southern Review*, 17/2, 115–146.

Easthope, A. (1983), *Poetry as Discourse*, London: Methuen.

Eco, U. (1979), *The Role of the Reader: Explorations in the Semiotics of Texts*, Bloomington: Indiana University Press.

Edwards, C. L. (1984), ' "Stop me if you've heard this one": narrative disclaimers as breakthrough into performance', *Formula*, 25/3–4, 214–28.

Ehrlich, V. (1973), 'Roman Jakobson: grammar of poetry and poetry of grammar', in Chatman, (ed.), 1973, 1–27.

Ehrmann, J. (ed.) (1970), *Structuralism*, New York: Doubleday Anchor.

Eisenstein, Z. R. (ed.) (1979), *Capitalist Patriarchy and the Case of Social Feminism*, New York: Monthly Review.

Eliot, T. S. (1920), *The Sacred Wood: Essays on Poetry and Criticism*, London: Methuen (7th edn 1950).

Ellis, J. (1982), *Visible Fictions*, London: Routledge & Kegan Paul.

Empson, W. (1928), 'Letter', *Experiment*, 1 (Nov), 4, reprinted in Empson, 1984.

Empson, W. (1930), *Seven Types of Ambiguity*, London: Chatto & Windus.

Empson, W. (1951a), *The Structure of Complex Words*, London: Chatto & Windus.

Empson, W. (1951b), 'Sense in the Prelude', *Kenyon Review*, 13/2, 282–302.

Empson, W. (1984), *Collected Poems*, London: The Hogarth Press.

Engler, B. (1982), *Reading and Listening. The Modes of Communicating Poetry and Their Influence on the Texts,* Cooper Monographs 30, Barn: A. Franke.

Enkvist, N. E. (1964), 'On defining style', in Spencer and Gregory (eds), 1964, 3–56.

Enright, D. J. and Chickera, E. de (eds) (1962), *English Critical Texts, Sixteenth Century to the Twentieth Century*, London: Oxford University Press.

Epstein, E. L. (1978), *Language and Style*, London: Methuen.

Fairclough, N. (1988), 'Register, power and socio-semantic change', in Birch and O'Toole (eds), 1988, 111–25.

Falck, C. (1986), 'Saussurean theory and the abolition of reality', *The Monist*, 69/1, 133–45.

Fawcett, R. P. (1980), *Linguistics and Social Interaction*, Heidelberg: Julius Groos and Exeter University.

Fawcett, R. P., Halliday, M. A. K., Lamb, S. M. and Makkai, A. (eds) (1984), *The Semiotics of Culture and Language I, Language as Social Semiotic*, London: Frances Pinter.

Felperin, H. (1985), *Beyond Deconstruction: The Uses and Abuses of Literary Theory*, Oxford: Clarendon Press.

Fetterley, J. (1978), *The Resisting Reader. A Feminist Approach to American Fiction*, Bloomington: Indiana University Press.

Fiedler, L. A. and Baker, H. A. Jr (eds) (1981), *English Literature: Opening up the Canon*, Baltimore: Johns Hopkins University Press.

Firth, J. R. (1957), *Papers in Linguistics, 1934–1951*, London: Oxford University Press.

Fish, S. (1970), 'Literature in the reader: affective stylistics', *New Literary History*, 2, 123–162, reprinted in Tompkins (ed.), 1980, 70–100.

Fish, S. (1972), *Self-Consuming Artifacts*, Berkeley: University of California Press.

Fish, S. (1973a), 'How ordinary is ordinary language?, *New Literary History*, 5, 41–54.

Fish, S. (1973b), 'What is stylistics and why are they saying such terrible things about it?', in Chatman (ed.), 1973, 109–52.

Fish, S. (1980), *Is There a Text in This Class? The Authority of Interpretive Communities*, Cambridge, Mass.: Harvard University Press.

Fiske, J. (1983), 'Surfalism and sandiotics: the beach in Oz culture', *Australian Journal of Cultural Studies*, 1/2, 120–49.

Flynn, E. (1983), 'Gender and reading', *College English*, 45, 236–53.

Fodor, J. D. (1980), *Semantics, Theories of Meaning in Generative Grammar*, Cambridge Mass.: Harvard University Press.

Fokkema, D. W. and Kunne-Ibsch, E. (1978), *Theories of Literature in the Twentieth Century*, London: Hurst.

Forgacs, D. (1982), 'Marxist literary theories' in Jefferson and Robey (eds), 1982, 134–69.

Foucault, M. (1971), *L'Ordre du Discours*, Paris: Gallimard; trans. as 'The Order of Discourse' in Young (ed.), 1981, 48–78.

Foucault, M. (1972), *The Archeology of Knowledge* (trans. A. M. Sheridan Smith), London: Tavistock.

Foucault, M. (1975), 'What is an author', *Partisan Review*, XLII/4, 603–14; reprinted in Harari (ed.), 1979, 141–60.

Foucault, M. (1980), *The Will to Truth*, London: Tavistock.

Fowler, R. (1966a), 'Linguistic Theory and the Study of Literature', in Fowler (ed.), 1966b, 1–28.

Fowler, R. (ed.) (1966b), *Essays on Style and Language, Linguistic and Critical Approaches to Literary Style*, London: Routledge & Kegan Paul.

Fowler, R. (1966c), 'Some stylistic features of the "Sermo Lupi" ', *Journal of English and Germanic Philology*, 65, 1–18.

Fowler, R. (1970), 'Against idealisation: some speculations on the theory of linguistic performance', *Linguistics*, 63, 19–50.

Fowler, R. (1971), *The Languages of Literature. Some Linguistic Contributions to Literature*, London: Routledge & Kegan Paul.

Fowler, R. (1972), 'Style and the concept of deep structure', *Journal of Literary Semantics*, 1, 5–24.

Fowler, R. (1975a), 'Language and the reader: Shakespeare's Sonnet 73', in Fowler, 1975b, 79–122.

Fowler, R. (ed.) (1975b), *Style and Structure in Literature. Essays in the New Stylistics*, Oxford: Basil Blackwell.

Fowler, R. (1977a), 'Cohesive, progressive, and localizing aspects of text structure', in van Dijk and Petöfi (ed), 1977, 64–84.

Fowler, R. (1977b), *Linguistics and the Novel*, London: Methuen.

Fowler, R. (1979), 'Linguistics and, versus, poetics', *Journal of Literary Semantics*, 8, 3–21, reprinted in Fowler, 1981, 162–79.

Fowler, R. (1981), *Literature as Social Discourse: The Practice of Linguistic Criticism*, London: Batsford.

Fowler, R. (1983), 'Studying Literature as Language', in D'haen (ed.) 1983, 171–84.

Fowler, R. (1986), *Linguistic Criticism*, London: Oxford University Press.

Fowler, R., Hodge, H., Kress, G. and Trew, T. (1979), *Language and Control*, London: Routledge & Kegan Paul.

Fowler, R. and Marshall, T. (1985), 'Language, text, discourse' in Chilton (ed.), 1985, 3–22.

Francis, W. N. (1967), 'Syntax and literary interpretation', in Chatman and Levin (eds), 1967, 209–16.

Freadman, A. (1986), 'Structuralist uses of Peirce: Jakobson, Metz *et al.*, in Threadgold *et al.* (eds) 1986, 93–124.

Freedle, R. (ed.) (1979), *New Directions in Discourse Processing*, Norwood, NJ: Ablex.

Freeman, D. C. (ed.) (1970), *Linguistics and Literary Style*, New York: Holt, Rinehart & Winston.

Friberg, I. (1982), 'The reflection in the mirror – an interpretation of Hemingway's "Cat in the Rain" ', *Moderna Språk*, LXXVI/14, 329–38.

Frow, J. (1983), 'Reading as system and as practice', *Comparative Criticism*, 5, 87–105.

Frow, J. (1984), 'Language, discourse, ideology', *Language and Style*, 17/4, 302–15.

Frow, J. (1986), *Marxism and Literary History*, Cambridge, Mass.: Harvard University Press.

Frye, N. (1957a), *Anatomy of Criticism, Four Essays*, Princeton: Princeton University Press.

Frye, N. (1957b), 'Polemical introduction, *Anatomy of Criticism*', in Polletta (ed.), 1973, 28–50.

Frye, N. (1959a), 'Literature as context: Milton's *Lycidas*' in Frye, 1959b, reprinted in Polletta (ed.), 1973, 404–12.

Frye, N. (1959b), *Fables as Identity: Studies in Poetic Mythology*, New York: Harcourt Brace Jovanovich.

Frye, N. (1970), *The Stubborn Structure*, London: Methuen.

Gallop, J. (1982), *Feminism and Psychoanalysis: The Daughter's Seduction*, London: Macmillan.

Garfinkel, H. (1967), *Studies in Ethnomethodology*, Englewood Cliffs, NJ: Prentice-Hall.

Garvin, P. L. (ed.), (1964), *A Prague School Reader on Esthetics, Literary Structure and Style*, Washington: Georgetown University Press.

Gauker, C. (1987), 'Language as tool', *American Philosophical Quarterly*, 24/1, 47–58.

Gee, J. Paul (1985), 'The structure of perception in the poetry of William Carlos Williams', *Poetics Today*, 6/3, 375–97.

Gelven, M. (1982), 'The Literary and the True', *Man and World*, 15/3, 311–22.

Genette, G. (1972), *Figures III*, Paris: Seuil.

Genette, G. (1980) *Narrative Discourse*, Oxford: Oxford University Press. (a translation of *Le Discours de Récit*, in Genette, 1972).

Gilbert, A. J. (1979), *Literary Language from Chaucer to Johnson*, London: Macmillan.

Gilbert, K. (1983), *Because a White Man'll Never Do It*, Sydney: Angus & Robertson.

Giles, S. (1987), 'Marxism and form: D. H. Lawrence's *St Mawr*', in Tallack (ed.), 1987, 49–66.

Gilham, D. G. (1980), 'Wordsworth's hidden figures of speech', in Green, 1980, 79–87.

Gill, R. (ed.) (1974), *William Empson, The Man and His Work*, London: Routledge & Kegan Paul.

Godard, B. (1985), 'Redrawing the circle. Power, poetics, language', in Kroker (ed.), 1985, 165–81.

Goffman, I. (1981), *Forms of Talk*, Oxford: Basil Blackwell.

Goldberg, D. (1986/7), 'Reading the signs: the force of language', *The Philosophical Forum*, XVIII/2–3, 71–93.

Gray, B. (1977), 'Is there a science of *parole?*', *Studies in Language*, 1/2, 223–36.

Green, B. (ed.) (1980), *Generous Converse. English Essays in Memory of Edward Davis*, Capetown: Oxford University Press.

Green, G. M. (1982) 'Linguistics and the pragmatics of language use', *Poetics*, 11, 45–76.

Greenwood, E. B. (1965), 'George Herbert's sonnet "Prayer": a stylistic study', *Essays in Criticism*, 15/1, 27–45.

Gregory, M. (1967), 'Aspects of varieties differentiation', *Journal of Linguistics*, 3/2, 177–98.

Gregory, M. (1974), 'A theory for stylistics – exemplified: Donne's "Holy Sonnet XIV" ', *Language and Style*, 7/2, 108–18.

Gregory, M. (1978), 'Marvell's "To His Coy Mistress": the poem as a linguistic and sociel event', *Poetics*, 7, 351–62.

Gregory, M. and Carroll, S. (1978), *Language and Situation: Language Varieties and Their Social Contexts*, London: Routledge & Kegan Paul.

Greimas, A. J. (1966), *Sémantique Structurale: Recherche de Méthode*, Paris: Larousse.

Greimas, A. J. and Courtés J. (1979), *Semiotics and Language. An Analytical Dictionary*, Bloomington: Indiana University Press.

Grice, H. P. (1975), 'Logic and conversation', in P. Cole and J. L. Morgan (ed.), 1975, 41–58.

Gronbeck, B. (1973), 'The rhetoric of social-institutional change: black action at Michigan', in Mohrmann (ed.), 1973, 96–123.

Groom, B. (1955), *The Diction of Poetry from Spenser to Bridges*, Toronto: University of Toronto Press.

Grundy, P. (1981), 'Linguistics and literary criticism: a marriage of convenience: a reply to Peter Barry's article in *English*, Summer 1980', *English* XXX/137, 151–69.

Guback, T. H. (1967), 'Reporting or distorting: broadcast network news

188 Bibliography

treatment of a speech by John F. Kennedy', in Skornia and Kitson (eds), 1967.

Gumperz, J. J. and Hymes, D. (eds) (1964), *The Ethnography of Communication*, Washington DC: American Anthropological Association.

Habermas, J. (1974), *Theory and Practice* (trans. John Viertel), Boston: Beacon Press.

Hak, T., Haafkens, J. and Nijhoff, G. (eds) (1985), *Working Papers on discourse and conversation analysis*, KONTEKSTEN, 6.

Halliday, M. A. K. (1964a), 'Descriptive linguistics in literary studies', in Freeman, 1970, 57–72.

Halliday, M. A. K. (1964b), 'The linguistic study of literary texts', in Lunt (ed.), 1964, 302–7, reprinted in Chatman and Levin (eds), 1967, 217–33.

Halliday, M. A. K. (1970a), 'Language structure and language function', in Lyons (ed.), 1970, 140–65.

Halliday, M. A. K. (1970b), *A Course in Spoken English: Intonation*, London: Oxford University Press.

Halliday, M. A. K. (1971), 'Linguistic function and literary style: an inquiry into the language of William Golding's *The Inheritors*', in Halliday, 1973, 103–43.

Halliday, M. A. K. (1973), *Explorations in the Functions of Language*, London: Edward Arnold.

Halliday, M. A. K. (1975), *Learning How to Mean*, London: Edward Arnold.

Halliday, M. A. K. (1976), 'The teacher taught the student English: an essay in applied linguistics', in Reich (ed.), 1976, 344–9.

Halliday, M. A. K. (1977), 'Text as semantic choice in social contexts', in van Dijk and Petöfi (eds), 1977, 176–225.

Halliday, M. A. K. (1978), *Language as Social Semiotic*, London: Edward Arnold.

Halliday, M. A. K. (1983), Foreword to Cummings and Simmons, 1983, vii–xvii.

Halliday, M. A. K. (1985a), *Spoken and Written Language*, Geelong: Deakin University Press.

Halliday, M. A. K. (1985b), *An Introduction to Functional Grammar*, London: Edward Arnold.

Halliday, M. A. K. (1988), 'Poetry as scientific discourse: the nuclear sections of Tennyson's "In Memoriam" ', in Birch and O'Toole (eds), 1988, 31–44.

Halliday, M. A. K. and Hasan, R. (1976), *Cohesion in English*, London: Longman.

Halliday, M. A. K. and Hasan, R. (1985), *Language, Context, Text: Aspects of Language in a Social-Semiotic Perspective*, Geelong: Deakin University Press.

Halliday, M. A. K., and McIntosh, A., Strevens, P. (1964), *The Linguistic Sciences and Language Teachings*, London: Longman.

Harari, J. V. (ed.) (1979), *Textual Strategies: Perspectives in Post-Structuralist Criticism*, New York: Cornell University Press.

Harland, R. (1987), *Superstructuralism: The Philosophy of Structuralism and Post-Structuralism*, London: Methuen.

Harris, S. (1984), 'Questions as a mode of control in magistrates' courts', *International Journal of the Sociology of Language*, 49, 5–27.

Harris, Z. (1952a), 'Discourse analysis', *Language*, 28, 1–30.

Harris, Z. (1952b), 'Discourse analysis: a sample text', *Language*, 28, 474–94.

Hartley, J. (1982), *Understanding News*, London: Methuen.

Hartley, J. and Montgomery, M. (1985), 'Representations and relations: ideology and power in press and TV news', in van Dijk, 1985, 233–69.

Hartman, G. (1969), 'The voice of the shuttle: language from the point of view of literature', in Hartman, 1970, 337–55.

Hartman, G. (1970), *Beyond Formalism: Literary Essays, 1958–1970*, New Haven: Yale University Press.

Hartman, G. (1975), *The Fate of Reading and Other Essays*, Chicago: Chicago University Press.

Hartman, G. (ed.) (1978), *Psychoanalysis and the Question of the Text. Selected Papers from the English Institute, 1976–1977*, Baltimore: Johns Hopkins University Press.

Hartman, G. (1979), 'Words, wish, worth: Wordsworth', in Bloom *et al.*, 1979, 177–216.

Hartman, G. (1980), *Criticism in the Wilderness: The Study of Literature Today*, New Haven: Yale University Press.

Hartman, G. (1981), *Saving the Text: Literature, Derrida, Philosophy*, Baltimore: Johns Hopkins University Press.

Hasan, R. (1967), 'Linguistics and the study of literary texts', *Etudes de Linguistique Appliquée*, 5, 106–12.

Hasan, R. (1971), 'Rime and reason in literature' in Chatman (ed.), 1971, 299–326.

Hasan, R. (1975), 'The place of stylistics in the study of verbal art', in Ringbom (ed.), 1975, 49–62.

Hasan, R. (1980), 'The identity of a text', *Sophia Linguistica*, VI, 75–89.

Hasan, R. (1984), 'Ways of saying: ways of meaning', in Fawcett *et al.* (eds), 1984, 105–62.

Hasan, R. (ed.) (1985a), *Discourse on Discourse Workshop Reports from the Macquarie Workshop on Discourse Analysis, 25 February 1983*, Applied Linguistics Association of Australia, Occasional Papers, 7.

Hasan, R. (1985b), *Linguistics, Language and Verbal Art*, Geelong: Deakin University Press.

Hasan, R. (1988), 'The analysis of the poem: theoretical issues in practice', in Birch and O'Toole (eds), 1988, 45–73.

Hawkes, T. (1977), *Structuralism and Semiotics*, London: Methuen.

Hawkes, T. (1985), 'Swisser-swatter: making a man of English Letters', in Drakakis (ed.), 1985, 26–46, reprinted in Hawkes, 1986, 73–91.

Hawkes, T. (1986), *That Shakespeherian Rag. Essays on a Critical Process*, London: Methuen.

Hawthorn, J. (1983), *Multiple Personality and the Disintegration of Literary Character From Oliver Goldsmith to Sylvia Plath*, London: Edward Arnold.

Hawthorn, J. (ed.) (1984), *The British Working-Class Novel in the Twentieth Century*, London: Edward Arnold.

Heath, S. (ed.) (1977), *Roland Barthes, Image, Music, Text*, London: Flamingo.

Heidegger, M. (1971), *Poetry, Language, Thought* (trans. A. Hoftadter), London: Harper & Row.

Hendricks, W. O. (1967), 'On the notion beyond the sentence', *Linguistics*, 37, 12–51.

Hendricks, W. O. (1974), 'The relation between linguistics and literary studies', *Poetics*, 11, 5–22.

Hill, A. A. (1955), 'An analysis of "The Windhover": an experiment in structural method', PMLA 70, 968–78.

Hill, A. A. (1958), *Introduction to Linguistic Structures*, New York: Harcourt.

Hill, G. (1984), *The Lords of Limit. Essays on Literature and Ideas*, London: André Deutsch.

Hirsch, E. D. Jr (1967), *Validity in Interpretation*, New Haven: Yale University Press.

Hirsch, E. D. Jr (1975), 'Stylistics and synonymity', *Critical Inquiry*, 1, 559–79.

Hirsch, E. D. Jr (1976) *The Aims of Interpretation*, Chicago: Chicago University Press.

Hjelmslev, L. (1969) *Prolegomena to a Theory of Language*, Madison: University of Wisconsin Press.

Hodge, R. (1979) 'Newspapers and Communities', in Fowler *et al.* (eds), 1979, 157–74.

Hodge, R. (1985), 'Getting the message across: a systemic analysis of media coverage of a CND march', in Chilton (ed.), 1985, 131–46.

Hodge, R. (1988) 'Halliday and the stylistics of creativity' in Birch and O'Toole (eds), 1988, 142–56.

Hodge, R. and Kress, G. (1974), 'Transformations, models and processes: towards a more usable linguistics', *Journal of Literary Semantics*, 3, 5–21.

Hodge, R. and Kress, G. (1982), 'The semiotics of love and power: *King Lear* and a new stylistics', *Southern Review*, 15/2, 143–56.

Hodge, R. and Kress, G. (1986), 'Rereading as exorcism: semiotics and the ghost of Saussure', *Southern Review*, 19/1, 38–52.

Hodge, R. and Kress, G. (1988), *Social Semiotics*, London: Polity Press.

Hoey, M. P. (1983), *On the Surface of Discourse*, London: Allen & Unwin.

Hoey, M. P. (1984), 'Persuasive rhetoric in linguistics: a stylistic study of some features of the language in Noam Chomsky', *Forum Linguisticum*, 8/1, 20–30.

Holden, J. (1986), *Style and Authenticity in Post-Modern Poetry*, Columbia: University of Missouri Press.

Holenstein, E. (1976), *Roman Jakobson's Approach to Language: Phenomenological Structuralism*, Bloomington: Indiana University Press.

Hornby, R. (1977), *Script into performance: a structuralist view of play production*, Austin: University of Texas Press.

Humphries, B. (1981), *A Nice Night's Entertainment, Sketches and Monologues 1956–1981*, London: Granada.

Hyland, P. (ed.), (1986), *Discharging the Canon: Cross Cultural Readings in Literature*, Singapore: Singapore University Press.

Hymes, D. (1964), 'Towards ethnographies of communication', in Gumperz and Hymes (eds), 1964, 1–34.

Ihwe, J. (1973), 'On the validation of text-grammars in the "study of literature" ', in Petöfi and Rieser (eds), 1973, 300–48.

Irigaray, L. (1977), *Ce sexe qui n'en est pas un*, Paris: Minuit.

Irigaray, L. (1985), *Speculum of the Other Woman* (trans. G. C. Gill), Ithaca: Cornell University Press.

Ives, S. (1962), 'Grammatical analysis and literary criticism', *Report of the Eleventh Annual Round Table Meeting, Linguistics and Language Studies*, Washington: Georgetown University Press.

Jacobus, M. (ed.) (1982), *Women Writing and Writing About Women*, London: Croom Helm.

Jahner, E. (1983), 'Cognitive style in oral literature', *Language and Style*, 16/1, 32–51.

Jakobson, R. (1960), 'Closing statement: linguistics and poetics', in Sebeok (ed.), 1960, 350–77.

Jakobson, R. and Bogatyrev, P. (1971), 'On the boundaries between studies of folklore and literature', in Matejka and Pomorska (eds), 1971, 91–3.

Jakobson, R. and Jones, L. (1970), *Shakespeare's Verbal Art in 'Th' Expense of Spirit'*, The Hague: Mouton.

Jakobson, R. and Lévi-Strauss, C. (1962), ' "Les Chats" de Charles Baudelaire', *L'Homme: Revue Française D'Anthropologie*, 2, 5–21; trans. K. Furness-Lane, reprinted in Lane, 1970, 202–21.

Jakobson, R. and Rudy, S. (1980), 'Yeats' "Sorrow of Love" through the years', *Poetics Today*, 2/1a, 97–125.

Jameson, F. (1972), *The Prison-House of Language*, Princeton: Princeton University Press.

Jameson, F. (1976), 'Criticism in history', in Rudick (ed.), 1976, 31–50.

192   Bibliography

Jameson, F. (1981), *The Political Unconscious, Narrative as a Socially Symbolic Act*, London: Methuen.

Jauss, H. R. (1974), 'Literary history as a challenge to literary theory', in Cohen (ed.), 1974, 11–41.

Jefferson, A. and Robey, D. (eds) (1982), *Modern Literary Theory. A Comparative Introduction*, London: Batsford.

Johnson, C. (1986), *The Song Circle of Jacky and Selected Poems*, Melbourne: Hyland House.

Jordan, M. P. (1984), *Rhetoric of Everyday English Texts*, London: Allen & Unwin.

Kachru, B. B. and Stahlke H. F. W. (eds) (1972), *Current Trends in Stylistics*, Edmonton: Linguistic Research Inc.

Kaiser, B. B. (1987), 'Poet as "female impersonator": the image of daughter Zion as speaker in biblical poems of suffering', *Journal of Religion*, 67/2, 164–82.

Kampf, L. and Lauter, P. (eds) (1970), *The Politics of Literature: Dissenting Essays on the Teaching of English*, New York: Pantheon Books.

Kantor, R. N., Bruce, B. C., Green, G. M., Morgan, J. L., Stein, N. L. and Webber, B. L. (1982), 'Many problems and some techniques of text analysis', *Poetics*, 11/3, 237–64.

Kelly-Gadol, J. (1976), 'The social relations of the sexes: methodological implications of women's history', *Sign*, 1, 809–24.

Kennedy, C. (1982) 'Systemic grammar and its use in literary analysis', in Carter (ed.), 1982c, 83–100.

Kenny, A. (1982), *The Computation of Style. An Introduction to Statistics for Students of Literature and Humanities*, London: Pergamon

Kermode, F. (1979), 'Institutional control of interpretation', *Salmagundi*, 43, 72–86.

Keyser, S. J. (1980), 'Wallace Stevens: form and meaning in four poems', in Ching *et al.* (eds), 1980, 257–82.

Keyser, S. J. (1983), 'There is method in their adness: the formal structure of advertisement', *New Literary History*, XIV/2, 305–34.

King, N. (1980), 'A reading of the literature-politics exchanges', *Critical Quarterly*, 22/1, 73–6.

Kintgen, E. R. (1983), *The Perception of Poetry*, Bloomington: Indiana University Press.

Kirstein, B. (1982), 'Piercean semiotic concepts applied to stylistic analysis', *KODIKAS-CODE, Ars Semiotica*, 4/5, 9–20.

Koelb, C. (1984), *The Incredulous Reader, Literature and the Function of Disbelief*, Ithaca: Cornell University Press.

Kress, G. (ed.) (1976), *System and Function in Language*, London: Oxford University Press.

Kress, G. (1978), 'Poetry as anti-language: a reconsideration of Donne's "Nocturnall" ', *Poetics and Theory of Literature*, 3, 327–44.

Kress, G. (1979), 'The social values of speech and writing', in Fowler *et al.*, 1979, 46–62.

Kress, G. (1982), *Learning to Write*, London: Routledge & Kegan Paul.

Kress, G. (1985a), *Linguistic Processes in Sociocultural Practice*, Geelong: Deakin University Press.

Kress, G. (1985b), 'Discourses, texts, readers and the pro-nuclear arguments', in Chilton (ed.), 1985, 65–88.

Kress, G. (ed.) (1988a), *Communication and Culture: An Introduction*, Sydney: New South Wales, University Press.

Kress, G. (1988b), 'Textual matters: the social effectiveness of style', in Birch and O'Toole (eds), 1988, 127–41.

Kress, G. (1988c), 'Language as Social Practice' in Kress (ed.), 1988a, 79–130.

Kress, G. and Hodge, R. (1979), *Language as Ideology,* London: Routledge & Kegan Paul.

Kress, G. and Trew, T. (1978), 'Transformations and discourse: A study in conceptual change', *Journal of Literary Semantics*, 7, 29–48.

Kristeva, J. (1974), *La Revolution du Langage Poétique*, Paris: Seuil.

Kristeva, J. (1980), *Desire in Language: A Semiotic Approach to Literature and Art*, New York: Columbia University Press.

Kroker, M. (ed.) (1985), *Feminism Now: Theory – Practice*, Montreal: Culture Texts.

Kuhn, T. S. (1962), *The Structure of Scientific Revolutions*, Chicago: Chicago University Press.

Labov, W. (1972a), *Language in the Inner City*, Philadelphia: University of Pennsylvania Press.

Labov, W. (1972b) *Sociolinguistic Patterns*, Philadelphia: University of Pennsylvania Press.

Lacan, J. (1977) *Ecrits*, Paris: Seuil.

Lakoff, R. (1975), *Language and Woman's Place,* New York: Harper & Row.

Lane, M. (ed.) (1970), *Structuralism: A Reader*, London: Jonathan Cape.

Larkin, P. (1955), *The Less Deceived* (5th edn 1962), London: Marvell Press.

Latre, G. (1983), 'Realist or romantic? Philip Larkin's modes of writing', in D'haen (ed.), 1983, 185–99.

Lawless, E. J. (1983), 'Shouting for the Lord. The power of women's speech in the Pentecostal religious service', *Journal of American Folklore*, 96/382, 434–59.

Leach, E. (1973), 'Structuralism in social anthropology', in Robey (ed.), 1973, 37–5.

Leavis, F. R. (1936), *Revaluation*, London: Chatto & Windus.

Leavis, F. R. (1954), *The Great Tradition*, Garden City: Doubleday.

Leavis, F. R. (1975), *The Living Principle. 'English' as a Discipline of Thought*, London: Oxford University Press.

Leech, G. (1965), ' "This bread I break" – language and interpretation', *A Review of English Literature*, 6, 66–75; reprinted in Freeman, 1970, 119–28.

Leech, G. (1966), *English in Advertising. A Linguistic Study of Advertising in Great Britain*, London: Longman.

Leech, G. (1969), *A Linguistic Guide to English Poetry*, London: Longman.

Leech, G. (1977), 'Literary criticism and linguistic description', *The Dutch Quarterly Review of Anglo-American Letters*, 7/1, 2–22.

Leech, G. and Short, M. H. (1981), *Style in Fiction. A Linguistic Introduction to English Fictional Prose*, London: Longman.

Leech, G. and Svartvik J. (1975), *A Communicative Grammar of English,* London: Longman.

Leitch, V. (1983), *Deconstructive Criticism*, New York: Columbia University Press.

Lessing, D. (1971), *Briefing For a Descent into Hell*, London: Jonathan Cape.

Lévi-Strauss, C. (1955), *Tristes Tropiques*, Paris: Plon.

Lévi-Strauss, C. (1958) *Anthropologie Structurale*, Paris: Plon.

Lévi-Strauss, C. (1962), *Pensée Sauvage*, Paris: Plon.

Lévi-Strauss, C. (1969), *The Elementary Structures of Kinship*, London: Eyre & Spottiswoode.

Lévi-Strauss, C. (1970), *The Raw and the Cooked*, London: Harper & Row.

Levin, S. R. (1962), *Linguistic Structures in Poetry*, The Hague: Mouton.

Levin, S. R. (1970), 'Coupling in a Shakespeare Sonnet' (pp. 51–8 in Levin, 1962), reprinted in Freeman (ed.), 1970, 197–205.

Lofaro, M. A. (1976), 'The mask with no eyes: Yeats's vision in "Per Amica Silentia Lunae" ', *Style*, 10/1, 51–66.

Lotman, J. M. (1977), *The Structure of the Artistic Text*, Ann Arbor: University of Michigan Press.

Love, G. A. and Payne M. (eds) (1969), *Contemporary Essays on Style*, Glenview, Illinois: Scott, Foresman & Co.

Lukács, G. (1978), *Writer and Critic and Other Essays* (trans. and ed. A. Kahn), London: Merlin.

Lumsden, R. (1987), 'Is practical criticism practical?', *Journal of Literary Semantics*, XVI/1, 30–55.

Lunt, H. G. (ed.) (1964), *Proceedings of Ninth International Congress of Linguistics*, The Hague: Mouton.

Lyons, J. (ed.) (1970) *New Horizons in Linguistics,* Harmondsworth: Penguin.

Macherey, P. (1978), *A Theory of Literary Production* (trans. G. Wall), London: Routledge & Kegan Paul.

Machin, R. and Norris, C. (eds) (1987), *Post-Structuralist Readings of English Poetry*, Cambridge: Cambridge University Press.

Malinowski, B. (1935), *Coral Gardens and Their Magic*, New York: American Book Company.

Man, P. de (1979a), *Allegories of Reading: Figural Language in Rousseau, Nietzsche, Rilke and Proust*, New Haven: Yale University Press.

Man, P. de (1979b), 'Shelley disfigured' in Bloom et al. 1979, 39–73.

Man, P. de (1984), *The Rhetoric of Romanticism*, New York: Cornell University Press.

Marks, E. and Courtivron, I. de (eds) (1981), *New French Feminisms* Brighton: Harvester Press.

Marshall, A. (1944), *These Are My People*, Melbourne: Gold Star Publications. 1972 edn.

Martin, J. R. (1985), *Factual Writing: Exploring and Challenging Social Reality*, Geelong: Deakin University Press.

Mason, M. (1982), 'Deixis: a point of entry to *Little Dorrit*', in Carter, 1982c, 29–40.

Massey, I. (1970), *The Uncreating Word. Romanticism and the Object,* Bloomington: Indiana University Press.

Matejka, L. and Pomorska, K. (eds) (1971), *Readings in Russian Poetics: Formalist and Structuralist Views*, Cambridge, Mass: Harvard University Press.

Mays, W. (1970), Introduction to Mays and Brown (eds), 1970, 1–26.

Mays, W. and Brown S. C. (eds) (1970), *Linguistic Analysis and Phenomenology*, Lewisburg: Bucknell University Press.

McCarl, R. S. (1984), ' "You've come a long way – and now this is your retirement": an analysis of performance in fire-fighting culture', *Journal of American Folklore*, 97/386, 492–521.

McHoul, A. W. (1982), *Telling How Texts Talk: Essays on Reading and Ethnomethodology*, London: Routledge & Kegan Paul.

Mcintosh, A. and Halliday, M. A. K. (1966), *Patterns of Language: Papers in General, Descriptive and Applied Linguistics*, London: Longman.

McLain, R. L. (1976), 'Literary criticism versus generative grammars', *Style*, 10, 231–51.

McLain, R. L. (1977), 'The problem of "style": another case in fuzzy grammar', *Language and Style*, 10, 52–65.

McLain, R. L. (1979), 'Semantics and style – with the example of quintessential Hemingway', *Language and Style*, 12/2, 63–78.

McLellan, J. and Heather, P. R. (1951), *Exercises in Appreciation*, London: G. Bell and Sons.

McNamara, E. (ed.) (1969), *The Interior Landscape. The Literary Criticism of Marshall McLuhan, 1943–1962*, New York: McGraw-Hill.

Medhurst, M. J. (1987), 'Eisenhower's "atoms for peace" speech: a case study in the strategic use of language', *Communication Monographs*, 54, 204–20.

Medvedev, P. N. and Bakhtin, M. (1978), *The Formal Method in Literary*

Scholarship: An Introduction to Sociological Poetics, Baltimore: Johns Hopkins University Press.

Melchiori, G. (1976), *Shakespeare's Dramatic Meditations: An Experiment in Criticism*, Oxford: Clarendon Press.

Mepham, J. (1973), 'The structuralist sciences and philosophy', in Robey (ed.), 1973, 104–37.

Michels, J. (1982), 'The role of language as consciousness: a structuralist look at "Proteus" in *Ulysses*', *Language and Style*, 15/1, 28–32.

Miller, D. L. (1981), 'Language and theory', *International Journal for the Sociological Study of Language*, 31, 43–64.

Miller, J. H. (1971), 'The still heart: poetic form in Wordsworth', *New Literary History*, 2, 297–310.

Millett, K. (1969), *Sexual Politics*, London: Virago.

Mitchell, J. (1975), *Psychoanalysis and Feminism*, Harmondsworth: Penguin.

Mohrmann, G. P. (ed.) (1973) *Explorations in Rhetorical Criticism*, Michigan: Pennsylvania State University Press.

Moi, T. (1985), *Sexual/Textual Politics: Feminist Literary Theory*, London: Methuen.

Moss, P. (1985), 'Rhetoric of defence in the United States: language, myth and ideology', in Chilton (ed.), 1985, 45–64.

Mukařovský, J. (1964), 'Standard language and poetic language' in Garvin (ed.), 1964, 17–30.

Mulhern, F. (1979), *The Moment of Scrutiny*, London: New Left Books.

Nash, W. (1980), *Designs in Prose. A Study of Compositional Problems and Methods*, London: Longman.

Nash, W. (1982), 'On a Passage from Lawrence's "Odour of Chrysanthemums",' in Carter (ed.), 1982c, 101–22.

Nash, W. (1985), *The Language of Humour. Style and Technique in Comic Discourse*, London: Longman.

Newmeyer, F. (1983), *Grammatical Theory: Its Limits and Its Possibilities*, Chicago: University of Chicago Press.

Ngara, E. (1982), *Stylistic Criticism and the African Novel*, London: Heinemann.

Norris, C. (1976), 'Theory of language and the language of literature', *Journal of Literary Semantics*, 5, 90–7.

Norris, C. (1978), *William Empson and the Philosophy of Literary Criticism*, London: Athlone Press.

Norris, C. (1980), 'Deconstruction and the limits of sense', *Essays in Criticism*, XXX/4, 281–92.

Norris, C. (1982), *Deconstruction, Theory and Practice*, London: Methuen.

Norris, C. (1983), 'Perpetuum mobile', *PN Review*, 32, 61–2.

Norris, C. (1984a), *The Deconstructive Turn. Essays in the Rhetoric of Philosophy*, London: Methuen.

Norris, C. (1984b), 'On Marxist deconstruction problems and prospects', *Southern Review*. 17, 203–11.

Norris, C. (1985a), 'The importance of Empson (II): the criticism'. *Essays in Criticism*, 35/1, 25–44.

Norris, C. (1985b), *The Contest of Faculties. Philosophy and Theory after Deconstruction*, London: Methuen.

Nowottny, W. (1962), *The Language Poets Use*, London: Athlone Press.

Nuttall, A. D. (1974), *A Common Sky. Philosophy and the Literary Imagination*, London: Chatto & Windus: Sussex University Press.

Ogden, C. K. and Richards, I. A. (1923), *The Meaning of Meaning*, London: Routledge & Kegan Paul.

Ohmann, R. (1964), 'Generative grammars and the concept of literary style', *Word*, 20, 424–39; reprinted in Freeman, 1970, 258–78.

Ohmann, R. (1966), 'Literature as sentences', *College English*, 27, 261–7; reprinted in Chatman and Levin (eds), 1976, 231–40.

Ohmann, R. (1970), 'Studying literature at the end of ideology', in Kampf and Lauter, 1970, 130–59.

Ong, W. (1976), 'From rhetorical culture to New Criticism: the poem as closed field', in Simpson (ed.), 1976, 150–67.

O'Toole, L. M. (1971), 'Speech Functions and the Study of Style', *Melbourne Slavonic Studies*, 5/6, 106–23.

O'Toole, L. M. (1975), 'Analytic and synthetic approaches to narrative structure. Sherlock Holmes and "The Sussex Vampire" ', in Fowler (ed.), 1975, 143–76.

O'Toole, L. M. (1982), *Structure, Style and Interpretation in The Russian Short Story*, New Haven: Yale University Press.

O'Toole, L. M. (1988), 'Henry Reed and what follows the "Naming of Parts" ', in Birch and O'Toole (eds), 1988, 12–30.

Parrinder, P. (1977), *Authors and Authority. A Study of English Literary Criticism and its Relations to Culture, 1750–1900*, London: Routledge & Kegan Paul.

Pateman, T. (1975), *Language, Truth, Politics, Towards a Radical Theory for Communication*, Lewes: Jean Stroud.

Pavel, T. G. (1973), 'Some remarks on narrative grammars', *Poetics*, 8, 5–30, reprinted in Ching *et al.* (eds), 1980, 187–212.

Pêcheux, M. (1975a), *Language, Semantics and Ideology*, (trans. H. Nagpal, London: Macmillan, 1982).

Pêcheux, M. (1975b), *Analyse du Discours. Langue et Idéologies*, Paris: Dider-Larousse.

Petitt, P. (1977), *The Concept of Structuralism: A Critical Analysis*, Berkeley: University of California Press.

Petöfi, J. S. (1973), 'Towards a grammatical theory of verbal texts', in Petöfi and Rieser (eds), 1973, 205–75.

Petöfi, J. S. and Rieser, H. (eds) (1973), *Studies in Text Grammars*, Dordrecht: Reidel.

Peyre, H. (1967), *The Failure of Criticism*, Ithaca: Cornell University Press.

Polletta, G. (ed.) (1973), *Issues in Contemporary Literary Criticism*, Boston: Little, Brown.

Posner, R. (1976), 'Poetic communication *v*. literary language, or the linguistic fallacy in poetics', *Poetics and the Theory of Literature*, 1, 1–10.

Posner, R. (1982), *Rational Discourse and Poetic Communication: Methods of Linguistic, Literary and Philosophical Analysis*, Berlin and New York: Mouton.

Poythress, V. S. (1982), 'A framework for discourse analysis: the components of a discourse from a tagmemic viewpoint', *Semiotica*, 38/3–4, 277–98.

Pratt, M. L. (1976), *Towards a Speech Art Theory of Literary Discourse*, Bloomington: Indiana University Press.

Pratt, M. L. (1981), 'The Ideology of Speech Act Theory', *Centrum* 1/ 1

Pratt, M. L. (1982/3) 'Interpretive strategies/strategic interpretations: on Anglo-American reader response criticism', *Boundary 2*, XI/1/2, 201–31.

Presley, J. (1979), 'D. H. Lawrence and the Resources of Poetry', *Language and Style*, 12/1, 3–12.

Prince, G. (1973), *Grammar of Stories: An Introduction*, The Hague: Mouton.

Propp, V. (1958), *Morphology of the Folktale* (ed. S. Pirkova-Jakobson, trans. L. Scott), Bloomington: Indiana University Research Centre.

Pulgram, E. (1967), 'Sciences, humanities and the place of linguistics', *Linguistics*, 53, 70–92.

Quinn, C. Jr (1982), ' "Literary" language. Is it different?' *University of Michigan Papers in Linguistics*, 4/1, 29–56.

Quirk, R. (1986), *Words at Work. Lectures on Textual Structures,* London: Longman.

Rader, R. (1974a), 'Explaining our literary understanding', *Critical Inquiry*, 1, 901–11.

Rader, R. (1974b), 'Fact, theory, and literary explanation', *Critical Inquiry*, 1, 262–72.

Ragland-Sullivan, E. (1984), 'The magnetism between reader and text: prolegomena to a Lacanian poetics', *Poetics*, 13, 381–406.

Rasmussen, D. (1971), *Mythic-Symbolic Language and Philosophical Anthropology: A Constructive Interpretation of the Thought of Paul Ricoeur*, The Hague: Nijhoff.

Raval, S. (1986), 'Philosophy and the Crisis of Contemporary Literary Theory', *The Monist*, 69/1, 119–31.

Reeves, J. (1956), *The Critical Sense, Practical Criticism of Prose and Poetry*, London: Heinemann.

Reich, P. A. (ed.) (1976), *The Second LACUS Forum*, Columbia: Hornbeam Press.

Reinhart, T. (1980), 'Conditions for text coherence', *Poetics Today*, 1/4, 161–80.

Richards, I. A. (1924), *Principles of Literary Criticism*, London: Routledge & Kegan Paul.

Richards, I. A. (1929), *Practical Criticism. A Study of Literary Judgement*, London: Routledge & Kegan Paul.

Richards, I. A. (1970), 'Jakobson's Shakespeare: the subliminal structures of a sonnet', *Times Literary Supplement*, 28 May, 589–90.

Richardson, K. (1985), 'Pragmatics of speeches against the peace movement in Britain: a case study', in Chilton (ed.), 1985, 23–44.

Ricks C. (1984), *The Force of Poetry*, Oxford: Clarendon Press.

Ricoeur, P. (1971), 'What is a text? Explanation and interpretation', in Rasmussen, 1971: reprinted in Ricoeur, 1981, 145–64.

Ricoeur, P. (1981), *Hermeneutics and the Human Sciences* (ed. and trans. J. B. Thompson), Cambridge: Cambridge University Press.

Riding, L. and Graves R. (1928), *A Survey of Modernist Poetry*, New York: Haskell House (1969 edn).

Rieser, H. (1978), 'On the development of text grammar', in Dressler (ed.), 1978, 6–20.

Riffaterre, M. (1959), 'Criteria for style analysis', *Word*, 15, 154–74.

Riffaterre, M. (1960), 'Stylistic Context', *Word*, 16, 207–18.

Riffaterre, M. (1966), 'Describing poetic structures: two approaches to Baudelaire's "Les Chats" ', *Yale French Studies*, 36/7.

Riffaterre, M. (1971), *Essais de Stylistique Structurale*, Paris: Flammarion.

Riffaterre, M. (1973), 'The self-sufficient text', *Diacritics*, 3/3, 39–45.

Riffaterre, M. (1978), *Semiotics of Poetry*, Bloomington: Indiana University Press.

Ringbom, H. (ed.) (1975), *Style and Text: Studies Presented to Nils Erik Enkvist*, Stockholm: Skriptor.

Roberts, F. (1971), 'Being an Aboriginal in Australian Society' in *Racism in Australia. Tasks for General and Christian Education. A Report of the Southport Conference*, Nov 19–24, 1971, Melbourne: Division of Christian Education, 19–20.

Robey, D. (ed.) (1973), *Structuralism. An Introduction*, Oxford: Clarendon Press.

Robey, D. (1982), 'Anglo-American New Criticism' in Jefferson and Robey (eds), 1982, 65–83.

Rochester, S. and Martin, J. (1979), *Crazy Talk*, New York: Plenum.

Rodway, A. (1970), *The Truths of Fiction*, London: Chatto & Windus.

Rorty, R. (1979), *Philosophy and the Mirror of Nature*, Princeton: Princeton University Press.

Rosen, C. (1971), 'Art has its reason', *New York Review of Books*, June 17, 32–8.

Rosenblatt, L. (1978), *The Reader, The Text, The Poem: The Transactional Theory of the Literary Work*, Carbondale: Southern Illinois University Press.

Rosenfeld, M. (1984), 'The linguistic aspect of sexual conflict: Monique Wittig's *Le Corps lesbian*', *Mosiac*, XVII/2, 235–41.

Rudick, N. (ed.) (1976), *Weapons of Criticism, Marxism in America and the Literary Tradition*, Palo Alto: Ramparts Press.

Russell, L. M. (ed.) (1985), *Feminist Interpretation of the Bible*, Philadelphia: Westminster Press.

Ruthrof, H. (1981), *The Reader's Construction of Narrative*, London: Routledge & Kegan Paul.

Sagar, K. (1979), *The Art of Ted Hughes*, Cambridge: Cambridge University Press.

Saha, P. K. (1968), 'A linguistic approach to style', *Style*, 2/1, 7–31.

Said, E. (1975), *Beginnings: Intention and Method*, New York: Basic Books.

Said, E. (1978), *Orientalism*, New York: Pantheon.

Said, E. (1979), 'The text, the world, the critic', in Harari (ed.), 1979, 161–88.

Said, E. (1980), *Criticism Between Culture and System*, Cambridge, Mass.: Harvard University Press.

Said, E. (1983), *The World, The text, and the Critic*, Cambridge, Mass.: Harvard University Press.

Sapir, E. (1921), *Language: An Introduction to the Study of Speech*, New York: Harcourt Brace Jovanovich.

Saussure, F. de (1959), *Course in General Linguistics*, (trans. Wade Baskin; Bally, A. Sechehaye and A. Riedlinger, eds) New York: McGraw-Hill.

Sawyer, P. L. (1985), *Ruskin's Poetic Argument. The Design of the Major Works*, Ithaca: Cornell University Press.

Schauber, E. and Spolsky, E. (1981), 'Stalking a generative poetics', *New Literary History*, 12, 397–413.

Schauber, E. and Spolsky E. (1984), *The Bounds of Interpretations: Linguistic Theory and Literary Test*, Palo Alto: Stanford University Press.

Scheglov, Y. K. and Zholkovskii, A. K. (1975) 'Generating the literary text' (trans. L. M. O'Toole), *Russian Poetics in Translation, I*, Colchester: University of Essex.

Schmidt, S. J. (1978), 'Some problems of communicative text theories', in Dressler (ed.), 1978, 47–60.

Schwartz, M. M. (1978), 'Critic, define thyself', in Hartman (ed.), 1978, 1–17.

Schwenger, P. (1984), *Phallic Critiques. Masculinity and Twentieth-Century Literature*, London: Routledge & Kegan Paul.

Searle, J. R. (1969), *Speech Acts*, Cambridge: Cambridge University Press.

Sears, S. and Lord, G. W. (eds) (1972), *The Discontinuous Universe: Selected Writings in Contemporary Consciousness*, New York: Basic Books.

Sebeok, T. (ed.) (1960), *Style in Language*, Cambridge, Mass.: MIT Press.

Sedgwick, E. K. (1985), *Between Man, English Literature and Male Homosocial Desire*, New York: Columbia University Press.

Selden, R. (1985), *A Reader's Guide to Contemporary Literary Theory*, Brighton: Harvester Press.

Sharratt, B. (1982), *Reading Relations: Structures of Literary Production. A Dialectical Textbook*, Atlantic Highlands, NJ: Humanities Press.

Shelley, P. B. (1821), 'Defence of Poetry', in Enright and Chickera (eds), 1962, 225–55.

Short, M. H. (1972), ' "Prelude I" to a literary linguistic stylistics', *Style*, 6/2, 149–58.

Showalter, E. (ed.) (1985a), 'Toward a feminist poetics' in Showalter, 1985b, 125–43.

Showalter, E. (1985b), *The New Feminist Criticism, Essays on Women, Literature and Theory*, New York: Pantheon Books.

Showalter, E. (1985c), 'Feminist criticism in the wilderness', in Showalter, 1985b, 243–70.

Silverman, D. and Torode, B. (1980), *The Material Word. Some Theories of Language and Limits*, London: Routledge & Kegan Paul.

Simpson, L. P. (ed.) (1976), *The Possibilities of Order: Cleanth Brooks and his Work*, Baton Rouge: Louisiana State University Press.

Sinclair, J. (1968), 'A technique of stylistic description', *Language and Style*, 1, 215–42.

Sinclair, J. (1972a), *A Course in Spoken English: Grammar*, London: Oxford University Press.

Sinclair, J. (1972b), 'Lines about "Lines" ', in Kachru and Stahlke (eds), 1972, 251–61; reprinted in Carter, 1982c, 163–78.

Sinclair, J. (1984), 'Poetic discourse: a sample exercise', in Birch (ed.), 1984a, 9–28.

Sinclair, J. and Coulthard, M. (1975), *Towards an Analysis of Discourse*, Oxford: Oxford University Press.

Skinner, B. F. (1973), 'Reflections on meaning and structure' in Brower, Vendler and Hollander (eds), 1973, 199–209.

Skornia, H. J. and Kitson, J. W. (eds), *Problems and Controversies in Television and Radio*, New York: Pacific Books, 347–58.

Smith, C. (1961), 'A class of complex modifiers in English', *Language*, 37/3, 342–65.

Smith, F. J. (ed.), (1970), *Phenomenology in Perspective*, The Hague: Nijhoff.

Sola Pinto, de (ed.) (1946), *The Teaching of English in Schools*, London: Macmillan.

Sontag, Susan (1961a), 'Against Interpretation', in Sontag, 1961b, 3–14.

Sontag, S. (1961b), *Against Interpretation and Other Essays*, New York: Delta.

Spencer, J. and Gregory, M. (eds) (1964), *Linguistics and Style,* Oxford: Oxford University Press.

Sperber, D. (1979), 'Claude Lévi-Strauss', in Sturrock (ed.), 1979b, 19–51.

Spitzer, L. (1943), 'Why does language change?', *Modern Language Quarterly*, 4, 413–21.

Spitzer, L. (1948), *Linguistics and Literary History: Essays in Stylistics*, Princeton: Princeton University Press.

Spitzer, L. (1954), 'On Yeats's Poem, "Leda and the Swan" ', *Modern Philology*, 51, 271–6.

Spoerri, T. (1944), 'Style of distance, style of nearness', trans. C. Babb, in Babb (ed.), 1972, 62–78.

St Clair, R. (1978), 'The Politics of Language', *Word*, 29, 44–62.

St Clair, R. (1982) 'Language and the social construction of reality', *Language Sciences*, 4/7, 221–36.

Steiner, E. (1985), 'The concept of context and the theory of action', in Chilton (ed.), 1985, 215–30.

Stevens, W. (1955), *The Collected Poems of Wallace Stevens*, London: Faber & Faber.

Stevens, W. (1977), *Opus Posthumous* (ed. S. F. Morse), New York: Knopf.

Strong, L. A. G. (1946), 'Poetry in the schools', in Sola Pinto (ed.), 1946, 1–16.

Stuart, S. (1979), *New Phoenix Wings: Reparation in Literature.* London: Routledge & Kegan Paul.

Stubbs, M. (1980), *Language and Literacy. The Sociolinguistics of Reading and Writing*, London: Routledge & Kegan Paul.

Stubbs, M. (1983), *Discourse Analysis, The Sociolinguistic Analysis of Natural Language*, Oxford: Basil Blackwell.

Sturrock, J. (1979a), 'Roland Barthes', in Sturrock (ed.), 1979b, 52–80.

Sturrock, J. (ed.) (1979b), *Structuralism and Since. From Lévi-Strauss to Derrida*, London: Oxford University Press.

Suleiman, S. R. and Crossman, I. (eds) (1980), *The Reader in the Text: Essays on Audience and Interpretation*, Princeton, Princeton University Press.

Suttner, R. (1984), 'The ideological role of the judiciary in South Africa', *Philosophical Papers*, 13/2, 28–49.

Szondi, P. (1978), 'Introduction to literary hermeneutics', *New Literary History*, X/1, 17–30.

Tallack, D. (ed.) (1987), *Literary Theory at Work: Three Texts*, London: Batsford.

Tannen, D. (ed.) (1982), *Spoken and Written Language: Exploring Orality and Literacy*, Norwood, NJ: Ablex.

Taylor, T. J. (1980), *Linguistic Theory and Structural Stylistics*, London: Pergamon.

Thibault, P. (1986), 'Metaphors and political oratory in Ronald Reagan's acceptance speech' in Bosinelli, 1984, 149–68.

Thibault, P. (1988), 'Knowing what you're told by the agony aunts: language function, gender difference and the structure of knowledge and belief in the personal columns', in Birch and O'Toole (eds), 1988, 205–33.

Thompson, E. M. (1971), *Russian Formalism and Anglo-American New Criticism,* The Hague: Mouton.

Thorne, J. P. (1965), 'Stylistics and generative grammars', *Journal of Linguistics*, 1, 49–59.

Thorne, J. P. (1970), 'Generative grammars and stylistic analysis', in Lyons (ed.), 1970, 185–97.

Threadgold, T. (1986), 'Semiotics – ideology – language' in Threadgold *et al.*, 1986, 15–60.

Threadgold, T. (1988), 'Stories of race and gender: an unbounded discourse' in Birch and O'Toole (eds), 1988, 169–204.

Threadgold, T., Gros, E. A., Kress, G. and Halliday, M. A. K. (eds) (1986), *Semiotics, Ideology, Language*, Sydney: The Sydney Association for Society and Culture.

Thurley, G. (1983), *Counter-Modernism in Current Critical Theory*, London: Macmillan.

Todd, J. (ed.) (1983), *Jane Austen. New Perspectives*, New York: Holmes & Meier.

Todorov, T. (1968), *Grammaire du Decameron*, The Hague: Mouton.

Todorov, T. (1971), *Poetique de la Prose*, Paris: Seuil: trans. as *The Poetics of Prose*, London: Oxford University Press (1977).

Todorov, T. (1973a), 'Structuralism and literature', in Chatman (ed.), 1973, 153–68.

Todorov, T. (1973b), 'The structural analysis of literature: the tales of Henry James', in Robey (ed.), 1973, 73–103.

Todorov, T. (1981), *Introduction to Poetics* (trans. Richard Howard), Brighton: Harvester Press.

Tompkins, J. (ed.) (1980), *Reader-Response Criticism: From Formalism to Post-Structuralism*, Baltimore: Johns Hopkins University Press.

Tompkins, J. (1985), *Sensational Designs. The Cultural Work of American Fiction, 1790–1860*, Oxford: Oxford University Press.

Toolan, M. (1983), 'The functioning of progressive verbal forms in the narrative of "Go Down, Moses" ', *Language and Style*, 16/2, 211–30.

Toolan, M. (1984), 'Stanley Fish and the interpretive communities of responding readers', *The Dutch Quarterly Review of Anglo-American Letters*, 14/1, 62–73.

Toolan, M. (1988), 'Compromising positions: systemic linguistics and the locally managed semiotics of dialogue', in Birch and O'Toole (eds), 1988, 249–60.

204 Bibliography

Trew, T. (1979), ' "What the papers say": linguistic variation and ideological difference', in Fowler *et al*, 1979, 117–56.

Trudgill, P. (1974), *The Social Differentiation of English in Norwich*, Cambridge: Cambridge University Press.

Turner, G. W. (1973), *Stylistics*, Harmondsworth: Penguin.

Ullman, S. (1973), *Language and Style*, Oxford: Basil Blackwell.

Urban, G. (1984), 'Speech about speech about action', *Journal of American Folklore*, 97/385, 310–28.

Ure, J. (1982), 'Introduction: approaches to the study of register range', *International Journal for the Sociological Study of Language*, 35, 5–23.

van Dijk, T. A. (1971), 'Some problems of generative poetics', *Poetics*, 2, 5–35.

van Dijk, T. A. (1972), *Some Aspects of Text Grammars, A Study in the Theoretical Linguistics and Poetics*, The Hague: Mouton.

van Dijk, T. A. (1973), 'Text grammar and text logic' in Petöfi and Rieser (eds), 1973, 17–76.

van Dijk, T. A. (1977), *Text and Context. Explorations in the Semantics and Pragmatics of Discourse*, London: Longman.

van Dijk, T. A. (1981), *Studies in the Pragmatics of Discourse*, The Hague: Mouton.

van Dijk, T. A. (ed.) (1985), *Discourse and Communication. New Approaches to the Analysis of Mass Media, Discourse and Communication,* Berlin: de Gruyter.

van Dijk, T. A. and Petöfi, J. S. (eds) (1977), *Grammars and Descriptions*, Berlin: de Gruyter.

Van Peer, W. (1983), 'Pulp and purpose: stylistic analysis as an aid to a theory of texts', in D'haen (ed.), 1983, 229–48.

Vendler, J. (1973), 'Jakobson, Richards and Shakespeare's Sonnet CXXIX', in Brower, *et al.*, (eds), 1973, 179–98.

Verdonk, P. (1983), 'Poetic artifice and literary stylistics', in D'haen (ed.), 1983, 215–28.

Voloshinov, V. (1930), *Marxism and the Philosophy of Language* (trans. L. Matejka and I. R. Titunik) New York: Seminar Press (1973).

Vos, L. (1985), *Just the Other Day. Sutures of the Future*, Antwerp: Restant.

Watson, G. (1969), *The Study of Literature*, Harmondsworth: Penguin.

Watt, Ian (1964), 'The first paragraph of *The Ambassadors*: an explication', in Polletta (ed.), 1973, 70–86.

Weber, J. J. (1982), 'Frame construction and frame accommodation in a Gricean analysis of narrative', *Journal of Literary Semantics*, XI/2, 90–5.

Weber, R. W. (1982), 'What the literary critic can do for the linguist: an outsider's look at the English verb', *Poetics Today*, 3/4, 53–8.

Webster, R. (1984), ' "The Thought-Fox" and the poetry of Ted Hughes', *Critical Quarterly*, 26/4, 35–45.

Wendland, A. (1985), *Science, Myth and the Fictional Creation of Alien Worlds*, New York: UMI Research Center.

Werth, P. (1976), 'Roman Jakobson's verbal analysis of poetry', *Journal of Linguistics*, 12, 21–74.

Weston, H. (1934), *Form in Literature. A Theory of Technique and Construction*, London: Rich & Cowan.

Wetherill, P. M. (1974), *The Literary Text: An Examination of Critical Methods*, Oxford: Basil Blackwell.

White, H. (1974), 'Structuralism and Popular Culture', *Journal of Popular Culture*, 7/4, 758–75.

Whorf, B. L. (1956), *Language, Thought and Reality: Selected Papers* (ed. J. Carrol), New York: Wiley.

Widdowson, H. (1972), 'On the deviance of literary discourse', *Style*, 294–305.

Widdowson, H. (1975), *Stylistics and the Teaching of Literature*, London: Longman.

Widdowson, H. (1978), *Teaching Language as Communication*, London: Oxford University Press.

Widdowson, P. (ed.) (1982), *Re-reading English*, London: Methuen.

Wilbur, R., Nims, J. F., Berryman, J. and Lowell, R. (1973), 'On Robert Lowell's "Skunk Hour" ', in Polletta (ed.), 1973, 277–307.

Wimsatt, W. K. Jr (1954), *The Verbal Icon*, Lexington: University of Kentucky Press.

Wimsatt, W. K. Jr (1963), *Explication as Criticism*, New York: Columbia University Press.

Winter, W. (1965), 'Transformations without kernels?' *Language*, 41/3, 484–9.

Witherspoon, G. (1980), 'Language in Culture and Culture in Language', *International Journal of American Linguistics*, 46, 1–13.

Worpole, K. (1983), *Dockers and Detectives. Popular Reading: Popular Writing*, London: Verso.

Yap, A. (1984), 'An analysis of the thematic structure of Carl Sandburg's "Grass" ', in Birch (ed.), 1984a, 145–56.

Young, R. (ed.) (1981), *Untying the Text. A Post-Structuralist Reader*, London: Routledge & Kegan Paul.

Youngren, W. (1970), *Semantics, Linguistics and Criticism,* New York: Random House.

Index